ELECTING CHÁVEZ

PITT LATIN AMERICAN SERIES

John Charles Chasteen and Catherine M. Conaghan, Editors

Electing Chávez

THE BUSINESS OF ANTI-NEOLIBERAL POLITICS IN VENEZUELA

Leslie C. Gates

UNIVERSITY OF PITTSBURGH PRESS

Published by the University of Pittsburgh Press, Pittsburgh, Pa., 15260

Copyright © 2010, University of Pittsburgh Press

Manufactured in the United States of America

Printed on acid-free paper

10 9 8 7 6 5 4 3 2 1

Library of Congress Cataloging-in-Publication Data

Gates, Leslie C.

Electing Chavez : the business of anti-neoliberal politics in Venezuela / Leslie C. Gates.

   p. cm. — (Pitt Latin american series)

Includes bibliographical references and index.

   1. Neoliberalism—Venezuela. 2. Social movements—Venezuela. 3. Elections—Venezuela.

4. Venezuela—Politics and government—1974–5. Presidents—Venezuela—Election—

1998. 6. Chávez Frías, Hugo. I. Title.

   JC574.2.V4G38 2010

   324.987'064—dc22   2010002365

FOR KATE

CONTENTS

Contents

LIST OF TABLES

ACKNOWLEDGMENTS

This study would not have been possible without the initial support and assistance of many institutions and individuals. The Research Semester Award from the dean of the Harpur College of Arts and Sciences gave me the time to launch this project. David Smilde offered instructive comments and encouragement to push forward early on. The participants at the Contentious Politics Workshop in New York City helped steer this project, at the time of its inception, toward some of the more fruitful lines of inquiry. The Program on Latin America and the Caribbean at Syracuse University's Maxwell School of Public Affairs hosted me as a visiting research scholar one semester and provided a hospitable intellectual environment in which to develop a plan for research. I conducted my initial research in Venezuela with financial assistance from the dean of the Harpur College of Arts and Sciences and the United University Professionals' Individual Development Award at Binghamton University. Angelo Rivero-Santos, then at Georgetown University, and Rodolfo Magallanes of the Universidad Central de Venezuela shared valuable insights on Venezuelan politics that informed my research plan. Magallanes helped me make numerous contacts once I arrived in Caracas. Many others also assisted in this way, including David Holiday, Hilary Abell, Nancy Appelbaum, Maria Cook, Juanita Diaz, Ricardo Laremont, and David Smilde.

A Fulbright Scholar award made it possible for me to conduct research for ten months in Caracas. While in Caracas, the Universidad Central de Venezuela (UCV) and the Instituto de Estudios Superiores de Administración (IESA) hosted me. At UCV, I was affiliated with the graduate program in social sciences of the Facultad de Economía y Ciencias Sociales (FACES) thanks to Trino Márquez, Antonio de Venanzi, and Rafael Ramírez. De Venanzi helped establish my connection with the UCV and has since become a trusted critic of my work. At IESA, I became an affiliate of the public policy division of the school thanks to Rosa Amelia González. IESA generously provided office space and a congenial intellectual community. The library staff at IESA worked tirelessly on my behalf, dredging up obscure government documents and scouring the extensive archive for relevant works. I am especially grateful to Francisco Monaldi for his help with coding some of the political biographies, to Maximiliano González for sharing his database on board membership of publicly traded companies, and to Rosa Amelia González for sharing her list of all cabinet members. The students at both the UCV and IESA kept me on my toes and helped to sharpen my understanding of Venezuelan political life.

My research was made infinitely more efficient and enjoyable by several research assistants. I owe a huge debt to Clara Serfaty, who helped in particular with the database of political biographies. Her ingenuity and careful attention to detail have made the database so much better than it would have been without her. I am grateful to her for tolerating my wavering on coding decisions and my many long e-mails detailing an ever-expanding list of tasks to improve the database and, finally, for her friendship. The librarian, Edie Cardenas, at the Biblioteca Nacional facilitated data collection by allowing me to review and copy her private archive of biographies on and curriculum vitae of prominent political leaders. Joanna Borges also provided valuable assistance, helping to collect and code a sample of newspaper articles from which I constructed the corruption scandals database. The obliging staff at the Hemeroteca (the newspaper archive) of the Biblioteca Nacional cheered Joanna and me on in the otherwise tedious task of reviewing the reels of microfilmed newspapers.

I would especially like to thank all those who agreed to be interviewed. I appreciate, in particular, the business leaders who went out of their way to help me identify and contact others in the business community. Without their assistance, I would not have been able to glean the insider's perspective of the calculus that business leaders use during presidential campaigns, which informed chapters 5 and 6. I am particularly indebted to each member of the business community who took the time to review my list of nearly two thousand federal legislators. Similarly, I am grateful to the campaign insiders, those individuals who had close ties to Hugo Chávez during the 1998 presidential campaign and who agreed to meet with me. Their descriptions of the campaign and their willingness to identify elite outliers by name made the last part of the book possible.

Numerous individuals made life in Caracas easier and richer. Upon my arrival, Maria Eugenia Mendoza from the U.S. embassy in Caracas welcomed me and eased my transition. Urbi Garay and Patricia Márquez, from IESA, helped me find accommodations. Patricia's home, where I lived while she was in residence at Harvard, was an oasis in the city. It is also due to Patricia that I had the good fortune of meeting Delfina Casiani. Delfina became a friend and gave me a window into another life in Caracas. Rodrigo Navarrete adopted me, offering me friendship and, on numerous occasions, his informal services as tour guide of Caracas and beyond. The camaraderie formed over long lunches and a few late-night antics with fellow Fulbrighters Sue Taylor and Laura Graham kept my spirits up.

Various other kinds of assistance also improved this book. I owe a considerable debt to Brian Crisp for his continued willingness to offer guidance and even share data. It was at his suggestion that I collected biographical data on cabinet members and former federal legislators in Venezuela. Stephen Morris's work on corruption in Mexico served as an initial guide for how to study the political impact of corruption. In addition, he offered instrumental guidance on both my coding of corruption scandals and my design for how to collect data on that topic from newspapers. Roderic Camp's foundational work on Mexico's elite was my yardstick for how to construct a similar database. He readily answered my numerous questions about how to code political biographies in ways that paralleled his data. He also volunteered a previously unpublished analysis of his data to match the one I intended to conduct for Venezuela. Javier Corrales's work, too, was influential in shaping my argument, and I am grateful for his responsiveness to my queries on coding. Mike Mulcahy helped me conceive of how to transform the political biographies database into a format that I could analyze statistically, and he graciously agreed on many occasions to review my interpretations of statistical results. Jana Morgan helped me to gain access to the poll I use in chapters 3 and 4 (REDPOL98). Alfredo Vargas at the Universidad Simón Bolívar's Banco de Datos Poblacionales expeditiously responded to my petition for these data. I am grateful for permission to reprint here a modified version of a paper originally published as "The Business of Anti-globalization: Lessons from Venezuela's 1998 Presidential Elections," *Research in Political Sociology,* volume 15 (2007), © Emerald Group Publishing Limited.

This project has benefited from the critique and advice of numerous individuals. The members of the Dean and Deluca New York Writing Group, Mike Mulcahy, Liz Borland, Tim Bartley, and Rachel Sherman have suffered through numerous drafts and incarnations of this project. Without their advice on everything from the details of writing to the framing of a book-length manuscript, this book would certainly be less cogent and persuasive. Others have also taken the time to read my work at various stages of this project and to offer their valuable substantive guidance. They include Paul Almeida, Aaron Bobrow-Strain, Vonda Brown, Maria Cook, Fred Deyo, Jonathan Eastwood, Bill Martin, Martin Murray, Ravi Palat, Ann Pitcher, Harland Prechel, Kenneth Roberts, Benita Roth, Joel Stillerman, and Dale Tomich; participants in a workshop of the Program on Latin America and the Caribbean at Syracuse University's Maxwell School of Public Affairs; Richard Appelbaum and others in attendance at my American Sociological Association presentation in 2006; Stephen Morris, Chris Blake, and others who attended my presentation at the Latin American Studies Association meeting in 2007; and the anonymous reviewers for *Research in Political Sociology* and the University of Pittsburgh Press. I am also thankful to Josh Shanholtzer at the University of Pittsburgh Press for taking an interest in the project and shepherding it through the review process so expediently. The final prose benefited from judicious editing by my mother, Jann Gates, and the copyeditor, Maureen Creamer Bemko.

Thanks to the generous support of Binghamton University, I have had the time to complete this project. I owe a particular debt to the chairs of my department. Ricardo Laremont believed in this work from the beginning, endorsing my applications for external funding to take leave from teaching responsibilities. Michael West and Ravi Palat have been equally obliging. I began writing up this research with a Dr. Naula McGann Drescher Leave Award, made possible by the State of New York/United University Professions Affirmative Action/Diversity Committee. I have also benefited from the financial assistance provided by the dean's office of the Harpur College of Arts and Sciences during the period of my Fulbright award, the period when I was on Drescher award leave, and thereafter.

There are also less direct but nonetheless vital contributions that made this book possible. Kathleen Schwartzman helped me appreciate the value of puzzles and of eliminating barnacles. It is my hope that she will see her imprint on this work. Elisa Camiscioli introduced me to yoga, without which I am not so sure I would have finished this project. Annual visits to Lake George, with Nella VanDyke, Irenee Beattie, and their growing family have provided much-needed respite. The tasty meals and long dinner conversations at Common Fire nourished me. Seaside adventures with Hilary Abell, Paula Arnquist, Teresa Delgado, Caroline Isaacs, and Jenny Johnson and carousel rides with the Folans revived me. Exploring the old plazas from Santa Fe to Los Angeles with Susan Craig and Bear Ride kept me laughing. The days we spent with so many dear friends and family members who came to the Hudson Valley of New York in the summer of 2007 reminded me that there is, of course, much more to life than writing a book. Visits with Brian Philcox and Bonnie Buxton and their two energetic grandchildren injected some adventure into an otherwise all too sedate life. My parents have remained steadfast allies whose confidence in me has never wavered. Numerous wide-ranging conversations on Latin America with my father, Robert Gates, sharpened my argument and clarified what my contribution might be beyond Venezuela. One conversation in particular with my mother propelled me on the final push to write the book.

And finally, this book would surely not have happened were it not for my longtime partner and now spouse, Kate Griffith. At times a cheerleading enthusiast for my latest re-visioning of the book and at other times a discerning critic and editor, she has been a part of completing this book at every stage. It is for these, and many other reasons, that I dedicate this book to her.

LIST OF ACRONYMS

AD: Acción Democrática (Democratic Action)

CNE: Consejo Nacional Electoral (National Electoral Council)

CONINDUSTRIA: Confederación Venezolana de Industriales (Venezuelan Confederation of Industrialists)

COPEI: Comité de Organización Política Electoral Independiente (Independent Political Organizing Committee or the Social Christian Party)

CORDIPLAN: Oficina Central de Coordinación y Planificación (Central Office of Coordination and Planning)

CPI: Corruption Perception Index

CTV: Confederación de Trabajadores de Venezuela (Confederation of Venezuelan Workers)

FEDEAGRO: Confederación Nacional de Asociaciones de Productores Agropecuarios (National Confederation of Agricultural Producers)

FEDECAMARAS: Federación de Cámaras y Asociaciones de Comercio y Producción de Venezuela (Federation of Chambers of Commerce and Production of Venezuela)

FEDEINDUSTRIA: Federación de Cámaras y Asociaciones de Artesanos, Micros, Pequeños y Medianos Industrias y Empresas de Venezuela (The Venezuelan Federation of Chambers and Associations of Craftsmen, and Micro, Small, and Medium-sized Industrial Enterprises)

FIV: Fondo de Inversiones de Venezuela (Venezuelan Investment Fund)

FOGADE: Fondo de Garantía de Depósitos y Protección Bancaria (Government Guarantee and Financial Loan Fund)

JEF: Junta de Emergencia Financiera (Financial Emergency Committee)

MAS: Movimiento a Socialismo (Movement for Socialism)

MVR: Movimiento Quinta República (Movement for the Fifth Republic)

PCV: Partido Comunista de Venezuela (Venezuelan Communist Party)

PDVSA: Petróleos de Venezuela, S.A. (Venezuelan Oil Company, Inc.)

RECADI: Régimen de Cambios Diferenciales (Differential Exchange Rate Regime)

REDPOL: La Red Universitaria de Cultura Política (University Network of Political Culture)

TSSPP: Tribunal Superior de Salva Guarda del Patrimonio Público

URD: Unión Republicana Democrática (Democratic Republican Union)

PART I

◆

Introduction

1

·

THE UNLIKELY ELECTION OF

AN ANTI-NEOLIBERAL

I N 1998, Venezuelans elected a "staunchly anti-neoliberal" president (Ellner 2004, 11). During his ultimately victorious presidential campaign, Hugo Chávez, the former paratrooper and failed coup leader, "inveighed against neoliberalism and its tendency to exacerbate inequalities" (Ellner 2003, 16). He railed against neoliberalism's market-opening economic reforms, such as the privatizing of state-owned enterprises and the elimination of price controls, declaring such policies "savage" (Peña 1998). Instead, he called for a reversal of the many neoliberal policies introduced to Venezuela in the 1990s, for a partial moratorium on foreign debt payments (Cooper and Madigan 1998), and for an economy that "puts people first" (Gutkin 1998). He promised to "humanize Venezuela's economy" (Gutkin 1998) and "put an end to poverty" (Peña 1998).

Since Chávez won the Venezuelan presidency in 1998 with a decisive 56 percent of the vote, a "veritable left-wing tsunami" has hit Latin America (Castañeda

2006). As of January 2007, politicians who criticized neoliberal economic policies, prized "social justice and economic development" (Panizza 2005, 726), and upheld the political Left's traditional commitment of "confronting inequality" (Castañeda 2001) had swept to power in roughly two-thirds of Central and South America.[1] Interpreting this recent trend in Latin American politics depends on explaining why this tsunami first came ashore in Venezuela. This study offers an explanation for why it was Chávez in particular who emerged as the victor in Venezuela's 1998 presidential election.

Chávez's victory was, in some ways, not all that surprising. Venezuelans had already become disillusioned with their political establishment well before 1998. In particular, they lost their confidence in the two political parties, Acción Democrática (AD, or Democratic Action) and the Comité de Organización Política Electoral Independiente (COPEI, or the Independent Political Organizing Committee), which had dominated political life since the inception of Venezuela's democracy in 1958. By the early 1990s, voter abstention had risen (Buxton 2001, 59–73) and Venezuelans began to abandon the two establishment political parties. During the 1990s, many fewer Venezuelans voted for these two parties (Maingón and Sonntag 2000), let alone identified with them (Morgan 2007). Thus, in many respects, it is not surprising that a candidate like Chávez, one who vigorously denounced Venezuela's political establishment and promised to transform its political institutions and end corruption, would obtain widespread voter support.

Yet Chávez's victory was not a foregone conclusion. Chávez was not the only candidate who denounced Venezuela's widely discredited political establishment and rampant corruption. Indeed, in 1998, the vast majority of Venezuelans (94 percent) voted for political outsiders—candidates like Chávez who rejected the two historically dominant political parties. Less than half of 1 percent voted for the longtime leader of the historically more dominant establishment party (Coronil 2000).[2] Moreover, Chávez had to overcome the challenge of vocal opposition from the business community to win the election.

Soon after Chávez emerged as a serious contender for the presidency in March 1998, businesses of all sizes, industries, and nationalities mobilized and quickly set up meetings to strategize their response to a possible Chávez victory (Olivares 1998).[3] As one journalist put it bluntly, Chávez "scares Venezuela's business elite and foreign investors alike" (LaFranchi 1998). Even the business association that favored Chávez's protectionist economic policies saw him as a threat ("Fedeindustria" 1998). According to top Venezuelan economists, the prospect of a Chávez victory had led "people to take capital out of the country and stop investing in productive activities" because his victory would mean a return to "an interventionist economic program, based on controls and coercive regulations which would re-instigate state capitalism" (Márquez 1998). Major foreign investment firms also warned of a so-called "Chávez effect"— the negative effect his win would have on investment ("Investigarán" 1998).[4] As a representative of the British Chamber of Commerce in Caracas explained it, "People are afraid. Investments have ground to a halt while people wait to see what happens politically and economically" (quoted in Kovaleski 1998). A Merrill Lynch manager remarked ominously, "There is no question that investors are petrified of a Chávez victory. . . . It's impossible to imagine a positive spin to a Chávez win" (quoted in Colitt and Thurston 1998).

Business opposition should have made it more difficult for Chávez to win. Many believed that business opposition to an anti-neoliberal candidate like Chávez would arouse insurmountable fears among Latin American voters. Furthermore, business opposition should have made it more difficult for Chávez to secure the financial assistance critical to launching a viable presidential campaign. And yet, there were reports that some business executives had assisted Chávez. Venezuelan journalists noted, for instance, that one of Venezuela's few billionaires had arranged for his popular television network to give Chávez positive media coverage during the campaign (Santodomingo 1999, 36; Zapata 2000, 69). Major international newspapers even reported that this man had met with Chávez and had donated money to his campaign by mid-1998 ("Coup and Counter-coup" 2002; Marturet 2002; Romero 2002). During the campaign, Chávez also used a personal jet, which was reportedly on loan to him from the scion of one of Venezuela's oldest elite families (Zapata 2000, 132).

Thus, Chávez's victory in Venezuela's 1998 presidential elections poses two puzzles. First, how did Chávez overcome business opposition to win voter support so decisively? Second, how did Chávez manage to obtain assistance from a small coterie of well-heeled businesspeople willing to defy their community's vocal opposition to his candidacy? This study solves these two puzzles and thereby helps to explain the unlikely election of an anti-neoliberal candidate.

I concur with other scholars that we need to "rethink Venezuelan politics" by examining "important political and social actors that analysts have often excluded" (Ellner 2008, 13) in order to explain why Chávez won in 1998. Such scholars have contributed to this endeavor by rethinking both the state's relationship to Venezuela's Left and to its popular sectors (Ellner 2008) as well as Venezuela's state-military relations (Trinkunas 2005). But to explain how Chávez won both voter support and some business assistance despite generalized business opposition, and therefore to explain why Chávez emerged victorious in 1998, we must rethink Venezuela's state-business relations as well.

My research reveals that a previously overlooked facet of state-business relations in Venezuela, that of business prominence in politics, helps explain both puzzles. Many have discussed the ways that business in Venezuela depended economically on the Venezuelan state (Baptista 1997; Karl 1997; Naím 1984; Naím and Francés 1995). But no one has considered the political significance of the prominent, or visible, role many business leaders had within Venezuela's government throughout the political era of two-party dominance (1959–1998). This study shows how the combination of an economically dependent but politically prominent business community contributed to a political culture that discredited business and provoked some businesspeople to break away from the mainstream within the business community and assist Chávez. This new interpretation of state-business relations illuminates how Chávez defeated other candidates who, like Chávez, rejected the two parties that had dominated Venezuela's political establishment for forty years and who, like Chávez, promised to attack corruption. Chávez won voter support from those Venezuelans who had themselves lost confidence in the business community and who had likely been influenced by the business community's public association with corruption scandals and Venezuela's political establishment. Chávez gained business assistance from state-dependent business elites who feared losing access to the state if Chávez's main opponent won the election. It was, however, the political prominence of business, not just its state dependence, that stimulated these fears. This book sheds light on the conditions that offer fertile ground for anti-neoliberal electoral victories.

Two Puzzles Presented by Business Opposition

Business opposition to Chávez in 1998 represented one of the main challenges he had to overcome to win the presidential election. This challenge was particularly formidable because it should have made it more difficult for him to win two key ingredients of a successful election. Business opposition should have made it difficult for him to win both widespread voter support and some financial assistance from Venezuela's business elite. Thus, Chávez's victory, despite business opposition, poses both a "voter puzzle" and a "business assistance puzzle."

The Puzzle of Widespread Voter Support

Chávez's ability to win support from voters seemed unlikely, according to leaders of Latin America's Left and Venezuela's own historical experience with leftist candidates. In the wake of the Soviet Union's implosion in 1989 and the defeat of Nicaragua's Sandinistas in 1990, Mexican intellectual Jorge Castañeda called on Latin America's Left to devise "a totally new relationship with the private sector, . . . removed from the baiting and hostility of the traditional left" (Castañeda 1990, 482). The surprise electoral defeat of the Sandinistas' ten-year experiment with anti-neoliberal and anti-imperialist politics in the 1990 presidential elections forced many in Latin America's Left to recognize that even incumbent leftists could lose voter support when faced with opposition from domestic and foreign business elites (Harnecker 1999).[5]

Castañeda and others argued that leftist candidates should avoid provoking business opposition, in part, because business opposition might arouse among voters an insurmountable fear of leftist candidates. Castañeda cautioned, "If you go too far, they [the capitalists] will just decamp. Either there will be capital flight . . . or they'll overthrow the government" (Castañeda 2001, 32). In making this argument, Castañeda conjured the ghost of Chile's Salvador Allende, a democratically elected socialist party leader, and his short-lived presidency (1970–1973). Allende nationalized major industries such as copper, steel, and coal, and introduced price freezes and wage increases. Allende's policies, similar to those pursued by other leftist governments, "produced unsustainable bursts of growth followed by recession and rising inflation, harming the poor and destabilizing the governments" (Panizza 2005, 727). His presidency came to an uneremonious end in one of the region's bloodiest military coups just three years after it started and was followed by two decades of repressive military rule. Candidates from the Left who incite business opposition have since struggled to quell fears that their candidacies would result in similar economic turmoil or political repression. With his implicit reference to Allende,

Castañeda warned that the Left could win elections only if they built an alliance with the political Center in general (Castañeda 1990, 1993) and with sympathetic parts of the business community in particular.[6] He anticipated that certain domestic businesses, such as those that depend largely on the domestic market and that might be hurt by neoliberal economic policies (also referred to as the progressive bourgeoisie), would be sympathetic to such an alliance (Castañeda 1993).[7]

Many of the presidential candidates contributing to the "left-wing tsunami" since the 1990s appeared to confirm the wisdom of Castañeda's formula for success (Castañeda 2006). For example, Luiz Inácio "Lula" da Silva, a former union leader, won Brazil's presidency in 2002 after he issued his famous "Letter to the Brazilian People." In it, Lula reassured investors and his supporters that he would comply with the International Monetary Fund conditions of maintaining a budget surplus. Tabaré Vázquez, a former oncologist who represented a coalition of left-wing parties, won Uruguay's presidency in 2004 after he promised to install a moderate economist as finance minister (Panizza 2005, 725). Scholars thus concluded that moderate tendencies seemed to have enabled most of these left-of-center candidates to win over large swaths of the middle class and "even business, without whom it is difficult to gain office, let alone govern effectively" (Panizza 2005, 726). Analysts note approvingly that these leftists have been "only too aware that a radical discourse can frighten investors, provoke a catastrophic run on the currency, and lead to capital flight" and are therefore aware that they must "court . . . the financial markets" (Panizza 2005, 725). From the outset, these leftist presidents generally built pragmatic governing coalitions with parties to their right and sought to "bend and mould" to Washington's neoliberal consensus rather than attempt to construct alternative economic projects (Panizza 2005, 729).

Chávez's victory seems all the more curious given that Venezuela's Left had historically fared poorly in the face of strong business opposition. The first major foray of Venezuela's Left into building a popular basis for political power, that of forming Acción Democrática in 1941, provoked fear and uncertainty from business elites. The AD was like other populist parties in the region during the early twentieth century in that it employed "readily identifiable symbols" to appeal directly to the masses (Ellner 1999, 128) and built a multiclass party as a basis for governing through winning elections (Conniff 1999, 7, 193).

But, AD "stood to the left of most Latin American populist parties in the 1940s" (Ellner 1999, 132) as the only populist party with leaders who identified with communism and its commitment to long-term socioeconomic transformation.[8] It was also only one of two populist parties in Latin America that implemented land reform along with the more typical populist policies introducing labor rights (Collier and Collier 1991). Not surprisingly, then, AD provoked a fierce countermobilization in the form of a new conservative party (COPEI) and a military coup in 1948. During the AD's short three-year term in the 1940s, Venezuela's business community vociferously opposed AD's implementation of progressive labor legislation and proved indifferent to AD's plea for support to fend off the military intervention (Ellner 1999, 124–25; Moncada 1985).

Just as the overthrow of Allende cast a shadow over leftists in Chile, the overthrow of AD's Rómulo Gallegos in 1948 "left an indelible impression on . . . AD leaders" and Venezuela's Left more generally (Ellner 1999, 132). Even though the Venezuelan Communist Party (Partido Comunista de Venezuela or PCV) was Venezuela's fourth-largest party in 1959 and had played a heroic role in opposing the dictatorship, the political leaders who brokered Venezuela's transition to democracy in 1958 excluded the PCV (Karl 1987; Peeler 1992). The AD party leaders who convened the 1958 negotiations excluded the PCV, even as they included leaders from the two conservative parties, COPEI and the Unión Republicana Democrática (URD, or Democratic Republican Union), Catholic Church leaders, a traditional constituency of the elites, and leaders of the Venezuelan business community (Ellner 1999, 133; Myers 2004, 15).[9] The first post-1958 presidency sought to marginalize the PCV members of congress (representing 10 percent of the 1958 congress) by redirecting spending—away from PCV districts and toward COPEI districts (Myers 2004, 22). The first two presidencies of Venezuela's nascent democracy deployed the military to repress a Left-led insurgency that emerged in the face of the PCV's exclusion and marginalization.[10]

Venezuela's Left, similar to the Left elsewhere in Latin America, learned that it would have to moderate its positions if it hoped to be included in the formal political arena and win elections. Most former insurgents accepted amnesty when the government offered it to them in the early 1970s, and they subsequently formed a new, more moderate political party, the Movimiento a Socialismo (MAS, or Movement for Socialism).[11] This strategy appeared to pay off. MAS consistently won an important minority voice within Venezuela's national legislature, and one of MAS's leaders even ascended to a powerful cabinet-level position in the 1990s.

Thus, according to the received wisdom of the Left in Venezuela and across Latin America, Chávez was just the kind of leftist candidate who was unlikely to win widespread voter support from Venezuelans: he was a staunch anti-neoliberal who also faced stiff opposition from business. Because Chávez was a vociferous critic of the dominant economic policy in the region, we might expect voters to be particularly attuned to the way business reacted to his candidacy. The fact that business so vocally opposed him should have undermined voter confidence in his ability to govern without provoking economic distress. However, until now scholars have not squarely addressed how Chávez won widespread voter support in the face of considerable business opposition—they have not addressed the "voter puzzle" related to his victory.

The Puzzle of Assistance from Some Business Elites

It is equally hard to imagine how Chávez could have become a viable candidate for the presidency without significant financial assistance. Ever since the dawn of mass media in the 1970s, expensive media campaigns have become crucial to successful presidential campaigning in Venezuela (Alvarez 1995) and throughout Latin America (Weyland 1998). The increased importance of such campaigns has placed much greater pressure on candidates to attract financial assistance from business elites or favors from media tycoons. Venezuela's political leaders, particularly those less well known or who could not rely on party patrons, cultivated business patrons to finance their campaigns and political staffing (Coppedge 1999, 20). Thus, it is difficult to imagine how Chávez could have persuaded the public that he was a viable candidate without assistance from private media outlets. Chávez's ascent in the polls even corresponds to the positive media coverage he gained in the spring of 1998. His projected percentage of the vote increased from 30 percent in March to 41 percent in June (Buxton 2001, 200), a shift that occurred only after he had received positive attention in the news.

Business opposition should have made it even more difficult for Chávez to recruit major donors. Recent research conducted on campaign financing in Latin America confirms this conventional wisdom. It shows that left-leaning candidates, such as those who promise social justice and economic development and are critical of neoliberal policies, have greater difficulty obtaining business assistance (Samuels 2001). We thus naturally expect business to assist right-leaning politicians: those who favor fewer regulations on the private sector, more restrictions on unions, lower taxes, constrained wages, and reduced government spending on social services. As a staunch anti-neoliberal, Chávez seemed unlikely to secure such assistance, particularly in light of the evident opposition to his candidacy from business.

Nevertheless, by most accounts Chávez did in fact obtain business assistance, even without softening his critique of neoliberalism. His ability to secure some business assistance was particularly surprising given that many of those who reportedly assisted him during the campaign quickly abandoned him after the election. Thus far, however, business assistance to Chávez has been investigated by only a few journalists (Santodomingo 1999; Zapata 2000) and mentioned in passing by a few scholars (Hellinger 2003, 47; Ortiz 2004, 85). My own research represents the first systematic analysis of business assistance for Chávez. In this study, I extend my prior research (Gates 2007) and more fully account for the "business assistance puzzle" related to Chávez's victory.

Analyzing a Puzzle-Driven Case Study

Skeptics of case studies have claimed that the theoretical contributions of such studies are necessarily limited to generating hypotheses that must be tested in other cases to verify their generalizability (King, Keohane, and Verba 1994; Smelser 1976). These claims, however, have been convincingly refuted by others (e.g., Rueschemeyer 2003), who point out the widely recognized theoretical contributions of numerous single case studies, such as E. P. Thompson's (1964) study of the English working class. While single case studies may indeed be limited in their ability to verify the generalizability of a theory, case selection criteria and analytic strategies such as those employed here enable case studies to make theoretical contributions that other methods of research may even inhibit.

This particular case study is puzzle driven. In other words, it examines an unlikely case of a broader phenomenon: the recent electoral success of anti-neoliberal presidential candidates. Unlikely, deviant, or negative cases are the "ones in which a theoretically predicted outcome did not occur" (Emigh 1997, 665). Scholars widely recognize the value of resolving the puzzles that such cases present for extant theory (Emigh 1997; Mahoney 2000; Rueschemeyer 2003, 311; Seawright and Gerring 2008).[12] Thus, by explaining an unlikely case of anti-neoliberal victory—one that presents two puzzles—this study can shed new light on why anti-neoliberal candidates win elections.

I developed a broader interpretive framework for analyzing this unlikely case in part through interviews. During ten months of field research in Caracas, I interviewed fifty individuals (listed in appendix A by their qualifications). They included key members of Venezuela's business elite, insiders from the Chávez campaign in 1998, and individuals knowledgeable about Venezuelan corruption. The interviews with business elites included nearly all past presidents of Venezuela's peak business association, a critical mass of executives from Venezuela's biggest conglomerates, and influential former leaders in several of Venezuela's industry-specific, or sectoral, business associations. While the twenty-nine interviews with business executives are not the principal empirical basis of this study, they informed the thrust of my argument and were often helpful in securing other data or in confirming information obtained elsewhere.

While the broad goal here is to "interpret" or explain the unlikely outcome in this case, I use variable-oriented analyses to refine the argument and engage in a dialogue with alternative accounts. Variable-oriented analyses evaluate the relationship between variables within the case as they subdivide the case into subunits of analysis. The analytic strategy of combining a primarily case-oriented investigation with variable-oriented analyses permits a more rigorous assessment of competing theories (Ragin 1987, 69–84). For example, to analyze the sources of widespread voter support for Chávez, I conducted statistical analyses of a national opinion poll taken immediately prior to the presidential elections in 1998. The national opinion poll disaggregates the case into the subunits of individual respondents to the survey. Breaking up the case into these subunits makes it possible to test the relative importance of the sentiment that likely compelled people to favor Chávez versus those factors that others predicted would shape a voter's support for Chávez.

I also constructed several data sets that made it possible to further subdivide the case and assess relationships between variables within the case. For example, to analyze the historical association of business with corruption, I coded and analyzed more than three hundred Venezuelan corruption scandals (cases of corruption that received widespread media attention) by the type of actors implicated. This analysis represents the first systematic study of Venezuelan corruption scandals that spans the entire period of two-party dominance (1959–1998). (I describe how I collected and coded these scandals in appendix B.) Similarly, to analyze the historical association of business with the political establishment, I assembled an original database of the individual professional biographies of political leaders. The database includes biographies of nearly all economic cabinet members and a sample of federal legislators, identified as businesspeople, during the era of two-party dominance from 1959 to 1998. (Appendix C describes how I constructed the sample of ministers and federal legislators, how I collected their biographies, and how I coded each biography.) The sources included political dictionaries, biographical profiles published in newspapers, curriculum vitae, and interviews with business elites. The biographies enabled me to code each of the 162 economic cabinet posts and the sample of 195 legislative posts according to whether they were occupied by former business executives. When they were, it constituted an instance of business prominence in the political establishment. These biographies made it possible to disaggregate the case into subunits of individual political leaders. Similarly, to analyze the political calculus of the individual business elites who reportedly assisted Chávez, I identified a list of potential individual contributors. I then coded them according to their various potential rationales for assisting Chávez (as described in appendix D).

With these data sets I can evaluate prior accounts of Chávez's election as well as my proposed resolution to the puzzles. These evaluations reveal the need to re-specify prior approaches and support a new interpretation of this unlikely case of victory by an anti-neoliberal presidential candidate.

2

•

EXPLAINING CHÁVEZ'S ELECTION

WE CANNOT understand why Chávez won the 1998 presidential election in Venezuela without appreciating the factors that created an opening for candidates who, like Chávez, campaigned as political outsiders. Indeed, most scholars explaining the results of that year's presidential election focused on this issue. They have focused, that is, on why Venezuelans lost confidence in their two-party political establishment. Their explanations for the growing disillusionment with the political establishment can be grouped into three main theses: (1) the corruption thesis, (2) the failed institutions thesis, and (3) the social polarization thesis. Each thesis sheds light on why Venezuelans elected Chávez because each identifies factors that explain why Venezuelans voted against the political establishment.

Nonetheless, each thesis is also limited in its ability to explain why Venezuelans chose Chávez over other candidates who campaigned as political outsiders. None can fully answer this crucial question because none address how Chávez overcame a formidable obstacle: business opposition. Business opposition should have made it more difficult for Chávez both to win voter support and to obtain assistance from members of Venezuela's business elite. In short, business opposition made it unlikely that Chávez, an anti-neoliberal candidate, would win. But prior research has not addressed how Chávez overcame business opposition to win either voter support or assistance from some members of Venezuela's business elite. As a result, prior scholarship can not fully explain why Chávez defeated similar candidates. I propose an alternative argument that addresses both puzzles posed by Chávez's victory despite business opposition: the voter puzzle and the business assistance puzzle.

Contributions and Limits of Prior Research on Chávez's Election

To explain why Chávez won the presidential election in 1998, scholars most often cite one of the three main theses on why Venezuelans became disillusioned with what had seemed to be the region's model democracy. In short, these scholars sought first and foremost to explain why Venezuelans lost confidence in their political establishment—its leaders and its main organizations. Scholars have shown that widespread corruption, rigid political institutions, and neoliberal economic reforms eroded the public's confidence in Venezuela's political establishment prior to 1998. Such research helps us understand why there was a political opening in 1998 for candidates who disassociated themselves from Venezuela's traditional political leadership and its organizations. These scholars have thus attributed Chávez's victory to growing intolerance of corruption, rising frustration with Venezuela's failed political institutions, and mounting disillusionment with the neoliberal reforms introduced during the 1990s. Nevertheless, each of these theses is limited in its ability to fully explain why it was Chávez who emerged as the victor.

The Corruption Thesis

Many observers believe that the public's confidence in Venezuela's political establishment declined significantly and that public sympathy for political candidates not affiliated with the dominant political parties thus increased, "primarily because of the widespread perception of corruption" (Navarro 1994, 8). This view permeated Venezuela's media (Golden 1992; Olmos 1992b) and was advanced by pundits ("Impatience" 1992) and scholars alike throughout the 1990s (Constable 1992; Little 1996; Subero 2004). It is a view so widely held that it "constitutes the common sense explanation of the paradox" of the public's disillusionment with what was once Latin America's most celebrated democracy (Navarro 1994, 8).[1] There is ample evidence to support this argument, which I refer to as the corruption thesis.

First, experts on corruption have corroborated the premise of the thesis that corruption plagued Venezuela's two-party political establishment. Although there are no direct measures of the level of experience Venezuelans had with corruption before the 1998 election, there are some earlier measures based on expert opinion. For example, the international nongovernmental organization Transparency International compiles data derived from expert opinion on corruption around the world in its Corruption Perception Index (CPI). It began to assess the level of corruption in Venezuela in 1980. Out of 149 countries ranked by Transparency International's CPI between the years 1980 and 1985, Venezuela was only the 138th most transparent.[2] This position in the international ranking of corruption shows that most other countries in the survey were deemed less corrupt than Venezuela. Since then, Venezuela's CPI score and its related international ranking in perceived level of corruption has worsened.[3] By the mid-1990s, the percentage of nations rated "less corrupt" than Venezuela increased from 79 to 93 percent.[4]

Second, polls have affirmed the reasoning behind the corruption thesis. They reveal that the public perception of corruption as rampant went hand in hand with declining confidence in the political establishment. Although the public's confidence in the political establishment began to deteriorate in the 1970s (Baloyra 1986), it was not until the 1980s that "the government was not only seen as inefficient . . . [but] was also believed to be corrupt" (Templeton 1995, 90).[5] The turning point in the public's perceptions of corruption and support for Venezuela's political establishment seems to be 1983, which was the year of the first major currency devaluation.[6] Then, in 1989, the same year that Venezuelans participated in the region's most widespread protests of neoliberal reforms, corruption became "more than a single issue . . . [it] became a catch-all means of interpreting a wide range of problems, especially the economic crisis" (Romero 1997, 20). By 1992, Venezuelans viewed corruption as their country's number-one problem (Mine 1992; "Venezuela: Ex-president" 1992), and they supported drastic actions to attack corruption. Polls revealed broad support for junior military officers, including Chávez, who twice attempted to take over Venezuela's presidential palace in 1992 (on February 4 and again on November 27) on the grounds that no other action would eradicate corruption (Constable 1992; Olmos 1992a, 1992b). Polls also documented the public's overwhelming sympathy in 1993 with the successful campaign to remove Venezuela's once-popular president because of a number of corruption allegations. By 1995, nearly all Venezuelans (94 percent) thought that there would be more resources for everyone in society if corruption were eliminated (Romero 1997, 21). Furthermore, polls confirmed that Venezuelans increasingly blamed corruption for myriad economic and political crises.[7]

Third, political trends immediately prior to 1998 confirmed that discontent with corruption had become an important factor in the political preferences of Venezuelans. By the late 1980s, politicians from nontraditional political parties had begun to win elections by campaigning on anti-corruption platforms. For example, third-party candidates who ran on anti-corruption platforms unexpectedly won three governorships in 1989 ("Fewer Than Half" 1989). A politician who vowed to rid the country of both corruption and the traditional two-party political system won the presidency in 1993. Although the candidate elected president in 1993 had been one of the founders of the two-party system, he sought to distance himself from the political establishment by decrying corruption, even within his own former party. Polls conducted just after the presidential elections in December 1993 confirm that corruption was one of two top issues for voters in that election (Romero 1997, 22).

The apparent rise in corruption, the mounting public outrage at corruption, and the political events in the 1990s linked to this outrage together represent compelling evidence in support of the corruption thesis. Clearly, as posited by the corruption thesis, the public's growing preoccupation with corruption eroded public support for Venezuela's two-party political establishment. Corruption was, therefore, a critical factor in Chávez's electoral victory in 1998.

Nevertheless, the corruption thesis is limited in its ability to explain why Venezuelans chose Chávez in particular. According to the corruption thesis, Chávez garnered support from those who were principally concerned with rampant corruption within Venezuela's political establishment. The corruption thesis implies, then, that Venezuelans supported Chávez because they believed he would be the one most likely to address corruption. However, it is not obvious why the public would believe this, given that all of the leading candidates promised to rid the country of corruption and claimed to be political outsiders (Molina 2002, 231). Moreover, it is not obvious why the public would prefer the one anti-corruption candidate whom business opposed. As stated previously, business opposition should have made Venezuelans less likely to favor Chávez's anti-neoliberal candidacy.

The corruption thesis, however, represents just one of the three main arguments for why Venezuelans became disillusioned with their political establishment. After Venezuela's presidential election in 1998, a flurry of scholarship sought to go beyond the corruption thesis to explain the "unraveling of representative democracy" (McCoy and Myers 2004b) or "Venezuela's political difficulties" (Ellner 2003, 18) and, by extension, voter support for Chávez. Much of this scholarship coalesced around a common narrative that I refer to as the failed institutions thesis.[8]

The Failed Institutions Thesis

The failed institutions thesis posits that the public's confidence in Venezuela's political establishment (both its leaders and its organizations) declined principally because vast swaths of Venezuelan society felt excluded from the political process.[9] According to this view, Chávez's victory was a by-product of the voters' generalized frustration with the political establishment. This view is exemplified in the scholarship of Julia Buxton, who wrote that Chávez's victory "should more rightly be viewed as a rejection of the old system rather than a positive endorsement of the new Bolivarian vision" (Buxton 2001, 2). Similarly, Jennifer McCoy sums up the collective take of her coauthors, stating that Venezuelans "viewed their leaders as increasingly unresponsive and isolated. They looked elsewhere for leadership, and with the election of . . . Chávez . . . they sealed their rejection of Punto Fijo [Venezuela's two-party] representative democracy" (McCoy 2004, 263).

For scholars contributing to the failed institutions thesis, the public's preoccupation with corruption undoubtedly contributed, although it cannot fully explain the public's disillusionment with Venezuela's two-party political establishment. Such scholars therefore incorporate the corruption thesis in various ways. Many assert that public perceptions of rampant corruption contributed to the generally negative perception of the incumbent government and the traditional parties (Morgan 2007, 88). They then extend this view to explain why Venezuelans chose Chávez. For example, McCoy writes that Venezuelans, in selecting Chávez, "rejected all presidential candidates with ties to the traditional parties and voted for a leader who promised to eliminate the old parties, to end corruption, and to rewrite the constitutional rules to bring a new political and economic order to Venezuela"; they thus chose a leader who espoused "purging the country of what he saw as debilitating and pervasive corruption" (McCoy 1999, 66). Some scholars, though, explicitly share the premise of the corruption thesis, arguing that actual corruption contributed to general dissatisfaction with the political establishment (Buxton 2001, 30) or that "the instrumentations of inadequate policies, clientelism, and corruption" eroded party loyalty (Molina 2002, 244). Still others merely use the evidence amassed by corruption thesis scholars, such as the fact that Venezuelans increasingly viewed the two parties as "stifling and corrupting democracy" (Coppedge 1994b), as an indicator of the public's disillusionment with the political establishment.

Regardless, the main thrust of these scholars' research program has been to explain how the structure of Venezuela's political institutions undermined the public's support for the country's political establishment overall. With extensive research, scholars demonstrate the various ways that Venezuela's political institutions during the era of two-party dominance were overly rigid and exclusionary (Crisp 1996; McCoy and Myers 2004a, 7). These institutions, they show, created incentives for elected officials to value party loyalty over representation (Crisp 2000, 11) and to disregard their constituents (Buxton 2001, 222; Coppedge 1994b; Morgan 2005). These rigid political institutions, therefore, failed to provide ade-quate representation for a host of new political actors who emerged from major sociodemographic transformations in Venezuelan society during the 1980s and 1990s (Coppedge 1994a; Crisp 2000; Crisp and Levine 1998; Crisp, Levine, and Rey 1995). Specifically, they failed to represent societal interests (Morgan 2007), including the urban poor (Buxton 2001, 222; Buxton 2003; Canache 2004), intellectuals (Hillman 2004), an emergent civil society (Salamanca 2004), and junior military officers (Aguero 1995; Norden 1996; Trinkunas 2004).[10] It is these failed institutions, then, that they contend led voters in 1998 to reject candidates in any way associated with Venezuela's political establishment.

This scholarship helps us understand why Venezuelans so decisively rejected both parties and the ancillary political institutions that had anchored their stable democratic political system for nearly forty years. It details numerous ways that these political institutions contributed to their own demise by failing to satisfy a growing number of new constituencies. Nonetheless, this perspective cannot fully explain why voters chose Chávez over other candidates in 1998. True, Chávez formed a new political organization to guide his presidential bid, which defined itself in name and form as distinct from Venezuela's political establishment. The name of his new group, the Movimiento Quinta República (MVR, or Movement for the Fifth Republic), implied that his presidency would usher in political change so dramatic that it would constitute a new republic. The form of this new entity, a movement rather than a political party, conveyed his disdain for the political parties that were so intimately associated with the political establishment. It is also true that Chávez promised to transform Venezuela's political institutions via a means that would bypass existing legislators. He called for a constituent assembly to compose a new constitution.

Nonetheless, Chávez was not the only one campaigning as a political outsider in 1998 (Molina 2002, 231). All the main contenders in the 1998 presidential race identified as political outsiders. The early front-runner of the presidential field, Irene Sáez, was like Chávez in that she did not have previous electoral experience. Sáez, a former beauty queen, formed her own self-named IRENE Party to launch her candidacy. Like Chávez, she campaigned on a platform against corruption and for political change. Chávez's other leading opponent, Henrique Salas Römer, was yet "another charismatic and independent leader" (Molina 2004, 170). By July 1998, Salas Römer was the presidential candidate with the best chance of defeating Chávez. At that point, polls projected Salas Römer would win 20 percent of the vote, compared to a projected 41 percent for Chávez (Buxton 2001, 200). Like Sáez and Chávez, Salas Römer had also formed a new party, Proyecto Venezuela, to launch his presidential bid. As a leading business consultant explained, "The 1998 elections were elections about political rupture . . . [since] the two principal candidates [Chávez and Salas Römer] were both anti-system" (Interview 46, 4).

Moreover, in many respects, Salas Römer should have been a more viable candidate than Chávez. After all, Salas Römer had already twice been elected governor of Carabobo, Venezuela's second most important industrial state, and he had campaigned both times as a political independent and anti-corruption crusader. Chávez, in contrast, was the son of provincial schoolteachers (Gott 2005, 25–27). He had ascended to the rank of lieutenant colonel in Venezuela's military before he led a failed coup attempt in 1992 against a democratically elected president. He then spent two years in jail for his actions. Chávez's run for president in 1998 was his first foray into electoral politics.

Some speculate that Salas Römer only "presented an image of change" while Chávez "appeared as the more radical opposition alternative" (Molina 2002, 236) because Salas Römer accepted endorsements by the two traditional political parties right before the election (Molina 2002, 235). But Chávez's status as a political outsider was not unequivocal either. He accepted the official endorsement of parties that had participated in Venezuela's democratic system previously, although these were on the political Left, such as the Venezuelan Communist Party (PCV) and the Movement for Socialism (MAS). A former leader of MAS had even been a prominent member of the presidential cabinet in the then very unpopular outgoing government of Rafael Caldera. Furthermore, prominent political leaders who had been elected officials were active in key positions in Chávez's MVR.[11] Thus, some have argued that Salas Römer's so-called "'crisis of association' was equally applicable to Hugo Chávez" (Buxton 2001, 209).

Additionally, it is not clear that the last-minute endorsements accepted by Chávez's leading opponent actually hurt him (Christiansen 2000). Salas Römer reluctantly accepted the endorsement of the two traditional parties on November 30, two weeks before the election. But polls show that Salas Römer's projected vote tally went up from 26 percent on November 25 to 30 percent on the day after the endorsement, December 1. In the end, Salas Römer received an even greater share of the vote than projected before the endorsement, winning 40 percent (Buxton 2001, 207). Even if the endorsements cost Salas Römer some votes, they cannot fully explain why Chávez held and sustained a commanding lead over Salas Römer long before the two traditional parties endorsed Salas Römer (Koeneke R. 2000; Maingón 1999).

Thus, from a "failed institutions" perspective, it is not obvious why Chávez would have emerged as the decisive victor from this crowded field of political outsiders who similarly campaigned against corruption. While his promise to call for a constituent assembly no doubt appealed to those frustrated with the existing political establishment (Buxton 2003, 124), we must still understand why voters trusted Chávez more than others to carry out this political reform. In particular, we must explain why they believed that the anti-establishment candidate with powerful detractors in the business community would be able to carry out this plan. After all, we would expect such opposition to make voters fearful that his election would jolt the country into a downward spiral of economic and political chaos. I concur with others who urge us to more "carefully examine the sources of popular frustration" (Ellner 2003, 20) in order to determine why Chávez, in particular, emerged victorious in 1998. In an effort to do so, critics of the failed institutions thesis have developed the social polarization thesis.

The Social Polarization Thesis

The social polarization thesis, like the other two theses, examines why the public became so frustrated with Venezuela's political establishment. It contends that the public's growing frustration with the political establishment stemmed from the apparent indifference of political leaders to Venezuela's deepening social polarization beginning in the 1980s. This ascendant interpretation of the public's disillusionment incorporates some elements of the failed institutions thesis. For example, social polarization proponents acknowledge that Venezuela's political institutions failed to "serve as the fulcrum of popular political representation" (Roberts 2003b, 58). They differ, however, in their interpretation of the primary concerns that the public had with the political establishment and hence the primary concerns that led voters to choose Chávez in 1998.

Social polarization scholars contend that economic, not just political, issues preoccupied Venezuelans. They dispute the implication of the failed institutions perspective that the primary source of frustration with the political establishment was its exclusive political institutions. Instead, they argue that the problem was the political establishment's failure to curtail the onset of economic crisis in the 1980s and to avoid social polarization thereafter (Ellner 2003, 17). They point to the emergence of class-based political movements as indicative of this frustration. For decades, Venezuela conformed to the region's tendency of subverting class differences through multiclass parties (Myers 1998). In the 1990s, however, new movements, including Chávez's MVR and the labor union–based Causa R (Buxton 2001, 133–65; Hellinger 2003), mobilized economically marginalized populations around their class-based economic concerns. Social polarization scholars trace this re-politicization of class to the growing polarization of Venezuelan society.

According to these scholars, several socioeconomic trends that began in the 1980s converged to divide Venezuelan society and, hence, to create a social base for re-politicizing class. Indeed, Venezuela's debt crisis and the volatility in oil prices in the 1980s hurt the nation's economy. Plummeting oil prices in 1998 only accelerated these trends and their consequences for average Venezuelans (Buxton 2003, 121–22). By the 1990s, the social effects of this spiral included a 20 percent decrease in per capita gross domestic product (Crisp 2000, 175), a decline by nearly two-thirds in the purchasing power of the minimum wage, and a dramatic increase in poverty rates, from 36 percent in 1984 to 66 percent in 1995 (Roberts 2003b, 59). Neoliberal economic reforms, which eviscerated social spending and undermined productive capacity in agriculture and domestic manufacturing, compounded these effects (Roberts 2003b, 60). Some even argue that these reforms produced the world's sharpest increase in inequality (Naím 2001). For social polarization scholars, these trends presented the objective conditions that are ideal for class-politicizing movements (Roberts 2003b, 58–60).

Polls corroborate the implication of the social polarization thesis: that social polarization prompted the re-politicization of class. Venezuelans did indeed become ever gloomier about their own circumstances and the state of the economy as their society became increasingly unequal. Polls indicate that since the economic difficulties of the 1980s, "at least one-third of the population has always considered itself to be worse off than the year before" (Templeton 1995, 81). Furthermore, polls demonstrate that after Venezuela sank into a recession in 1997, respondents' negative economic assessments of their own circumstances and of the national economy intensified (Weyland 2003, 828).

Polls also confirm social polarization scholars' interpretation of the policy issues driving these movements. These scholars interpret the emergence of the new class-politicizing movements as evidence that economically marginalized members of Venezuelan society had largely disagreed with the political establishment's decision to implement neoliberal economic policies during the 1990s (Ellner 2003, 17; Roberts 2003b, 55). These scholars argue that the economically marginalized popular classes were critical of neoliberal reforms (Roberts 2003b, 64) and blamed the political establishment for permitting Venezuela to remain dependent on oil exports (Ellner 2003, 19). The marginalized popular classes, they posit, felt abandoned by their leaders, especially those on the Left, who had failed to resist neoliberal reforms and defend interventionist policies (Ellner 2003, 19; 2008, 9).[12] As Kenneth Roberts puts it, "The imposition of a strict neoliberal structural adjustment package in 1989 . . . ruptured both the programmatic consensus and the social pacts that had bound diverse constituencies to the established parties" (Roberts 2003b, 58). This interpretation was in line with earlier predictions (Hellinger 1984, 1991). Ironically, the nationalization of oil in 1976 would, they speculated, make it more difficult for political leaders to deflect blame for economic problems onto foreign oil companies. Instead, nationalization, they predicted, would force Venezuelans to look inward for the cause of their subsequent economic difficulties.

Pre-1998 polls confirm this claim. Venezuelans became increasingly dissatisfied with the political establishment's economic policies. In the mid-1990s, after the government had sought to liberalize trade and had privatized several major state-owned enterprises, only about a quarter of Venezuelans endorsed economic liberalization (Buxton 2001, 65). Opposition to privatizing the largest state-run enterprise, the oil industry, was particularly strong. In one study, 92 percent of respondents thought the oil industry should not be privatized (Molina 2002, 239). Instead, in the 1990s, most Venezuelans still favored state interventionism (Romero 1997, 21; Templeton 1995, 102–5). In the year leading up to the 1998 election, when oil prices again declined, Venezuelans became even less supportive of the government's economic policy, including its neoliberal policy of opening the oil industry to more private and foreign investment (Buxton 2003, 122).

The social polarization thesis offers important insight into the origins of declining public support for Venezuela's political establishment and, therefore, the social processes that paved the way for Chávez to win the 1998 election. In addition, unlike both the corruption and failed institutions theses, the social polarization thesis provides a powerful rationale for why Venezuelans might have preferred Chávez over the other candidates. As the only candidate with an anti-neoliberal policy position, Chávez could attract popular support from the growing ranks of Venezuela's economically marginalized, who were disillusioned with the establishment's decision to implement neoliberal economic reforms in the 1990s. This argument takes an important step toward explaining why Chávez, in particular, emerged as the winner in the presidential contest of 1998.

Nonetheless, a review of Latin America's most recent history raises questions about some of the underlying assumptions of this argument. For example, most Latin American nations introduced neoliberal economic reforms earlier than Venezuela and subsequently experienced intensifying poverty, inequality, and economic informalization, which in many instances were worse than Venezuela's. Even so, anti-neoliberal candidates failed to galvanize economically marginalized voters and win elections until the late 1990s, and these electoral successes did not necessarily occur in the countries that experienced the region's deepest social polarization. Mexicans, for example, have yet to elect an anti-neoliberal president, even though their government adopted one of the region's earliest and most comprehensive neoliberal projects in the 1980s. These reforms deepened social inequality, undermined union power (Gates 2001), lowered Mexican wages overall (Salas 2006), and dramatically expanded the ranks of Mexicans living in poverty (Jordan and Sullivan 2003; Public Citizen's Global Trade Watch 2006).

Furthermore, as many on Latin America's Left acknowledge, economic hard times have not always produced electoral victories for leftists nor have economically deprived populations always embraced the Left. In the 1990s, Latin America's Left largely concurred that the region's "objective conditions" of social polarization were those that had historically created opportunities for it to gain political power (Carr and Ellner 1993; Castañeda 1990, 485; Harnecker 2001, 87–89). But leftists also recognized that these objective conditions were merely conducive to winning elections and that leftist candidates would still have to realize the "subjective transformation" of their potential social base (Harnecker 2001, 87–89). They conceded that left-leaning candidates, particularly those like Chávez who were staunchly anti-neoliberal, would have to overcome a number of liabilities if they were to win elections. Many believed that business opposition constituted a chief liability for anti-neoliberal candidates.

Since scholars developing the social polarization thesis, like those contributing to both the corruption and failed institutions theses, have thus far not addressed how Chávez overcame business opposition, I offer my own argument below. It entails explaining how he won both voter support (the voter puzzle) and financial assistance from a few business elites (the business assistance puzzle).

Solving the Voter Puzzle

My solution to the voter puzzle draws on insights from all three theses discussed above. However, it amends, re-specifies, and extends these theses in new ways.

The Anti-business Thesis

I propose that Chávez won widespread support because he attracted voters who themselves lacked confidence in business. In other words, Chávez's supporters might have been what I refer to as "anti-business voters." Supporting a candidate opposed by business would not necessarily be a problem for those who themselves did not value the opinions of business. Such voters might be indifferent to business concerns. Alternatively, as some observers noted during the campaign, they might have supported Chávez in part *because* he seemed able and willing to unsettle the business community. Scholars have documented that Venezuelans had lower confidence in their principal business institutions compared with their other key institutions (Buxton 2001, 73–75; Romero 1997, 16; Templeton 1995, 89), but they have not investigated the potential effect of this view in the 1998 elections. We have yet to consider whether anti-business sentiment affected voter preference for Chávez independent of anti-corruption, anti-political establishment, and anti-neoliberal sentiments.

The possibility that Chávez might attract widespread voter support in part because of business opposition was a point made by private sector advocates as well as Chávez's own allies during the campaign. An economist warned business leaders that their shrill depiction of Chávez as an "authoritarian despot" was doing little to disqualify Chávez in the eyes of the public, especially the "poor sectors." Instead of "debilitating Chávez," the economist argued, their criticisms had "actually ramped him up to first place in the polls" (Márquez 1998).[13] Some of Chávez's political allies also seemed to believe that calling attention to business opposition could improve his popularity. In June 1998, a Chávez ally who served in Venezuela's national legislature, Carlos Melo, called on the congress to investigate the "national damage caused to the country by the 'political opinions' made by the foreign risk assessors" ("Investigarán" 1998). The opinions he referred to were those of risk assessors who had issued reports declaring Venezuela to be a greater investment risk once Chávez seemed likely to win.[14] As a result of Melo's request, the Interior Commission of Politics in the House of Deputies began to investigate "the reasons that these companies made these opinions, as well as the extent of damage they caused" ("Investigarán" 1998). Melo's request reveals that Chávez's allies did not fear drawing attention to the business community's opposition to Chávez. Like economist Trino Márquez, Melo suggested that this virulent business opposition actually had a positive effect when he commented that the business community's outcry was "far from provoking a decline for him [Chávez] in the polls" ("Investigarán" 1998).

That Chávez earned support from anti-business voters is also plausible given the electoral success of Latin American political leaders who court voters by denouncing elites more generally. Denouncing elites is widely recognized as an electoral strategy of populists in Latin America. Populists, and in particular those populists who are not leftists, stop short of calling for "far reaching structural change to overcome underdevelopment" (Carr and Ellner 1993, 15). However, populists are generally similar to leftist political figures in that they win with electoral support from popular sectors: the poor, the economically marginalized, and the working classes. They typically "promise, and sometimes delivered, a better life for the masses" (Conniff 1999, 6). They often proclaim an "amorphous or eclectic ideology, characterized by a discourse that exalts subaltern sectors or is anti-elitist and/or anti-establishment" (Roberts 1995, 88). Pointing to the importance of anti-elitist rhetoric as a key to populist electoral success, the scholars quoted here imply that populist leaders are either fostering or tapping into anti-elitist sentiment among voters. Such skepticism regarding elites could also explain why business opposition would not deter voters.

Therefore, I argue that Chávez won widespread voter support because there was already a pool of anti-business voters who were undeterred, and perhaps even encouraged by, business opposition. Chávez's leading opponent, Salas Römer, would have been unlikely to win over anti-business voters given that he was a "businessman-turned-politician" (Coronil 2000). Indeed, Venezuela's business community openly embraced Salas Römer, which led the media to dub him the "darling of businessmen" (Paulin 1998). It was this anti-business sentiment that helped Chávez lure voters away from his leading competition. In making this claim, I shift the focus away from Chávez's rhetoric and toward the pre-existing sentiments of voters that could be present in a wide range of social classes.[15]

Social polarization theorists have thus far overlooked anti-business sentiment as an element that could very well have facilitated the re-politicization of class. Anti-business sentiment is, after all, a feeling of distrust toward those who are quintessential members of the upper classes in society—those who own, invest in, and manage business enterprises. My argument is that those who, like Chávez, re-politicized class in the 1990s were successful not just because so many impoverished Venezuelans opposed neoliberal economic reforms, as thought by many social polarization theorists. Rather, they were successful because so many Venezuelans across diverse social classes distrusted their business leaders.

Nonetheless, the plausibility of the theory that Chávez's widespread voter support derived in large measure from those with anti-business sentiment also rests on establishing the likely origins of such anti-business sentiment. Undoubtedly, Venezuela's social polarization created conditions ripe for rising anti-business sentiment. Yet, as I noted earlier, social polarization is not sufficient to explain when and where movements that re-politicized class arise, let alone when and where the sentiments that facilitate such movements, such as anti-business sentiment, might arise. Thus, I look beyond the socioeconomic circumstances to identify plausible origins of anti-business sentiment.

Two Sources of Anti-business Sentiment

There are two likely sources of anti-business sentiment: the increased association of business with corruption and the increased prominence of business within the political establishment. In making this assessment, I do not reject the corruption or failed institutions theses. Rather, I draw on the insights of both to propose new ways that corruption and Venezuela's political institutions influenced the outcome of the presidential election of 1998. In my view, corruption's influence on that election had less to do with its perceived prevalence and more to do with its perceived role in giving business elites an unfair advantage. I propose that Venezuela's political institutions influenced the 1998 election not only by excluding so many Venezuelans but also by visibly including business elites. Anti-business sentiment, in other words, may originate in a historical association of business with both corruption and the political establishment.

We might expect voters to discredit both nongovernmental and governmental actors associated with corruption. This expectation builds on the corruption thesis, which posits that Venezuelans blamed corruption for the inefficacy of Venezuela's political establishment by 1998. There is good reason to believe, however, that business, more than any other nongovernmental actor, would have been publicly associated with corruption and thereby discredited. Studies suggest that it was hard to conduct business in Venezuela without engaging in various types of transactions that fit the legal definition of corruption (Francés 1989; Naím and Francés 1995; Pérez Perdomo 1991; 1999). These transactions typically involved securing state authorizations after paying a fee requested by a bureaucrat or voluntarily offering a bribe (Francés 1989, 111). These transactions sometimes involved receiving a favor after financing a candidate (Coppedge 2000, 118) or concocting elaborate collusion schemes with high-level government officials (Capriles Méndez 1992).

Corruption scandals that implicated business could have helped generate a pool of anti-business voters. Corruption *scandals* are by definition instances of corruption that the media publicizes and that are therefore likely to shape public opinion. No study that I am aware of, however, examines the degree to which business is *publicly* associated with corruption in Venezuela. The importance of corruption in the 1998 elections was, then, that it was viewed as intensifying social polarization and therefore unjust. In other words, business corruption, along with corruption's ubiquity, could help explain anti-business sentiment and hence the discrediting of business opposition to Chávez.

We might similarly expect voters to discredit nongovernmental actors who had acquired visibility, or prominence, within the political establishment. This expectation builds on the contention posited by the failed institutions thesis that there was widespread frustration with the political establishment by 1998. Just as the business community might have been discredited by becoming publicly associated with corruption, it might also have been discredited by becoming publicly associated with Venezuela's two-party political establishment.

Studies of Venezuela's policy-making process have already established that the business community had privileged access to decision making in Venezuela's two-party political establishment (Coppedge 2000; Crisp 2000). This privileged access was first evident as Venezuela's two-party democracy was being established, when individual business leaders helped broker agreements among rival political leaders and their followers (López Maya, Gómez Calcaño, and Maingón 1989). During the first several decades of the post-1958 democracy, policymakers established a special consulting relationship with the Federación de Cámaras y Asociaciones de Comercio y Producción de Venezuela (FEDECAMARAS), the voluntary business association that served as an umbrella organization for all of Venezuela's business groups (López Maya, Gómez Calcaño, and Maingón 1989, 67). This privileged access was then institutionalized in the main mechanisms through which Venezuela's political elites consulted with society: a maze of specialized ad hoc consultative commissions in which business groups were overrepresented (Crisp 2000). Other observers have similarly noted that individual business leaders historically penetrated Venezuela's extensive bureaucracy through informal networks (Gómez 1989, 105–6) or gained influence over political leaders through campaign financing (Coppedge 2000).

However, the forms of privileged access identified in prior research were largely invisible to the public. Even the ad hoc commissions that gave formal government access to the leading business association largely met behind closed doors. Individuals with significant prior business experience in prominent, high-profile positions of authority, however, would make this privileged access visible to the public. Thus, the prominence of business within the political establishment or business prominence could have helped to generate a pool of anti-business voters. A visible presence of business actors in politics could discredit business and lend credibility to a candidate whom the business community opposed. Other observers have noted that business elites did sometimes obtain high-level political appointments as ministers or gain nomination to represent political parties in the federal legislature. Michael Coppedge, for example, argues that business elites who financed political campaigns in Venezuela sometimes obtained "the ability to designate trusted associates to fill a few seats in Congress or a powerful cabinet post, such as Finance Minister" (Coppedge 1999, 22). Some have discussed a few high-profile cabinet ministers who had business ties (Corrales 1997, 2002), and others have even developed partial lists of the business ties of ministers during the two-party democratic era that lasted from 1959 to 1998 (Arroyo Talavera 1986, 363; Coppedge 1999, 24).[16] But no previous study has systematically examined the degree to which business was indeed prominent in Venezuela's political establishment throughout the two-party era.

We may therefore want to re-specify the role of Venezuela's political institutions in the origins of the public's disillusionment with the political establishment. The failed institutions scholars focus on how the structure of Venezuela's institutions provoked disillusionment by excluding a growing number of Venezuelans. This study instead focuses on how the types of societal interests embedded within these institutions eroded Venezuelan confidence in the political establishment. It was the increased identification of these institutions with elite business interests that stimulated antagonism toward Venezuela's business elite and political establishment. We may also want to re-specify the origins of class-based political movements. This study focuses on how business prominence, not just social inequality, facilitated the rise of movements that re-politicized class and thus generated voter support for an anti-neoliberal candidate opposed by business.

Solving the Business Assistance Puzzle

In order to solve the "business assistance" puzzle we must redirect our focus away from the sentiments of voters and toward the political calculus of business. In other words, we must understand the calculus of individual business elites who decided to assist Chávez and thereby become outliers within Venezuela's business community.

Scholars have not yet systematically studied the political calculations of the "elite outliers" who assisted Chávez. None of the theses described above, for instance, addresses this business assistance puzzle, although investigative journalists have pursued the subject (Santodomingo 1999; Zapata 2000). These investigations indicate that one of Chávez's closest advisors was probably a critical player in recruiting business assistance for Chávez's campaign.[17] Nevertheless, the complicated calculus individual businesspeople use to judge how likely they are to benefit from assisting a candidate limits even the most adept campaign fund raiser. Thus, it is important to identify how individual business elites might benefit by assisting Chávez. Theories on the political behavior of business actors and an extensive literature on state-business relations in Venezuela provide the starting point for that process of identification. I argue that both the business community's economic dependence on the state *and* the political prominence of business shaped the calculus of the "elite outliers" who assisted Chávez. This represents yet another way, not previously contemplated by failed institutions scholars, that Venezuela's political institutions may have shaped the 1998 elections.

The Politics of State-dependent Businesses

Studies on campaign financing suggest that some businesspeople may assist anti-neoliberal candidates like Chávez because their businesses are economically dependent on the state. These studies posit that business elites may be predisposed, by virtue of their structural or economic dependence on resources distributed by the state, to assist candidates who they believe would secure or ensure their access to the state. This prediction contrasts, however, with the conventional wisdom that business elites tend to support candidates who advocate the economic policies they are most likely to favor (Frieden 1991; Gourevitch 1986; Rogowski 1989; Shafer 1994; Silva 1996). It addresses the bigger puzzle of why some business elites would support candidates whose policy agendas ostensibly run counter to their particular economic interests (see Corrales and Cisneros 1999; Kingstone 1999).

Recent studies indicate that a willingness to finance candidates, regardless of their policy position, is associated with state dependence.[18] Studies of political action committees (PACs) in the United States and the companies that fund them reveal that some corporations are willing to support incumbents, regardless of the incumbent's espoused policies (Gopian, Smith, and Smith 1984; Grier, Munger, and Roberts 1994; Handler and Mulkern 1982). These corporations, according to the studies, tend to depend on the state in some way. Some rely on government contracts, while others may be dependent on the good graces of government regulators to operate or to generate profit. These corporations, they find, are the ones that are more likely to support policies like tax increases, wage increases, and higher social spending.

A study of campaign financing in Brazil (Samuels 2001) comes to a similar conclusion. It finds that some businesses in Brazil are more likely to be generous in their support of political leaders who control many of the most important resources the state distributes. In Brazil, these political leaders are the state governors, who tend to control the most lucrative contracts awarded to private companies. That study also reveals that companies depending on government contracts for their livelihood are the ones most likely to support candidates regardless of their policy preferences. Thus, research in the United States and Brazil reveals that *state-dependent* business actors have a structural predisposition to assist whichever candidate is most likely to grant them access to the state. This logic suggests that the outliers of the business community who assisted Chávez were dependent on the state. If so, then they may have assisted Chavez because they had a structural predisposition to pursue access to the state.

Prior descriptions of Venezuelan business affirm the prevalence of such a political calculus. Some scholars describe the business community there as being oriented toward "courting the state" (Naím and Francés 1995). More precisely, as Moisés Naím, a leading scholar and former cabinet member, put it, the Venezuelan state was like a "powerful, confused, preoccupied but easily influenced father" who obliged Venezuela's business elite "to seek out corrections, modifications, exceptions to decisions and rules adopted by the government" (Naím 1984, 175). Antonio Francés describes these state-courting behaviors of business elites in further detail: "The Venezuelan business[person] feels the presence of the state practically at every turn. To establish an industry, sign a union contract, import inputs, export products, the businessperson must obtain official permissions and engage in transactions which can be complex and expensive. The businessperson must ask the state . . . for purchase orders for their products, credits to expand their factory, subsidies to increase consumption, [state investment in] infrastructure construction, provision of every kind of public service and inputs for their products manufactured by state enterprises" (Francés 1989, 103).

Scholars variously trace the state-centric orientation of business to state interventionism (Pérez Perdomo 1991, 1999) to Venezuela's small, oligopoly-dominated economy (Naím and Francés 1995) or, more generally, to Venezuela's oil economy (Karl 1997). The studies on campaign finance cited above, however, suggest that this orientation of Venezuela's business community can be traced most immediately to its economic dependence on the state, regardless of whether this dependence originated in a particular economic policy, firm structure, or resource base. While others have amply demonstrated how Venezuela's business community has historically depended on the state (Baptista 1997; Briceño-León 1990), they have not elucidated how this dependence also shaped the political calculus of business elites in 1998. And yet, the economic dependence of many businesses in Venezuela likely shaped their leaders' political calculus such that they favored the candidates through whom they believed they would be most likely to obtain access to the state.

Although most of the business elites who assisted Chávez were in state-dependent sectors (Gates 2007), clearly the vast majority of Venezuela's state-dependent business elites did not assist Chávez. Moreover, those who did support him could not have done so for the same reasons that Brazilian construction companies assisted left-leaning governors. The latter assisted leftist candidates merely because they were incumbents. But Chávez was not an incumbent. Why, then, did some state-dependent elites become outliers and assist Chávez while others did not? To explain variation in the political calculus of similarly economically dependent business elites, we must look more closely at the access-based rationales of elite outliers.

The Politics of Ensuring Business Access to the State

Intuitively, we might expect state-dependent business actors to assist presidential candidates with whom they have a personal connection, regardless of the candidate's policy persuasion. Such a connection would give them a reason to trust a particular candidate (Gates 2007, 107, 111). That connection would supposedly ensure access to the state under that president's administration and thus result in benefits such as state contracts for that business.

It is also plausible, nonetheless, that state-dependent elites would assist candidates who they feared might limit their access to the state were they not to fund them, regardless of the candidate's policy orientation. This reasoning makes sense when we consider the nature of economic dependence on the state. Dependence on the state forces businesses to compete for the same set of coveted state favors in their sector. Therefore, it is reasonable to expect that acute fears of losing access to the state would have shaped the political calculus of the elite outliers in 1998 (Gates 2007, 106, 110). However, it was likely the political prominence of business that intensified the fears of losing access and led some elites to assist Chávez. This political prominence could come into play in two ways.

First, when individual state-dependent businesses appear to accrue conspicuous benefits from being a patron of a leading political figure, they might fear reprisals from that person's political competitors. As Coppedge has argued, business leaders in Venezuela cultivate relationships with politicians, much as they do in the United States, by financing their political campaigns (Coppedge 2000, 118). Although becoming a patron of a candidate might yield a windfall, such as the nomination of a trusted ally for a top economic policy position, securing such a conspicuous windfall could also make the favored business elite a convenient target for reprisals by their client's political enemies. Thus, we would expect that business executives who suspected they had become publically identified as patrons of a particular political leader to have an acute fear of losing access under a new administration. Such a fear would convince them to assist the candidate most likely to win the next elections, no matter what their political persuasion, in order to offset the risk of political reprisals.

Second, individual state-dependent business elites might fear the victory of a candidate who seems likely to confer coveted state favors on one of their business competitors (Gates 2007, 107, 112). Candidates with close ties to a business competitor would likely provoke this kind of fear. Or, more often, certain business elites may fear a particular candidate because that candidate is likely to appoint one of their business competitors to a chief economic policy post. The presence of these prospective business executives–turned-bureaucrats, whom I call *businocrats*, could constitute a reason to fear loss of access if that candidate won. Thus, I propose that the prospective businocrats of Chávez's leading political opponent, Salas Römer, might have evoked acute fears of losing access. These fears may have been strong enough to lead some business elites to become outliers and assist Chávez.

To some, it may not be readily apparent that the visible presence of business in Venezuela's political establishment would be decisive in generating acute fears of losing access to the state. After all, a leading theory of economic development posits that the ideal developmental state is not only autonomous enough, or sufficiently independent of any particular business's influence, to act in the nation's general interest but also sufficiently embedded within the business community to inspire business trust and cooperation (Evans 1995). There is a similar argument that this type of productive collaboration depends on factors such as a free flow of information between the state and business and the state's ability to inspire the trust of the business community (Schneider and Maxfield 1997). These factors must be present to avoid "degenerating into the unproductive exchange of favors for bribes" (Schneider and Maxfield 1997, 15).

Nevertheless, a careful analysis of Venezuela's neoliberal reforms during the 1990s reveals that the economic cabinet members (ministers) who faced the fiercest opposition from business ironically had the most intimate and therefore most visible professional connections to business (Corrales 1997; 2002, 163–66). Rather than inspire greater confidence in their reforms, the ministers who had previously served as top managers and board members of major corporations fueled suspicions that their policies would favor their own businesses at the expense of others in their sector. Javier Corrales thus identified a potential problem with embeddedness not contemplated by Peter Evans (1995): that of policymakers being "overly linked" to business. Policymakers who were overly linked to business, Corrales argues, could evoke fears of bias being embedded in policy proscriptions, particularly among businesses that occupied the same economic sector as the minister.

I extend Corrales's insight to a new context: that of the political calculus of business actors during electoral campaigns. The business ties of candidates and their allies are just as likely to evoke business elites' fears of losing access as to inspire trust in a particular political candidate. For this reason, we need to take into consideration how the prominence of business within Venezuela's political arena shaped the political calculus of the elite outliers in 1998.

PART II

◆

Voter Support for Chávez

3

•

THE ROLE OF

ANTI-BUSINESS SENTIMENT

WHY WOULD Venezuelans vote to place their nation in the hands of a presidential candidate who provoked strong opposition from the business
community? The reasons why Venezuelans were willing to do so are not obvious. One might naturally assume that business leaders opposed to Chávez
could have dissuaded voters from supporting Chávez by convincing them that
a Chávez government would severely destabilize the economy the way that
Allende's democratically elected socialist government destabilized Chile during
the early 1970s. Business leaders might also have persuaded voters that electing
Chávez would provoke a political reaction that would result in the restriction
of democratic freedoms, like the coup against Allende and subsequent martial
law or the 1948 coup against the first left-leaning government in Venezuela and
the subsequent decade of authoritarian rule.[1] That Venezuela's voters still supported Chávez thus poses a puzzle.

One answer to this puzzle is that Chávez specifically attracted voters who lacked confidence in business. Such voters would be indifferent to business concerns. Thus, we might expect those with lower confidence in business to be more likely to favor Chávez, even after taking into consideration other factors, such as those voter concerns identified by the three existing explanations for Chávez's election: the corruption, failed institutions, and social polarization theses.

Anti-business voters may even have been encouraged by a candidate who disturbed business. As others have demonstrated, Chávez's supporters had "pronounced optimism" about the nation's prospects (Weyland 2003, 843). This finding is consistent with research showing that unless economic discontent is accompanied with optimism for a specific opposition candidate, it may lower voter turnout and therefore decrease, rather than increase, the chances that opposition candidates will defeat traditional political leaders (Radcliff 1994). Kurt Weyland attributes this optimism among Chávez supporters to the candidate's charisma and the generalized propensity for wishful thinking among voters faced with dire economic circumstances. But Weyland fails to specify why Chávez, more than other candidates, might have inspired this greater optimism. He writes, "It seems many citizens simply felt compelled to believe in Chávez' charisma, independent of realistic assessments of his likely success" (Weyland 2003, 825).

Perhaps Chávez inspired greater optimism so seemingly "divorced from concrete performance assessments" (Weyland 2003, 843) in part because of his antagonistic relationship with the Venezuelan business community. In making this argument, I do not dispute the evident role charisma played in Chávez's popularity or Weyland's interpretation that Chávez's supporters exhibited the "exaggerated risk aversion" posited by cognitive psychological theory (Kahnemann and Tversky 2000) rather than the "simple materialistic" cost-benefit calculation (Weyland 2003, 825) posited by economic voting theories (Key and Cummings 1966; Lewis-Beck 1988). Nonetheless, such an interpretation still depends on a rationale for why voters pinned their hopes on Chávez as the candidate best qualified to be their "savior" (Weyland 2003, 840). The rationale I propose derives from an argument more in line with one (Stokes 2001) arguing that economic cost-benefit calculations are mediated by the judgments that voters make about who should be blamed for current problems. To examine this possibility, one can determine whether the optimism of voters who favored Chávez is related, at least in part, to their skepticism regarding business. In other words, is the effect of an individual's anti-business sentiment on an intention to vote for Chávez indirect, via their optimism?

This study represents the first systematic test of all three leading theories and thereby advances Steve Ellner's agenda to "prioritize the importance of sources of the discontent in order to understand why system legitimacy was questioned" (Ellner 2003, 17). Using the same national opinion poll I have employed, José Molina (2002) identifies a number of sociodemographic changes, political identities, and opinions on campaign themes that characterized Chávez's supporters but does not conduct a systematic test of the three leading theses on the election. Similarly, Weyland (2003) tests leading theories of economic voting but does not test the three theories on Chávez's election. Damarys Canache's (2002) analysis of this same poll helps solve the puzzle of why voters supported Chávez even though he was a former military officer and leader of a failed coup attempt but does not address the puzzle of voter support for a candidate that business leaders opposed. A systematic examination of leading theories on Chávez's election, however, reveals that Chávez did not just appeal to anti-corruption, anti-political establishment voters or voters concerned with the dire circumstances of the economy; he also appealed to anti-business voters. Furthermore, the present analysis shows that this anti-business sentiment contributed to voters' optimism regarding Chávez.

Anti-business Sentiment

There is good reason to think that Chávez drew support from those who had misgivings about business. As prior analyses of opinion polls show (Buxton 2001; Romero 1997; Templeton 1995), Venezuelans had lost confidence in business by the late 1990s and increasingly blamed business for their problems.

Table 3.1 summarizes the level of confidence Venezuelans had in various institutions between 1985 and 1998. It shows that the percentage of Venezuelans with little or no confidence in business increased 47 percentage points between 1985 and 1998. This increase was greater than the increase in the percentage of Venezuelans with little or no confidence in any other major Venezuelan institution during that time frame. In 1985, less than half (44 percent) of Venezuelans polled nationally had little or no confidence in business, while well over half already had little or no confidence in public administration (67 percent), the congress (57 percent), the police (52 percent), and trade unions (64 percent)

TABLE 3.1. Percentage of Venezuelans having little or no confidence
in various institutions, 1985–1998

Institution	Percentage change, 1985–1998	1985[a]	1991	1995	1998
Business[b]	47	44	63	68	91
Congress	36	57		75	93
Police	36	52	85	76	88
Military	36	28	42	46	64
Government[c]	25	67	87	66	92
Trade unions[d]	25	64	82	75	89
Judiciary	25[e]			65	90
Universities	15	33	34	31	48
Catholic Church	11[f]		33	29	44
Political parties	3[f]		91	82	94

Sources: For 1985, Pulso Nacional conducted by Datos, C.A., as cited in Templeton 1995, 89; for 1991, Instituto Venezolano de Opinión, March 1992, 53, as cited in Buxton 2001, 73; for 1995, Conciencia 21, "Estudio sobre valores del venezolano," June 1995, 217, as cited in Romero 1997, 17; for 1998, REDPOL98, Banco de Datos Poblacionales, Universidad Simón Bolívar.

Note: Some cells are empty because the lists of institutions differed across polls.

[a] In 1985, respondents were asked how much confidence they had in the honesty of those who managed various institutions. In all other years, respondents were asked how much confidence they had in various Venezuelan institutions.

[b] In 1998, respondents were asked specifically about FEDECAMARAS rather than about business more generally.

[c] In 1985, respondents were asked about public administration rather than about government in general.

[d] In 1992 and 1998, respondents were asked only about Venezuela's main union, the Confederación de Trabajadores de Venezuela (CTV).

[e] Percentage increase between 1995 and 1998.

[f] Percentage increase between 1992 and 1998.

(Buxton 2001, 73).[2] Even before Chávez led the first of two coup attempts in 1992, the proportion of the public with little or no confidence in business had increased to nearly two-thirds (63 percent). This decreasing confidence in business contrasts with Venezuelans' continued confidence in other nongovernmental entities, such as universities and the Catholic Church. Only about a third of respondents had little or no confidence in universities or the Church in 1991. While it may not be surprising that confidence in business did not improve between 1991 and 1995, it is surprising that the proportion with no or little confidence in business in 1995 is about the same as that for government and the judiciary. At the time of the June 1995 poll, Venezuelans had endured a year and a half of the nation's worst financial crisis ever, one in which half of the private banking sector failed. The judiciary, in particular, was widely perceived as being

TABLE 3.2. Percentage of Venezuelans blaming various institutions for crises in 1984 and 1992

Institution	Economic crisis, 1984[a]	Political crisis, 1992
Previous government	77	
Business[b]	72	75/60[b]
Present government[c]	66	84
Venezuelan people[d]	65	35
World economic situation	65	
Oil industry[e]	63	50
Trade unions	61	
AD political party		82
National congress		78
Economic crisis		74
Judiciary		70
COPEI political party		65
Privatization		62
Left-wing political parties		48
News media		36

Sources: For 1984, Pulso Nacional, conducted by Datos, C.A., as cited in Templeton 1995, 88; for 1992, Consultores 21, "Estudio de Temas Económicos," 1992, second trimester, in-house report, as cited in Romero 1997, 16.

[a] The survey prompted respondents to consider whether institutions should bear some or a lot of responsibility.

[b] In 1984, the survey prompted respondents to consider businesspeople. In 1992, the survey prompted respondents to consider FEDECAMARAS (first figure given) as well as private enterprise (second figure given).

[c] In 1992, the survey prompted respondents to consider the current president.

[d] In 1984, the survey prompted respondents to consider the egoism of Venezuelan people.

[e] In 1984, the survey prompted respondents to consider international petroleum prices.

an ineffective adjudicator of the numerous corruption scandals that emerged in the midst of the financial crisis.

The proportion of respondents with little or no confidence in business also rose sharply between 1995 and 1998, with government overall and the judiciary eliciting similar levels of disdain. The proportion who had little or no confidence in business increased more than 22 percentage points, from 68 to 90.5 percent, almost as much of a percentage point increase as the two institutions with the highest percentage point increase (government and the judiciary). It is remarkable that in 1998, for the first time, confidence in business was lower than in the highly stigmatized peak labor union federation, the Confederación de Trabajadores de Venezuela (CTV).[3]

According to polls, Venezuelans also increasingly believed that business bore significant responsibility for Venezuela's economic and political crises (table 3.2). For example, in a poll taken in 1984, immediately after the first major currency devaluation in several decades, Venezuelans blamed businesspeople more than all other actors, except the previous government. While 77 percent of respondents said the previous government had some or a lot of responsibility, 72 percent thought businesspeople bore some or a lot of responsibility for the economic crisis, with 49 percent assigning businesspeople a lot of responsibility (Templeton 1995, 88). Similarly, several months after the first of the two 1992 coup attempts, 75 percent of Venezuelans blamed the peak business association, FEDECAMARAS, for the crisis; only 16 percent said it should not be blamed at all (Romero 1997, 16). The depth of condemnation of FEDECAMARAS was surpassed only by leading political entities such as the sitting president, his party, and the national congress. Furthermore, in the midst of the financial crisis in 1994, three-fourths of those surveyed agreed with the statement that "all businessmen were thieves" (76 percent), even as 84 percent blamed politicians for their country's problems (Romero 1997, 23). We might therefore anticipate that anti-business sentiment affected the public's presidential preferences in 1998.

Chávez's Support among Voters with Anti-business Sentiment

A national opinion poll conducted shortly before the presidential elections in 1998 reveals that Chávez's supporters did indeed have distinctly low levels of confidence in business. This affirms my hypothesis that voters were willing to support Chávez—a candidate opposed by business—at least in part because they themselves did not have confidence in business.

To determine the level of confidence in business reported by Chávez's supporters, I used a national opinion poll that is widely viewed as ideal for assessing the motivations of voters in this presidential election. This poll was conducted by the research organization DATOS, C.A., on behalf of a team of Venezuela's leading political scientists collectively called the Red Universitaria de Cultura Política (referred to hereafter as REDPOL). It was conducted between November 13 and 27, 1998, just prior to the December 6 election and just after the November 8 special election for national legislators (both deputies and senators), governors, and state legislatures. It is based on a national representative sample of fifteen hundred adults.[4]

The poll asked respondents whether they intended to vote and, if so, for which of all possible presidential candidates they intended to vote. In addition, the poll asked about their level of confidence in Venezuela's peak business association, FEDECAMARAS, which has historically been the official voice of business in dealings with the government. For instance, FEDECAMARAS has represented the business community on the myriad ad hoc commissions that have served as a principal locus of policy making in Venezuela (Crisp 2000). We might therefore expect the public's opinion of FEDECAMARAS to be indicative of its assessment of the leaders in the broader business community. I subsequently refer to this variable as indicating confidence in business or measuring the degree of anti-business sentiment.

So did the 36.3 percent of respondents who intended to vote for Chávez differ in their degree of confidence in business from anyone else (including undecided voters)? Table 3.3 indicates that they did. Of those who intended to vote for Chávez, more than half (54.3 percent) had no confidence in business. Furthermore, most (41.2 percent) of the others who intended to vote for Chávez only had some or a little confidence in business.[5] The level of confidence in business that Chávez's supporters had differed significantly from that of those who did not intend to vote for Chávez. Only 46 percent of those who did not intend to vote for Chávez, for instance, had no confidence in business. This supports my explanation for Chávez's success despite business opposition. It demonstrates that Chávez's supporters were largely anti-business and therefore less likely to have confidence in the opinions of the business community.[6]

We can now turn to the question of whether confidence in business among Chávez's supporters was lower than it was among supporters of the other presidential contenders. As the last italicized row in table 3.4 shows, about a quarter (28.4 percent) of the respondents favored Chávez's leading opponent, Henrique Salas Römer, while another quarter (24.9 percent) were unsure or thought they might abstain from voting. The other 10.5 percent intended to vote for a candidate other than those two, including Luis Alfaro Ucero, the candidate supported for most of 1998 by the establishment party, Acción Democrática.[7] The proportion of Chávez's supporters who had no confidence in business (54.3 percent) is even slightly higher than that of those who thought they might not vote or were undecided voters (52.1 percent). While the difference is not large,

TABLE 3.3. Level of confidence in business by intention to vote for Chávez, 1998

Level of confidence in business	Intention to vote for Chávez		
	No	Yes	Total
None	430	286	716
	46.4%	54.3%	49.3%
Some	425	217	642
	45.9%	41.2%	44.2%
Much	71	24	95
	7.7%	4.6%	6.5%
Total number of respondents	926	527	1,453
Total percentage	100%	100%	100%
Chi²(2) = 10.8543 p = 0.004			

Source: REDPOL98, Banco de Datos Poblacionales, Universidad Simón Bolívar.
Note: Percentages pertain to the data in that column.

it does highlight the fact that Chávez's supporters were even less confident in business than those so disaffected from the political process as to be unlikely to vote. The first italicized row in table 3.4 shows that the largest proportion of those who had no confidence in business intended to vote for Chávez (39.9 percent). In contrast, the third italicized row indicates that the largest proportion of those with a great deal of confidence in business intended to vote for Salas Römer (32.6 percent).

To establish the relative importance of anti-business sentiment among Chávez's supporters, we must examine whether anti-business sentiment remains significant even after taking into consideration the other concerns predicted by the corruption, failed institutions, and social polarization theories.

Chávez's Potential Support among Voters with Other Concerns

The three theories on why voters elected Chávez suggest that factors other than anti-business sentiment characterized Chávez's supporters. These include attributes that voters might possess and opinions they might reasonably be expected to hold. Table 3.5 lists each of these variables as well as the control

TABLE 3.4. Level of confidence in business
by preferred presidential candidate, 1998

Confidence in business	Vote intention				
	Chávez	Salas Römer	Other candidates	Intend to abstain or don't know	Total
None	286	181	61	188	716
	39.9%	*25.3%*	*8.5%*	*26.3%*	*100%*
	54.3%	*43.8%*	*40.1%*	*52.1%*	*49.3%*
Some	217	201	71	153	642
	33.8%	*31.3%*	*11.1%*	*23.8%*	*100%*
	41.2%	*48.7%*	*46.7%*	*42.4%*	*44.2%*
Much	24	31	20	20	95
	25.3%	*32.6%*	*21.1%*	*21.1%*	*100%*
	4.6%	*7.5%*	*13.2%*	*5.5%*	*6.5%*
Total	527	413	152	361	1,453
	36.3%	*28.4%*	*10.5%*	*24.9%*	*100%*
	100%	*100%*	*100%*	*100%*	*100%*

$Chi^2(6) = 26.26$ $p = 0.000$

Source: REDPOL98, Banco de Datos Poblacionales, Universidad Simón Bolívar.
Note: Percentages for each row are in italics.

variable of education, which is widely applied in public opinion research predicting candidate preferences.

According to the corruption thesis, we would expect that Chávez's supporters would be anti-corruption voters. In other words, the thesis predicts that the greater an individual's anti-corruption sentiment, the more likely that individual would favor Chávez for president. As table 3.5 illustrates, the corruption thesis is tested with a measure indicating whether respondents mentioned "the fight against corruption" as one of the most important tasks for the next government.

According to the failed institutions thesis, we would expect that Chávez's supporters would be not only anti-corruption but also more generally dissatisfied with the political establishment. This thesis posits that Venezuela's political institutions produced a generalized frustration with the political establishment because their rigid structure excluded a growing number of constituents from the political process. It is these failed institutions, scholars argue, that led voters to reject the political establishment in 1998 and vote for Chávez.

TABLE 3.5. Variable definitions and summary statistics for national opinion poll, 1998

Variable	Definition	Mean	Std. dev.	No. of observations
Intention to vote for Chávez	0=no intention to vote for Chávez 1=intend to vote for Chávez	0.359	0.480	1500
Control variable				
Education level	1=low, did not complete primary 5=high, completed higher education	2.658	1.125	1492
Corruption thesis				
Corruption as priority for next government	0="fight against corruption" not mentioned as priority 1="fight against corruption" mentioned as priority	0.529	0.499	1500
Failed institutions thesis				
Satisfied with existing democracy	0=not satisfied (15.7%) 1=little satisfied (39.7%) 2=satisfied (38.9%) 3=very satisfied (5.8%)	1.347	0.810	1493
Social polarization thesis				
Social class	1=low (39.8%) 5=upper (2%)	1.865	0.880	1500
Support privatization	0=shouldn't privatize anything (31.5%) 1=only those that do not work (58.5%) 2=should privatize all (9.8%)	0.783	0.605	1414
Support state intervention	0=less (7.9%) 1=same (15.9%) 2=more (76.1%)	1.682	0.612	1407
Retrospective sociotropic	"Country's situation is . . . than last year" 0=worse (69.9%) 1=same (26.2%) 2=better (3.9%)	0.339	0.549	1481
Retrospective pocketbook	"You are doing . . . than last year" 0=worse (35.4%) 1=same (45.1%) 2=better (19.5%)	0.841	0.724	1486
Anti-business sentiment thesis				
Confidence in FEDECAMARAS (business)	0=none (49.3%) 1=some (44.2%) 2=much (6.5%)	0.573	0.613	1453
Optimism variable				
Prospective sociotropic	"Within a year, the country's situation will be..." 0=worse (34.8%) 1=same (28.3%) 2=better (36.9%)	1.022	0.847	1056

Source: REDPOL98, Banco de Datos Poblacionales, Universidad Simón Bolívar.

Thus, this failed institutions thesis predicts that the greater an individual's anti-political establishment sentiment, the more likely that individual would be to favor Chávez. We can test the failed institutions thesis with the REDPOL survey question that asks respondents to assess their general satisfaction with the existing democracy.[8] This "provides the best available indicator for popular assessments of the performance of the political class" as a whole (Weyland 2003, 834).[9]

According to the social polarization thesis, we would expect that Chávez's supporters had not only political but also economic concerns. Social polarization theorists contend that Chávez's supporters were not merely motivated by a generalized frustration with the political establishment, let alone corruption. They contend instead that a "genuine commitment to change was defined by opposition to neoliberal economic policies and not by anti-party rhetoric" (Ellner 2008, 105). They explain that Chávez built his base of support by denouncing the "deleterious social consequences of the neoliberal model" (Roberts 2003b, 66). Thus, they predict that the more an individual supported privatization, the less likely such individuals would be to favor Chávez. To measure support for privatization, I use the question on the REDPOL survey that assesses an individual's broad opinion of privatization: whether they support privatizing all enterprises, some of them, or none of them. Social polarization scholars predict that, in similar fashion, the more an individual supports state interventionism, the more likely such individuals would favor Chávez. To measure voter support for state intervention, I use the polling question that asks respondents to evaluate their support for state intervention (table 3.5).

According to the social polarization thesis, however, several other variables affect voting decisions. For example, social polarization scholars contend that voters from lower socioeconomic strata were more likely to favor Chávez because, objectively speaking, these Venezuelans had experienced the greatest degree of decline in their material circumstances. In other words, they argue that Chávez's supporters were more economically deprived voters as well as more anti-neoliberal. Thus, they predict that the higher an individual's socioeconomic status, the less likely a voter would favor Chávez. There is a class status index on the REDPOL survey that can be used to assess this prediction. It combines measures of income, educational attainment, housing, and occupational positions into a five-category ordinal variable, with the highest status coded as 5.

The social polarization argument implies that there are several additional variables that may have affected voter preference for Chávez. The thesis suggests that Chávez's supporters were more likely to have a negative assessment of their own and the nation's overall situation. These scholars' prediction—that those from the popular sectors (lower socioeconomic strata) were more likely to support Chávez—implies that those from the popular sectors are likely to have a more negative assessment of their own economic circumstances. Similarly, their contention—that those opposed to neoliberal economic reforms were more likely to support Chávez—implies that those opposed to neoliberal reforms have a more negative assessment of the country's economic circumstances. However, the failure of anti-neoliberal candidates to galvanize voters in countries experiencing comprehensive neoliberal reforms and deep social polarization shows that we cannot assume that someone's worsening economic circumstances will necessarily be perceived as such. The effect of objective circumstances on the likelihood of favoring Chávez may be mediated by an individual's subjective perceptions of his or her economic circumstances. We also cannot assume that a nation's worsening economic circumstances will necessarily be perceived as being the result of neoliberal economic policies. Thus, to fully test the social polarization thesis, we also need to examine whether those persons with negative assessments of their own and the nation's circumstances were, indeed, more likely to favor Chávez. I use two widely accepted measures of how individuals assess their own circumstances as well as the nation's overall condition in the recent past: the retrospective pocketbook and retrospective sociotropic variables, respectively.

The Relative Importance of Anti-business Sentiment among Chávez's Supporters

Binomial logistic regression analysis (Long 1997) is a statistical technique that can be used to weigh the importance of anti-business sentiment relative to that of other potential reasons for voters to choose Chávez as predicted by the three leading arguments. With this technique, I examine how each of these factors affects the likelihood that respondents intended to vote for Chávez versus any other intention. Model 1 in table 3.6 presents the results of the first analysis predicting an intention to vote for Chávez (coded as 1). The percentage change in odds (in parentheses) helps us interpret the estimated parameters (not in parentheses) of the model (Long and Freese 2006, 129–81).[10]

TABLE 3.6. Logistic regression effects of anti-business sentiment and other concerns on intention to vote for Chávez

Variables	Model 1	Model 2
Control variable		
Level of education	0.036	0.036
	(3.7%)	(3.7%)
Corruption thesis		
Corruption mentioned as priority	0.252*	0.239*
	(28.7%)	(27.0%)
Failed institutions thesis		
Satisfaction with democracy	-0.423***	-0.399***
	(-34.5%)	(-32.9%)
Social polarization thesis		
Social class	-0.152*	-0.154*
	(-14.1%)	(-14.3%)
Support privatization	0.068	0.067
	(7.0%)	(7.0%)
Support state interventionism	0.104	0.109
	(11.0%)	(-11.5%)
Retrospective sociotropic	-0.338**	-0.325**
	(-28.7%)	(-27.7%)
Retrospective pocketbook	-0.214*	-0.217*
	(-19.3%)	(-19.5%)
Anti-business sentiment thesis		
Confidence in business		-0.227*
		(-20.3%)
Constant	0.126	0.227
Number of observations	1296	1296
Chi²	69.005	74.335
Pseudo R²	0.0404	0.0436
Likelihood-ratio test Chi²(1)		5.33
Prob > Chi²		0.021

Source: REDPOL98, Banco de Datos Poblacionales, Universidad Simón Bolívar.
Note: Percentage change in odds of intending to vote for Chávez versus not intending to vote for Chávez in parentheses.
* $p < 0.05$; ** $p < 0.01$; *** $p < 0.001$

Table 3.6 demonstrates that both economic and political concerns affected the likelihood that an individual would vote for Chávez. As the corruption thesis predicts, those poll respondents who mentioned that corruption should be a priority for the incoming government were 28.7 percent more likely to favor Chávez. Similarly, as the failed institutions thesis predicts, those who were satisfied with the state of the national democracy were significantly less likely to favor Chávez. With each degree of increasing satisfaction with the democracy, respondents were 34.5 percent less likely to favor Chávez. The fact that this effect is highly significant affirms the contention of the failed institutions thesis that Chávez captured the anti–political establishment voters in disproportionately high numbers. The joint significance of both anti-corruption and anti–political establishment sentiment also affirms those failed institutions scholars who incorporate the corruption thesis as part of their argument. Moreover, the model illuminates the fact that political concerns were not the only factors that characterized Chávez's supporters.

There is some evidence to support the social polarization argument. As this thesis predicts, voters' objective economic condition influenced their presidential preference. Those voters with higher social class status were less likely to favor Chávez.[11] I find that for each increasing degree of social class status, a person's likelihood of favoring Chávez decreased by 14.1 percent. The significance of this effect could help explain why Chávez's margin of victory was so significant. There was a dramatic increase in voter turnout among the poor that narrowed the voting rate gap between the poor and upper income respondents from 15 percentage points in 1993 to 6 percentage points in 1998 (Canache 2004, 46).[12] The enthusiasm for Chávez among the poor, and among the urban poor in particular, undoubtedly helped him win.

Furthermore, as the social polarization thesis implies, Venezuelans' assessments of their own and the nation's economy overall influenced their vote intention. Those with more favorable assessments of the economy overall (the retrospective sociotropic variable) and their own situation in particular (the retrospective pocketbook variable) were less likely to favor Chávez. Those who thought the economy overall had been doing better were 28.7 percent less likely to favor Chávez than those who thought it was doing about the same, holding other factors constant. Similarly, those who thought they had been doing about the same as a year ago were 19.3 percent less likely to favor Chávez than those who thought they were doing worse than a year ago. In other words, those who favored Chávez tended to have a more negative assessment of the nation's economic condition and their own current economic circumstances, just as the social polarization thesis implies they would.

Nonetheless, the results for model 1 in table 3.6 do not support the social polarization contention that the economic policy preferences of voters led them to favor Chávez. Neither support for privatization nor support for state intervention affected their intention to vote for Chávez.[13] In other words, Chávez's supporters were not more anti-neoliberal or more pro–state intervention than others, on average. This confirms what other studies have shown: that neither views on privatization nor those on state interventionism affected presidential preferences in 1998.[14] This result probably reflects the overwhelming concurrence of Venezuelans on the economic policies they did and did not want for their country.[15] It may also reflect the fact that Venezuelans were confronted with myriad new political actors, which made it more difficult to discern their policy positions (Morgan 2007, 92).[16] These results confirm the central contention of the social polarization thesis: economic concerns, not just political concerns, were important to Chávez's supporters. The results also demonstrate, however, that Chávez's supporters were not distinct from others in their economic policy preferences. They were not, then, as the social polarization scholars have argued, anti-neoliberal voters.

The results for model 2, as shown in table 3.6, represent the test for the question of whether confidence in business affected voters' likelihood of favoring Chávez (controlling for the other concerns that might have motivated people to favor Chávez). Those with greater confidence in business were indeed less likely to favor Chávez (controlling for their other possible concerns). Furthermore, the test for whether this additional variable significantly improves the overall fit of the model (and therefore improves our ability to predict the distinguishing characteristics of Chávez's supporters) is significant. For each increasing degree of confidence in business, respondents were on average 20.3 percent *less* likely to favor Chávez for president (controlling for their political and economic concerns). These results indicate that, on average, Chávez's supporters were undeterred by business opposition because they themselves did not have confidence in business. Their lower level of confidence in the leadership of the business community suggests that they were skeptical that business's opinion would be good for them or the country. We can infer, then, that Chávez's supporters were likely to have been either indifferent to business concerns or perhaps even particularly optimistic about a candidate who provoked business opposition.

Anti-business Sentiment and Chávez's Optimists

The above analysis confirms the hypothesis that those who favored Chávez were not deterred by business opposition, in part, because they did not have confidence in business's opinion. Nevertheless, it leaves open the question of whether they were indifferent to business opposition or whether business opposition may have influenced their optimism regarding a future governed by Chávez.

Prior studies have shown that voters are often reluctant to favor opposition candidates, like Chávez, unless they are also optimistic about them being able to improve the country's situation (Radcliff 1994). The historical trends in assessments of the near future (that is, prospective sociotropic opinions) in Venezuela are consistent with the argument that a shift toward greater optimism took place in 1998.[17] Moreover, prior research has already demonstrated that Chávez's supporters were not only frustrated with the economy or the political leadership but also "strikingly hopeful" about the future of their country (Weyland 2003, 826). According to Weyland's study, neither those who favored Chávez's leading opponent, Salas Römer, nor those who favored any other candidate were so optimistic about the future of their country. Weyland's study therefore demonstrates the intriguing paradox that "under dire circumstances, citizens do not prefer prudent, less costly measures" but instead "have particularly exalted hopes in prominent political leaders" (Weyland 2003, 825). In coming to this conclusion, his study contributes to broader debates about how economic considerations shape voter preferences.[18]

Yet Weyland fails to specify what it was about Chávez that might have inspired this greater optimism. For example, he writes that more and more Venezuelans, "fed up with the incapacity of the established regime to resolve the country's problems, . . . opted for a *radical outsider* who promised a profound political transformation" and "who . . . called for drastic political house-cleaning and promised a social revolution" (Weyland 2003, 828). He speculates that Salas Römer's lagging popularity was due to the fact that "he projected a more moderate image than Chávez." Weyland further casts Chávez's criticism of neoliberal policies and the fact that he was the only candidate who "attacked the political class and its oligarchical regime" as additional factors that qualified Chávez as a radical political outsider (Weyland 2003, 828). However, the greater optimism of those who intended to vote for Chávez, while it may reflect unrealistic hopes for Chávez (Weyland 2003, 825), still demands an explanation.

To identify why optimism typified Chávez's supporters, we can examine which, if any, of the concerns already established above as having a direct effect on the intention to vote for Chávez loses its significance after controlling for assessments of the nation's future (or relative optimism). I use a measure of relative optimism (see table 3.5) that is commonly referred to as a prospective sociotropic variable because it asks respondents to speculate about the general status of their nation in the future. Those concerns that lose significance after controlling for the degree of optimism can be interpreted as having an indirect effect on an intention to vote for Chávez via their effect on relative optimism. Using this measure thus allows us to identify the issues that Chávez's supporters were most optimistic about having him address. We can make this inference, in part, because at the time of the survey, Venezuelans would have expected Chávez to win. The national polls indicated that Chávez would win, and candidates allied with Chávez swept the federal legislature and state governor elections on November 8, 1998. Thus, the sunny outlook on the future harbored by those who intended to vote for Chávez is inextricably linked to their belief that he would win. After controlling for an individual's relative optimism, we would expect that variables contributing to his or her optimism would have a reduced direct effect on an intention to vote for Chávez. We can, therefore, interpret such variables as indicating the issues or concerns that Chávez's supporters were most hopeful he would address.

Table 3.7 presents the findings of the binomial logistic regressions predicting the likelihood that a person would favor Chávez for president. The second model presented in the table demonstrates the powerful effect that optimism about Chávez had on a person's intention to vote for him. For each additional degree of optimism among respondents, they were 78.6 percent more likely to favor Chávez for president. Overall, the model is also significantly more powerful than the model without the prospective sociotropic variable.[19] This confirms that Chávez's supporters were euphoric about the future.

More importantly, the second model permits an examination of whether anti-business sentiment contributed to the optimism of Chávez's supporters. The model reveals that it did. The confidence that respondents had in business

TABLE 3.7. Logistic regression effects of optimism (controlling for other concerns) on intention to vote for Chávez

Variables	Model 1	Model 2
Control variable		
Level of education	0.036	0.049
	(3.7%)	(5.0%)
Corruption thesis		
Corruption mentioned as priority	0.239*	0.231
	(27.0%)	(26.0%)
Failed institutions thesis		
Satisfaction with democracy	-0.399***	0.400***
	(-32.9%)	(-33.0%)
Social polarization thesis		
Social class	-0.154*	-0.183*
	(-14.3%)	(-16.7%)
Support privatization	0.067	0.029
	(7.0%)	(2.9%)
Support state interventionism	0.109	0.11
	(-11.5%)	(11.6%)
Retrospective sociotropic	-0.325**	-0.241[+]
	(-27.7%)	(-21.4%)
Retrospective pocketbook	-0.217*	-0.361***
	(-19.5%)	(-30.3%)
Anti-business sentiment thesis		
Confidence in business	-0.227*	-0.209+
	(-20.3%)	(-18.9%)
Degree of optimism		
Prospective sociotropic		0.580***
		(78.6%)
Constant	0.227	-0.209
Number of observations	1296	927
Chi²	74.335	89.733
Pseudo R²	0.0436	0.0727
Likelihood-ratio test Chi²(1)		44.77
Prob > Chi²		0.0000

Source: REDPOL98, Banco de Datos Poblacionales, Universidad Simón Bolívar.

Notes: Percentage change in odds of intending to vote for Chávez versus not intending to vote for Chávez in parentheses. Likelihood-ratio test compares model 2 with another version of model 1 (not shown) that is restricted to the smaller sample of model 2.

[+] $p < .10$; * $p < 0.05$; ** $p < 0.01$; *** $p < 0.001$

still had a significant direct effect on their intention to vote for Chávez in model 2, but it is less significant when controlling for their optimism. Furthermore, respondents with greater confidence in business were only 18.9 percent less likely to favor Chávez, after controlling for their optimism (model 2), compared to being 20.3 percent less likely to favor Chávez without controlling for their optimism (model 1). The decline in significance level and in the power of the effect after controlling for the degree of optimism can be interpreted as demonstrating that anti-business sentiment had an indirect effect on the intention to vote for Chávez, via individual voters' striking optimism for the future. It affirms the idea that Chávez's supporters were not only indifferent to business but actually inspired to trust him because he seemed likely to check the political influence of business.

Optimism about a future in which Chávez governed also seemed related to respondents' frustration with the economy overall and their concern regarding corruption. The effect of their assessment of how well the country had been doing over the past year on their intention to vote for Chávez is much less significant once we take into consideration their optimism. The coefficient for the retrospective sociotropic variable in model 2 is statistically significant at a much lower level than in model 1. Those who thought the country was doing better were only 21 percent less likely to favor Chávez than those who thought the country was doing about the same as it had been a year ago, after controlling for relative optimism. This suggests that those who were optimistic about a future governed by Chávez were, in part, optimistic about his ability to address their concerns about how the country was doing overall. Similarly, the effect of their concern regarding corruption on their intention to vote for Chávez loses significance altogether once we take into consideration their relative optimism. This suggests that those who were optimistic about the future in 1998 were also, in part, optimistic about Chávez's ability to address their concerns regarding corruption.

How Business Opposition Backfired

While others have studied the opinions of Chávez's supporters, they have not addressed why Chávez might have been able to overcome fears business opposition should have provoked in voters. The analysis here suggests that Chávez's supporters were undeterred by business opposition in part because they lacked confidence in business and that some Venezuelans may even have been optimistic about Chávez *because* he appeared likely to disconcert business. These findings vindicate the worries expressed during the campaign by some close to the business community that their vocal opposition might backfire. Instead of dissuading Venezuelans from supporting Chávez, business opposition might actually have encouraged Venezuelans to support Chávez.

These findings also suggest that anti-business sentiment, not just anti-neoliberalism, facilitated the re-politicization of class in new political movements during the 1990s. The fact that anti-business sentiment, independent of an individual's class status, affected how likely an individual was to favor Chávez suggests another reason why such movements had broad appeal. Their leaders did not have to rely exclusively on the economically marginalized to build their movement. They could draw on sympathy for such a movement from voters across the social spectrum, from Venezuelans who, like the economically marginalized, distrusted business.

This chapter thus demonstrates that views of business played a previously overlooked role in the 1998 presidential election. However, the analysis does not necessarily explain why Venezuelans would have been so distrustful of business or why their anti-business sentiment would have factored into their political behavior as voters. It is to those questions that we now turn.

4

•

THE SOURCES OF

ANTI-BUSINESS SENTIMENT

THERE ARE at least two plausible sources of anti-business sentiment in Venezuela other than Chávez's own rhetoric. One is Venezuela's long history of corruption scandals that implicate business (i.e., business corruption), and another is the visible, or prominent, role of business in Venezuelan politics (i.e., business prominence). Since I have demonstrated that the public's lack of confidence in business had an impact on the outcome of the 1998 election, it is important to establish the plausible origins of anti-business sentiment and whether they affected that dwindling level of confidence in business in 1998. Doing so reveals several new ways that corruption and Venezuela's political institutions could have shaped the 1998 presidential election.

Business Corruption

Corruption by definition involves government agents. Whether elected or not, government agents can siphon off public funds for their own private gain in myriad ways. They can embezzle funds or engage in various schemes that defraud the public but do not involve private citizens. Sometimes, however, corruption also involves nonstate actors such as business executives. Corruption involving businesspeople can entail agents of a business bribing government actors to secure a license or contract or government actors extorting fees from business actors in exchange for government authorizations that businesses may require in order to operate. I refer to such instances of corruption as "business corruption." In the corruption scandals that emerge from such cases, formal allegations of corruption may implicate not only government actors but also executives or other agents of a business.

Corruption scandals are the cases of corruption most likely to have a political impact because they are the cases that have received widespread media attention. Corruption scandals are not necessarily the most egregious cases of corruption, and, in the vast majority of cases, those implicated in scandals are never declared guilty in a court of law. But corruption scandals can affect and/or reflect the public's opinion of the individuals and institutions allegedly involved in corruption. They therefore serve as an important barometer of the type of corruption that dominates the public's attitude toward corruption and, therefore, its stance toward the actors most often blamed for corruption.

A systematic analysis of corruption scandals reveals that business corruption has a long history in Venezuela but that it escalated during the 1990s. Furthermore, it demonstrates that corruption became associated with one of two major policy arenas: foreign exchange controls and financial sector regulations. This pattern implicated business in what appeared, to many, to be systemic corruption.

The Rise of Corruption Scandals
Implicating Business

With the beginning of Venezuela's two-party democracy in 1958, Venezuela's political leaders became committed to the development of a private sector. They promoted programs that effectively transferred wealth from the state to the private sector. However, the scale and range of such programs expanded considerably during Carlos Andrés Pérez's first stint as president (1974–1979). Along with these changes came a wave of corruption scandals that implicated business. During Pérez's administration, it is widely acknowledged that a few political leaders oversaw a massive and direct transfer of state resources to their private supporters (Capriles Méndez 1992, 213). Corruption scandals that came to the public's attention at the time suggested that large-scale bribery (the exchange of money from private actors for favors from state officials) or fraud (collusion between private actors and state officials to defraud the government) had become more common (Capriles 1993, 212). Indeed, Pérez's administration became associated with boosting the economic fortunes of a new group of business elites, whom one observer sarcastically dubbed Pérez's twelve apostles (Duno 1975), in exchange for their campaign support.

The Pentacom scandal illustrated this new type of corruption: one in which private actors seemed to be successfully pressing state officials to make their special interests a matter of public policy, regardless of whether doing so served the public good. Reports began to circulate in March 1975 that a handful of the country's major conglomerates—many of which had been among Pérez's largest campaign donors in 1973—had presented the Ministry of Energy and Mines with a glossy feasibility study for how they might develop the soon-to-be government-controlled petrochemical sector ("Venezuela: This Little Pig" 1975). These conglomerates had formed a petrochemical company, Pentacom, and made a significant amount of capital available for the company. The feasibility study presented to the government included a proposal to allocate a large sum of government resources to build major petrochemical plants. The plan seemed to confirm widespread suspicion that Pérez would grant private industry the right to develop the petrochemicals sector to repay those who had supported his presidential candidacy in 1973. Under intense scrutiny, however, Pérez rejected the proposal ("Venezuela: This Little Pig" 1975).

The Pentacom scandal, which did not lead to any convictions, made visible what appeared to be a shift in the private sector's orientation from being an initiator of new production to becoming a supplicant for favors from the state (Bond 1987). It also revealed what appeared to be a state on the verge of being captured by these powerful business interests. But Pérez's administration in the 1970s was not the only one in which business was widely implicated.

While business corruption has a long history in Venezuela, it escalated in the 1990s. I use two samples of corruption scandals to show this trend. As mentioned above, the first of the two samples consists of those described in a three-volume summary of all corruption scandals from 1959 to 1992 painstakingly assembled by one of Venezuela's leading corruption scholars (Capriles Méndez 1990a, 1990b, 1992). The second is one I constructed for the remaining years of the two-party democratic era (i.e., 1992–1998) using sampling criteria similar to those of Ruth Capriles. Following leading corruption scholars (Morris 1991), I identified corruption scandals reported in one of Venezuela's leading newspapers, *El Universal,* on a random sample of dates. In both samples, I coded each corruption scandal according to whether the scandal included formal allegations (legal proceedings) against a business actor for corruption. (Appendix B describes more fully these sampling and coding procedures.) As reported in the media, the scandals involved a wide range of alleged violations of Venezuela's anti-corruption laws. Of these, the most common during the 1959–1992 period were instances of the government overpaying a private citizen for a product or a service (approximately one-third of the cases), a company not following through on a contract, the government awarding contracts without a competitive bidding process, and the sale of underpriced government products to businesses.

Table 4.1 presents the number and percentage of the corruption scandals that implicated business by presidential administration. Table 4.1's presentation of the Capriles data set (1959–1992) shows that the only administration in which the percentage of corruption scandals implicating business was higher than the overall average was the second administration of Carlos Andrés Pérez (1989–1992).[1] On average, 34 percent of the corruption scandals between 1959 and 1992 implicated business. In the first three years of the second Pérez administration (1989–1992), however, 46 percent of the corruption scandals implicated business. While table 4.1 also shows that corruption scandals implicating business represented 40 percent of all corruption scandals during the first Caldera administration (1969–1974), we should be careful about inferring too much from this comparatively high percentage. Although the percentage of corruption scandals that implicated business was indeed high, the total number of corruption scandals during Caldera's first administration is too low to make the rate significantly different from the overall average of 34 percent during the period covered in the Capriles data set (1959–1992).

Table 4.1 reveals that the number of corruption scandals implicating business remained high throughout the 1990s. During the second Caldera administration, a full 45 percent of the corruption scandals that occurred between

TABLE 4.1. Corruption scandals by whether they implicated business, 1959–1998

President (term)[a]	Percentage of corruption scandals implicating business	Number of corruption scandals
Capriles data set		
Betancourt (1959–1964)	0	3
Leoni (1964–1969)	25	8
Caldera (1969–1974)	40	10
Pérez (1974–1979)	38	21
Herrera Campins (1979–1984)	28	86
Lusinchi (1984–1989)	35	77
Pérez (1989–1992)[b]	46[+]	41
Total for 1959–1992	34	246
Gates data set		
Pérez (1992–1993) / Velásquez (1993–1994)[c]	22	41
Caldera (1994–1998)[d]	45	105
Total for 1992–1998	38	146
Both data sets		
Total for 1959–1998	36	392

Sources: For 1959–1992 period, Capriles Méndez 1990a, 1990b, 1992. For 1992–1998, see appendix B for details on the data set I compiled from articles in *El Universal*.

[+] $p < .10$

[a] I assign each corruption scandal to the year when it first emerged in the public eye, that is, the year it was denounced. In Venezuela, presidents are elected in December of the year before they begin office but do not take office until February of the following year. Hence, the years of each administration overlap.

[b] Represents the first three years of the Pérez administration based on the Capriles sample. The rate of implicating business in corruption scandals during this period was significantly higher (at the .10 level) than the average rate of 34 percent for the entire 1959–1992 period.

[c] Represents the remainder of the Pérez administration (from January 1992 to May 1993) and the Velásquez presidency (from May 21, 1993, to February 1994).

[d] The sample does not include any cases that may have surfaced during his final month in office (January 1999).

1994 and 1998 implicated business. This is higher than the overall average of 38 percent during the period of this data set (1992–1998) as well as the overall average of 36 percent for the era of two-party dominance (1959–1998).[2]

My analysis of the Capriles data also shows a general shift toward allegations against business actors as opposed to allegations against other actors. I compared the percentage of corruption scandals that implicated business to the

TABLE 4.2. Corruption scandals by type of actor implicated, 1959–1992

Political period	Type of actor implicated (%)			Number of corruption scandals
	Government official	Politician	Business actor	
1959–1974	47.6	23.8	28.6	21
1974–1979	38.1	28.6	38.1	21
1979–1984	46.5	23.3	27.9	86
1984–1989	41.6	23.4	35.1	77
1989–1992	43.9	22.0	46.3	41
Total	43.9	23.6	34.1	246

Sources: Coding based on Capriles Méndez 1990a, 1990b, 1992.

percentage that implicated other actors (table 4.2). As noted earlier, we expect corruption allegations to implicate some type of government actor, whether they be unelected (appointed or career) government officials or elected politicians. Table 4.2 affirms the widely held characterization of the first Pérez administration (1974–1979) as one in which corruption scandals tended to implicate business actors and their ties to high-level politicians. During that administration, the rate of scandals implicating business actors reached the same level as those implicating government actors, or 38.1 percent. Moreover, it is during that administration that the percentage of corruption scandals implicating politicians reached its peak of 28.6 percent. Table 4.2 also reveals that the second Pérez administration (1989–1992) was the only one in which the percentage of corruption scandals implicating business actors is higher than the level implicating government officials. This further corroborates the public's growing focus on corruption scandals that involved allegations against business actors, or business corruption.

Implicating Business in Systemic Corruption

The present analysis of corruption scandals also reveals how business became associated with Venezuela's corruption problem through two instances of what appeared to be systemic corruption. In the 1980s and 1990s, there was a seemingly endless cascade of individual corruption scandals related to two policy arenas: foreign exchange controls and financial sector regulations. The clustering of so many corruption allegations around these two policy arenas and the alleged involvement of government officials at the highest levels led many experts to conclude that there had been a shift in the nature of Venezuela's corruption. Historically, corruption scandals implicating business had pointed to a few bad apples (Capriles Méndez 1992, 572). They typically implicated business executives for procuring contracts to construct public works or provide services for the state (Pérez Perdomo 1992, 5) through special "arrangements" in which they "shared" the profits with the government officials authorizing the contract. In other instances, such as the Pentacom scandal, the allegations against business involved individual campaign financiers who allegedly expected government favors in return for their contributions. These two policy arenas, however, appear to be institutional environments that generated powerful incentives for both state actors and business executives to pursue illicit avenues of transferring public wealth to the private sector (Pérez Perdomo 1992, 5).

One of the policy arenas in which business was implicated in systemic corruption was that of price and exchange rate controls. The government implemented the Régimen de Cambios Diferenciales (RECADI, or Differential Exchange Rate Regime) in 1983, after Venezuela's debt crisis and subsequent currency devaluation. Under this policy, the government bought foreign currency, typically the dollar, at a lower rate than was available to the general public. Businesses, however, could apply for authorization to have access to the lower-than-market foreign monetary exchange rate for certain types of international transactions. The government introduced this multitiered exchange rate system because the devaluation had threatened to cripple Venezuela's industrial producers, whose enterprises relied on importing parts and raw materials. Thus, to obtain authorization for the most preferential exchange rate, businesses had to justify their petition on the grounds that they were importing *necessary* goods and services or that they would use the cheaper foreign currency to pay the interest on foreign debt (Beroes 1990, chap. 2). RECADI remained in place from 1983 through the initial days of the second Pérez presidential administration, in 1989.

To many, the RECADI-related corruption scandals revealed that Venezuelan public policies increasingly, even if unintentionally, facilitated systemic corruption (Capriles Méndez 1992, 572). A book-length investigation into RECADI estimates that, of the roughly US$34 billion RECADI authorized for the preferential exchange rate, US$11 billion financed corrupt transactions (Beroes 1990, conclusion). This US$11 billion figure is nearly equal to the national reserves at the time (Capriles Méndez 1992, 554). Others have deemed RECADI a "magnet for corruption," "an exchange rate fiasco" (Naím 1993b), and "the culminating expression of a process in which Venezuela's contemporary morality had been degraded" (Capriles Méndez 1992, 559). Another scholar confers on RECADI the dubious honor of being the worst of Venezuela's top ten corruption scandals during the two-party era (Coronel 1997). By 1989, most Venezuelans (69 percent) had heard of RECADI, and 79 percent of them believed it involved corruption. RECADI brought widespread corruption to mind more than had any previous corruption scandal (Templeton 1995, 91).

The impression that RECADI-related corruption was indicative of a new, more systemic form of corruption grew, in part, from the fact that RECADI's allegedly corrupt elements included all levels of government. They included low-level government officials accused of taking commissions to authorize preferential rates and members of the National Guard or customs agents who allegedly accepted bribes to verify imports as qualifying for the preferential rate (Capriles Méndez 1992, 561, 591–613). They also included nearly all cabinet ministers, the directors of the Central Bank, and the president himself (Capriles Méndez 1992, 553, 560, 633).[3] Some high-level officials were charged with using their influence to push through authorizations of preferential exchange rates for friends and business associates.[4] Some were even detained for authorizing $8 billion more than the budgeted limit for preferential exchange rates in 1987 and 1988 (Capriles Méndez 1992, 636, 658–59).

The RECADI indictments brought to light numerous ways that Venezuela's business executives had allegedly deceived the public or bribed government officials.[5] Many businesses were accused of swindling the public by exaggerating the price of the goods they were importing in order to obtain authorization for a larger sum of dollars at the preferred rate than was actually warranted (Capriles Méndez 1992, 562). For example, in May 1989, a judge ordered the detention of executives from a wheat importing firm for allegedly having exaggerated the cost of the wheat that they imported to sell domestically (Capriles Méndez 1992, 554–56, 614–24). In a few instances, businesspeople had allegedly swindled the public by setting up phantom companies (Capriles Méndez 1992, 561). For example, the lone businessperson whom the government convicted on RECADI corruption charges created seven phantom companies through which he had applied and obtained authorization for more than US$26 million via RECADI (Capriles Méndez 1992, 554, 579–83).[6] Numerous court-ordered investigations in 1989 alleged that businesspeople had bribed government officials to obtain preferential exchange rate authorization (Capriles Méndez 1992, 553, 560–61, 564). For example, one businessperson allegedly bribed a customs official to qualify an airplane he was bringing into the country as a new import even though it had already been in the country. Another businessperson allegedly bribed officials to verify, as new, merchandise that was actually old. To secure authorization for a preferential exchange rate, yet another businessperson allegedly bribed an official to falsely qualify liquor as a necessary import (Capriles Méndez 1992, 557, 561, 567).

These RECADI-related corruption scandals had humiliating consequences for some of Venezuela's most high-profile business leaders. For example, in 1989, a Venezuelan judge "issued 47 arrest warrants for foreign or local business executives and more than 100 orders restricting travel for executives and former Government officials," which resulted in at least fourteen Venezuelan business officials being temporarily jailed (Brooke 1989). One of the first RECADI-related corruption investigations involved allegations that foreign car assemblers operating in Venezuela had overestimated, by US$125 million, the value of their imports (Capriles Méndez 1992, 589).[7] It was thought that the auto industry had collectively received approximately 40 percent of RECADI authorizations (Capriles Méndez 1992, 588), so a corruption court judge ruled that executives of General Motors, Ford, and Renault could not leave the country (Capriles Méndez 1992, 589). Executives who worked at other multinational firms were investigated ("'Judicial Terror'" 1989), prompting many to flee the country. Some deemed these executives to be victims of a "witch hunt" (Brooke 1989). Even the president of Venezuela's leading business organization, FEDECAMARAS, was jailed for eight days after he declared that the real culprits of RECADI-based corruption scandals were in the former Lusinchi government (1984–1989), not in the business community (Brooke 1989). While many of the business executives ordered to be detained managed to leave the country before being apprehended, the fourteen who were initially jailed included "two big fish" ("Scandal Grows" 1989), businessmen from two of Venezuela's most established and elite families (Capriles Méndez 1992, 618).

Thus, RECADI-related corruption implicated business in what appeared to be systemic corruption. In fact, nearly all of the corruption scandals that involved the RECADI program implicated business. All four of the RECADI corruption scandals in my newspaper sample and all but three of the fourteen RECADI corruption scandals described by Capriles involved formal allegations against business. Even those three cases that did not involve formal allegations against business implicated business indirectly. In one of those three cases, a local governor was accused of having "advised" a group of liquor importers who shared his Syrian-Lebanese heritage about how to submit requests for authorization in such a way as to secure authorizations for an exceedingly large sum of dollars (Capriles Méndez 1992, 576). In the other two cases, judges were accused of acting unprofessionally by protecting government officials who had favored businesses.[8] Moreover, while there were about three thousand companies that were formally charged, "practically all traders and industrialists who import merchandise, machines, or primary materials" had probably participated in similarly corrupt transactions (Capriles Méndez 1992, 553).

RECADI-related corruption scandals represented 50 percent of the corruption scandals (in the Capriles sample) implicating business during the first three years of that administration. They represented 44 percent of the corruption scandals (in my newspaper sample) implicating business during in the final years of the truncated Pérez administration and the interim Velásquez administration (January 1992 through February 1994). RECADI-related cases were particularly dominant in 1989, the first year of Pérez's second administration. Nine of the thirteen corruption scandals implicating business in 1989, or 69 percent, related to RECADI. All of these RECADI-related corruption scandals gave the impression that the policy had facilitated systemic corruption and that business had been involved. But RECADI was not the only policy that brought to light what appeared to be systemic corruption implicating business.

Venezuela's banking crisis in 1994 placed a spotlight on the second policy arena that appeared to provoke systemic corruption and that implicated business. As I describe elsewhere (Gates 2007, 112), the banking crisis began when Venezuela's second-largest bank, Banco Latino (Krivoy 2003, 1) informed the government on January 13, 1994, that it would not be able to honor the checks endorsed by its clients. The government took a number of steps in response, one being that it froze the savings accounts of Banco Latino's depositors on January 16. Collectively, these accounts were worth US$1.4 billion. In freezing the accounts, the government prevented 1.3 million depositors from accessing their assets and provoked Venezuelans to withdraw their money from numerous other banks ("Venezuela: Arrests Begin" 1994). The Government Guarantee and Financial Loan Fund, commonly referred to by its acronym FOGADE (Fondo de Garantía de Depósitos y Protección Bancaria), provided loans to some banks to try to keep them open. Within three weeks, nearly a third of the nation's banks remained in operation as a result of government loans. Meanwhile, capital flight surged to an estimated US$2 billion. By August 1995, when the financial system was finally stabilized, nineteen financial institutions (all but one were commercial banks) had failed and 7 million depositors, almost a third of Venezuela's population, had suffered uncertainty and financial loss (Krivoy 2003, 1, 3). To save the system, the government seized numerous commercial banks, the combined assets of which amounted to 70 percent of the total funds in the financial sector (Fidler 1994).[9] The loans, repayment of insured depositors, and public recapitalization efforts cost the government an estimated US$7.3 billion in 1994 alone (Krivoy 2003, 7). This sum represented around 75 percent of the government's 1994 revenue and roughly 11 percent of the gross domestic product that year (Krivoy 2003, 7; "Unexpected Moves" 1994). It was Latin America's fifth-largest bank crisis in three decades and, as of 2002, it was the world's thirteenth most costly bank crisis (Krivoy 2002, 220).

Like the RECADI program, the bank crisis of 1994 unleashed a torrent of corruption scandals that implicated business, and it was foremost among the scandals implicating business, just as RECADI had been. Indeed, in my newspaper sample 60 percent of the individual corruption scandals implicating business that emerged between 1994 and 1998 (during Caldera's administration) related to the bank crisis. In 1994, when the crisis began, nearly all (fourteen of sixteen) of the business corruption scandals related to troubled banks.

As in the RECADI-related scandals, many of the corruption allegations had humiliating consequences for those business executives accused of wrongdoing. In the bank crisis scandal, the initial allegations involved accusations of "irregularities" in the activities of former executives and board members at troubled banks; detention orders and travel restrictions resulted. Early in the year, newspapers reported allegations that Banco Latino was a "centrifuge of dollars" (C.S. 1994a). The first formal allegations were announced in March 1994, when a criminal court judge ordered the detention of eighty-three board members and managers of Banco Latino along with just one former government official. The judge charged the bankers with a number of irregularities in their managing of the banks. He accused the former superintendent of banks of "being complicit with allowing Banco Latino to publish deceitful information" (Krivoy 2002, 153). At the same time, the government issued an order prohibiting all managers and board members at eight troubled banks receiving government aid (FOGADE aid) from leaving the country (Krivoy 2002, 153).[10] At the end of March, the superintendent of banks gave all directors of financial institutions a month to submit a notarized declaration of their personal assets (Chiappe 1994). In May, five other individuals associated with Banco Latino—the former external auditor and several directors of the bank—were also denounced for corruption (Vargas 1994c).

By June 1994, people increasingly suspected that the directors left in charge of the banks receiving government aid were corrupt ("Venezuelan Banking; Chaos in Caracas" 1994) and had stolen government money (Krivoy 2002, 186). Venezuelan newspapers reported that the government's FOGADE aid seemed to have fallen into a black hole ("Unexpected Moves" 1994). Instead of being used for its intended purpose—to help bank depositors—the money was reportedly "recycled to other weak banks" or used for other illegitimate purposes (Gates 2007, 112; Mann 1994b). At the behest of the superintendent of banks, in mid-1994, a criminal court judge investigated former bank executives and board members for a host of "possible irregularities in the use of financial assistance granted by FOGADE" (Hernández 1994). Venezuela's superintendent of banks publicly blamed bankers for the "delicate situation," arguing that the banks were in crisis due to "inefficient administration" and "bank operations off the balance sheets" (Vargas 1994d). On June 9, another judge ordered about thirty bank directors to stay in the country. A day later, the same judge ordered the detention of the president and three top executives of another financial institution that had received FOGADE assistance. He did so because it appeared that this institution had improperly designated FOGADE money for "interbank loans or to cancel obligations to companies that were affiliated with the conglomerate" (Vargas 1994d).

The Caldera government took an increasingly hard-line approach with troubled banks at risk of failure. President Caldera even suspended constitutional guarantees that allowed him to arrest people without charges and to confiscate property without the otherwise necessary legal instruments (Krivoy 2002, 187–89).[11] The attorney general declared this action "a law against heists committed by bankers" ("Procurador Petit da Costa" 1994). He explained that undoing the bankers' "financial engineering" would require "judicial engineering." On behalf of the administration, he then used these new legal provisions to take over a vast network of companies affiliated with government-seized banks (Krivoy 2002, 189). Venezuela's interior minister publicly blamed bankers for the crisis, declaring that "the main cause of the problem [with banks] is white collar delinquency" ("El Ministro del Interior" 1994). Even the new state-appointed administrator of one of the seized banks called for criminal investigations against the former board members of the bank he administered after numerous unauthorized transactions came to light (Vargas 1994b). The former bankers were subsequently investigated for embezzlement and irregular management of large sums of money. In early 1995, new bank tribunals, which exclusively focused on bank-related corruption charges, resulted in a new wave of allegations against former bank executives and board members (Mendoza 1995a, 1995b).

As reports of the corruption related to the bank crisis increasingly alleged the improper use of government funds, they alerted the public to the systemic nature of apparent corruption in the financial sector. In March 1994, for example, rumors had circulated of arrest warrants being issued for many high-level government officials. Three months later, in the midst of heated public condemnation of the alleged misuse of government loans and aid extended through FOGADE, formal legal proceedings against those with authority to regulate the financial sector began (Krivoy 2002, 220). These investigations eventually included complaints against the former finance minister, the superintendent of banks, the president of FOGADE, and the Central Bank (García 1998). It was alleged that only 20 percent of FOGADE's loan assistance funds had been used appropriately (Krivoy 2002, 218).[12] The scandal even extended to those who were appointed to supervise and manage the banks after the government took them over.[13]

Thus, to the extent that business had a visible role in corruption scandals during the 1990s, RECADI and the bank crisis were largely the reason. Even though the vast majority of the scandals associated with these policies did not result in a formal showing of culpability in the courts, it is hard to imagine that they did not undermine the public's confidence in business more generally. Indeed, it seems likely that the apparent involvement of business in what seemed to be systemic corruption effectively fueled anti-business sentiment.

Business Prominence in Politics

Another likely reason for declining public confidence in business and, therefore, the increase in anti-business sentiment, was the visible presence of business actors within Venezuela's widely discredited two-party political establishment. To identify individuals who held powerful political positions and also had significant business experience, I examined the membership of both the federal legislature and the presidential cabinet's economic posts. As elected officials, federal legislators are the public face of the political establishment around the country, and, in Venezuela, they must also earn the trust of those at the helm of the country's dominant political institutions: the political parties. During the two-party era, Venezuela's political parties nominated individuals to serve in the federal legislature and voters chose parties, not individuals, when they cast their ballots. Thus, to be nominated, a candidate had to secure the support of party leaders. I also examined those who accepted presidential appointments to become ministers at Venezuela's leading economic policy–related ministries. (See appendix C for list of those six ministries.) As ministers responsible for economic policy, these individuals were among the most visible political leaders in any administration. Ministers also earned their positions by securing the trust of party leaders. In the case of ministers, though, they owed their position to the president.

I collected professional biographies of all economic ministers and a select sample of federal legislators (see appendix C for details). Out of all the federal legislators whom the interviewees identified as businesspeople, 69 could be verified as having had significant prior business experience. Collectively, these 69 legislators held 118 posts in the federal legislature during Venezuela's era of two-party dominance (1959–1998). As table 4.3 demonstrates, these 118 posts held by federal legislators with significant prior business experience represented 6.2 percent of all 1,899 federal legislative positions during that era. On its surface, this figure does not seem remarkably high. However, this proportion does stand out once it is compared to that of all federal legislators with prior significant business experience in a similar country. Mexico is similar to Venezuela in that it, too, had multiclass parties that incorporated both the laboring and the peasant classes into the formal political process and that dominated a relatively stable political system for several decades (Collier and Collier 1991). Numerous scholars have invoked this similarity to justify the usefulness

TABLE 4.3. Percentage of federal legislators in Venezuela and Mexico with significant prior business experience, 1958–2000

Venezuela		Mexico	
President (term)	Percent (n)	Percent (n)	President (term)
Betancourt (1959–1964)	4.4 (184)	3.0 (67)	López Mateos (1958–1964)
Leoni (1964–1969)	5.8 (225)	2.1 (97)	Díaz Ordaz (1964–1970)
Caldera (1969–1974)	8.7 (226)	2.8 (106)	Echeverría (1970–1976)
Pérez (1974–1979)	7.3 (247)	1.9 (105)	López Portillo (1976–1982)
Herrera Campins (1979–1984)	5.8 (243)		
Lusinchi (1984–1989)	9.0 (244)	1.9 (107)	De la Madrid (1982–1988)
Pérez (1989–1993)	3.7 (246)	1.1 (93)	Salinas (1988–1994)
Caldera (1994–1999)	4.5 (244)	8.7 (127)	Zedillo (1994–2000)
Total	6.2 (1899)	3.3 (702)	

Sources: See appendix C for sampling procedure and biographical sources on Venezuelan legislators. Total number of Venezuelan legislators calculated based on *Los partidos políticos y sus estadísticas electorales, 1944–1984*, vol. 1 (Caracas: Consejo Supremo Electoral, 1987), 145, and an electronic list of all elected officials in 1993 obtained from the Venezuelan Secretaría General, Dirección de Estadísticas Electorales, División de Geografía Electoral. Roderic Camp provided me with the data for Mexico. It is based on his comprehensive study of Mexican elites (Camp 2002).

Note: Number of federal legislators indicated in parentheses.

of comparing the politics of these two countries (Burgess 1999; Coppedge 1993; Murillo 2000). Even state-business relations in these two countries have been interpreted as similarly combining corporatist inclusion of business associations with informal channels of communication between political leaders and individual business actors (Camp 1989; Coppedge 1993; 2000). Thus, we might expect both countries to have business actors similarly represented among public figures.

Nonetheless, as table 4.3 illustrates, the proportion of individuals with significant prior business experience in the federal legislature in Mexico was only 3.3 percent overall. This proportion is derived using the same definition of business experience as the one I used to assess the business experience of political leaders in Venezuela. Furthermore, in every administration, except Caldera's, the last one of the two-party era, the proportion of legislators with significant prior business experience was higher in Venezuela than it was in Mexico. Not until the Zedillo administration in Mexico (1994–2000) did Mexican political parties recruit directly from within the ranks of business leaders to find nominees for the federal legislature. This move reflected the declining power of Mexico's historically dominant multiclass party, a shift facilitated by a series of political reforms. Specifically, this larger presence of business-affiliated legislators reflected the increased representation of PAN (Partido Acción Nacional), a conservative party that had historically been tied to business and that, in the 1980s and 1990s, increasingly drew its leadership from the business community (Chand 2001; Luna 1992; Puga 1993; Trevizo 2003). Unlike Roderic Camp, however, I do not have information on *every* legislator in Venezuela. Thus, Venezuela's percentages of business-affiliated legislators, as shown in table 4.3, reflect what should be considered the lowest probable figures or a minimum rate. These figures would likely be higher if one considered biographical information on every legislator.

Similarly, I found that business executives had a long and increasing presence in Venezuela's most visible economic policy-making positions: cabinet posts that deal with economic issues. These individuals had become bureaucrats by virtue of accepting a ministerial appointment. Nevertheless, they were distinct from typical *bureaucrats,* who build their careers primarily within the state bureaucracy, and from typical *technocrats,* those bureaucrats with extensive technical training (Centeno 1995; Centeno and Maxfield 1992; Centeno and Silva 1998). These bureaucrats might be better described as *businocrats* because of their significant business experience prior to taking a government post.

As table 4.4 shows, half (50.6 percent) of Venezuela's economic policy-making positions were occupied by individuals who had significant prior business experience and who therefore qualify as businocrats. Such individuals had a strong presence in Venezuela's economic policy-making positions in the first six administrations of the two-party era. They become even more prevalent, however, beginning with the second Pérez administration (1989–1993). In that administration, 56.0 percent of the ministers occupying economic cabinet posts had significant business experience. The proportion of businocrats in economic cabinet positions was also higher than average in the final two administrations of the period: that of the interim presidency of Ramón Velásquez, who took over after Pérez stepped down, and that of Rafael Caldera. In other words, the proportion of economic policy makers who were businocrats was significantly higher during the six years preceding the 1998 presidential elections than it had been at any other time during the two-party era.

Comparing the relative prominence of business leaders among Mexico's cabinet ministers with the relative prominence of such individuals in Venezuela's

TABLE 4.4. Percentage of cabinet posts in Venezuela and Mexico occupied by businocrats, 1958–2000

	Venezuela		Mexico	
President	Percentage in economic cabinet posts	Percentage in all cabinet posts	Percentage in all cabinet posts	President
Betancourt (1959–1964)	37.5 (16)	17.1 (35)	8.3 (24)	López Mateos (1958–1964)
Leoni (1964–1969)	37.5 (16)	17.1 (35)	8.3 (24)	Díaz Ordaz (1964–1970)
Caldera (1969–1974)	46.2 (13)	18.8 (32)	16.4 (55)	Echeverría (1970–1976)
Pérez (1974–1979)	45.0 (20)	17.7 (51)	14.7 (34)	López Portillo (1976–1982)
Herrera Campins (1979–1984)	50.0 (16)	17.8 (45)		
Lusinchi (1984–1989)	35.0 (20)	12.5 (56)	6.9 (29)	De la Madrid (1982–1988)
Pérez (1989–1993)	56.0 (25)	20.0 (70)	9.1 (33)	Salinas (1988–1994)
Velásquez (1993–1994)	81.7* (11)	33.3 (27)		
Caldera (1994–1999)	68.0+ (25)	27.9 (61)	13.6 (22)	Zedillo (1994–2000)
Total	50.6 (162)	19.9 (412)	11.8 (221)	

Sources: See appendix C for sampling procedure and biographical sources on Venezuelan ministers. Total number of Venezuelan cabinet posts calculated based on data provided by Rosa Amelia González, which I adjusted to include all economic policy positions. Roderic Camp provided the data on Mexico. It is based on his comprehensive study of Mexican elites (Camp 2002).

Notes: Number of posts (n) indicated in parentheses. The asterisk and cross refers to results of Chi^2 tests, which assess whether the percentage for each particular administration was significantly different than the percentage overall. The Mexico data did not permit a separate analysis by economic ministries.

+ $p < 0.10$; * $p < 0.05$

cabinet posts further illustrates the prominence of business in Venezuela's political arena. Table 4.4 compares the percentage of all cabinet members who were businocrats in Mexico with the percentage of cabinet posts occupied by businocrats in Venezuela.[14] Even this minimum measure of business prominence in Venezuela's ministries is higher than Mexico's. Table 4.4 shows that the proportion of cabinet members who were businocrats is 11.8 percent in Mexico. In contrast, businocrats filled 19.9 percent of all (412) Venezuelan cabinet-level posts during the same period. The table further demonstrates that in every administration, the minimum rate of businocrats was higher in Venezuela than it was in Mexico. In other words, Venezuela had a long and escalating trend of having ministers with significant prior business experience.

We might expect that government officials with backgrounds in Venezuela's powerful conglomerates would be very visible to the public. As table 4.5 shows, nearly a quarter (22.8 percent) of all Venezuelan economic cabinet posts were occupied by those who had significant prior ties to major economic conglomerates, or *grupos económicos,* before they became ministers. This trend seemed to accelerate in the 1990s. The economic cabinet members in the second Pérez administration (1989–1993), for instance, had a higher-than-average rate of ties to conglomerates (36 percent). This increasing political prominence of conglomerates would have further tied business to Venezuela's political establishment.

The Prevailing Concerns of Anti-business Voters

If the public's anti-business sentiment did, in fact, originate in the long and escalating association of business with both corruption and the political establishment, we would expect anti-business sentiment in 1998 to be related to both anti-corruption and anti-political establishment sentiments. Given the public association of business with corruption, particularly in the 1990s, we would expect those who were preoccupied with the problem of corruption in 1998 to have had less confidence in business. We would also expect that those who were preoccupied with corruption had the impression that business was intimately involved with the country's corruption problem. This is the business corruption hypothesis. Furthermore, given the prominence of business within the political establishment, particularly in the 1990s, we would expect that those who were less satisfied with the political establishment in 1998 had less

TABLE 4.5. Percentage of Venezuelan economic cabinet posts with prior ties to conglomerates, 1959–1999

President (term)	Percentage with prior tie to conglomerate	Number of economic cabinet posts
Betancourt (1959–1964)	18.8	16
Leoni (1964–1969)	6.3[+]	16
Caldera (1969–1974)	23.1	13
Pérez (1974–1979)	15.0	20
Herrera Campins (1979–1984)	12.5	16
Lusinchi (1984–1989)	25.0	20
Pérez (1989–1993)	36.0[+]	25
Velásquez (1993–1994)	27.3	11
Caldera (1994–1999)	32.0	25
Total	22.8	162

Sources: See appendix C.

Note: Crosses ([+]) refer to Chi^2 tests of significant difference between the rate for each administration and the rate for all administrations.

[+] $p < 0.10$

confidence in business. Again, we would expect that those dissatisfied with the political establishment had the impression that business was intimately connected to the country's current political establishment. This is the business prominence hypothesis.

I examine these hypotheses using the 1998 national opinion poll conducted immediately prior to the presidential elections (REDPOL). This analysis controls for a number of factors we might expect to affect voter confidence in business. They include all of the factors predicted to affect a voter preference for Chávez (see chapter 3). Thus, I control for education and the factors predicted to influence an intention to vote for Chávez by the social polarization thesis. For example, we might expect those from lower social strata to have less confidence in business for a similar reason that social polarization scholars expect them to have more favorable attitudes toward Chávez: those from lower social strata experienced the brunt of Venezuela's economic decline in the 1990s. Following a similar logic, we might expect those who oppose privatization (one of the central planks of the neo-liberal economic reform agenda) to be less sympathetic toward business. Alternatively, we might expect that those who considered their own circumstances (the retrospective pocketbook variable) and the nation's situation (the retrospective sociotropic variable) to be worse than in the previous year would have less confidence in business.

A statistical technique called multinomial logistic regression can be used to test what affects confidence in business.[15] It permits an analysis of the effects of various factors on each of the three levels of confidence in business (none, some, and much) independently. Table 4.6 presents the results. The column in table 4.6 headed "Some confidence in business" presents the effects of each independent variable (listed to the left) on the likelihood of having some confidence in business versus having no confidence in business. In other words, we can think of this column as showing how the group of individuals with some confidence in business compares with the group of people who had no confidence in business. The column to the right of the "some confidence" column presents the relative effects of each variable on the likelihood of having much confidence in business versus having no confidence in business. Thus, in this analysis, the reference group for both columns is the group of individuals who reported having no confidence in business.

Table 4.6 shows some support for the business corruption hypothesis. Those who mentioned corruption as a priority for the next government were just as likely to have some confidence in business as they were to have no confidence in business. As expected, however, those who mentioned corruption as a priority for the next government were less likely to have much confidence in business than to have no confidence, controlling for other factors. More precisely, they were 36.7 percent less likely to have a lot of confidence than to have no confidence, independent of other variables.[16] These results suggest that those who most wanted the government to address the corruption problem were less confident in business, at least in part because they believed business was intimately involved with the country's corruption problem.

Table 4.6 also shows strong support for the business prominence hypothesis. The first column of data reveals, after I control for other factors that might influence confidence in business, that those who were more satisfied with the existing democracy were more likely to have some confidence in business than to have none. Indeed, those who were more satisfied with the existing democracy were 40.4 percent more likely to have some confidence than to have no confidence. Similarly, the second column of data reveals that those who were more satisfied with the existing democracy were even more likely to have much

TABLE 4.6. Multinomial logistic regression effects on level of confidence in business

Variables	Some confidence in business	Much confidence in business
Control variables		
Level of education	0.066	-0.134
	(6.9%)	(-12.5%)
Social class	-0.006	-0.087
	(-0.6%)	(-8.3%)
Support privatization	0.075	-0.301
	(7.7%)	(-26.0%)
Support state intervention	0.031	0.198
	(3.2%)	(21.9%)
Retrospective sociotropic	0.279*	0.204
	(32.2%)	(22.6%)
Retrospective pocketbook	-0.089	0.059
	(-8.5%)	(6.1%)
Business corruption hypothesis		
Corruption mentioned as priority	-0.177	-0.457*
	(-16.2%)	(-36.7%)
Business prominence hypothesis		
Satisfaction with democracy	0.339***	0.539***
	(40.4%)	(71.4%)
Constant	-0.724*	-2.211***
Statistics		
Log likelihood	-1131.99	
Likelihood ratio test (d.f.)	56.378 (16)	
Prob > Chi²	0.0000	
Pseudo R²	0.0243	
Number of observations	1296	

Source: REDPOL98, Banco de Datos Poblacionales, Universidad Simón Bolívar.

Notes: The dependent variable reference category is "no confidence in business." Numbers in parentheses refer to percentage change in odds for a unit increase in the independent variable.

$* p < 0.05; ** p < 0.01; *** p < 0.001$

confidence in business than to have none, holding other factors constant. They were 71.4 percent more likely to have a lot of confidence in business than no confidence in business.[17] These results suggest that those less satisfied with the political establishment were also less confident in business at least in part because they connected business to the country's ill-reputed political establishment.[18]

How Business Corruption and Business Prominence
Paved the Way for Chávez

In Venezuela, business clearly had a long and increasingly visible association with both corruption and the political establishment. The point here is not that Venezuela's business executives were actually corrupt or were more corrupt than their counterparts in other countries. Such a claim would in any case be difficult to support given the clandestine nature of corruption. Rather, my aim here is to show that there were reasons for the public to *perceive* business as corrupt. The mounting scandals implicating business and the association of business with what appeared to be systemic corruption likely contributed to the gathering storm, not just against Venezuela's long-dominant traditional political parties but also against business. Furthermore, the ample presence, or prominence, of business elites within Venezuela's political establishment likely tied business to a discredited political establishment. This history of business corruption and business prominence in politics paved the way for Chávez by fueling anti-business sentiment.

Business corruption and business prominence represent ways not previously contemplated by scholars contributing to the corruption and failed institutions theses, that both corruption and Venezuela's political institutions influenced the 1998 presidential elections. While the perception of corruption as rampant no doubt influenced the election, this perception could not explain why Venezuelans chose Chávez over any of the other anti-corruption candidates. Rather, corruption's more critical influence on the elections may have been its increasingly more apparent role as a vehicle for business elites to secure unfair privileges. It is the growing visibility of *business* corruption in the media that could have stoked the public's ire with business and hence its willingness to vote for an anti-neoliberal candidate who business opposed.

Similarly, Venezuela's political institutions may very well have influenced the elections because their rigid structures led many Venezuelans to feel excluded from the political process and generated widespread sympathy for candidates who, like Chávez, ran as political outsiders. Nevertheless, resentment toward Venezuela's political establishment cannot explain why so many Venezuelans chose Chávez over the other anti–political establishment candidates. We need to look beyond the structure of the institutions and instead consider the societal interests with which the institutions became identified to explain why Venezuelans chose Chávez. It is the identification of Venezuela's political institutions with business that could have stimulated resentment toward not only the political establishment but also the business community. It may be in this way, then, that Venezuela's political institutions shaped the willingness of voters to elect an anti-neoliberal candidate whom business opposed.

My analysis of anti-business sentiment in 1998 thus underscores the value of uncovering these two previously overlooked aspects of Venezuelan politics —Venezuela's political culture, rife with corruption allegations against business actors, and the political prominence of business. Without them, it would be difficult to solve the puzzle of why voters in 1998 overwhelmingly supported a candidate whom business so vehemently opposed. In particular, without them, it is hard to understand what generated the pool of anti-business voters that helped Chávez win. Given the widespread skepticism regarding business, it seems that business opposition helped to qualify Chávez as the candidate most likely to break with the political establishment and the corruption it engendered.

PART III

Business Assistance
for Chávez

5

·

DEPENDENT PROMINENCE

AND ELITE OUTLIER CALCULUS

TO ASSIST CHÁVEZ

MANY OF the business elites I interviewed had no difficulty remembering their disdain for Chávez during the 1998 presidential election. For example, one of Caracas's real estate barons scoffed, "I thought he didn't have any idea about economics. And, he had three or four socialist ideas that came from Marxism" (Interview 19, 9). A titan of Venezuelan industry explained why he dismissed Chávez, saying, "I didn't see anything in Chávez's policies that inspired me to think that, with his government, we would have sustainable development. Indeed, I saw the opposite" (Interview 24, 8). Another conglomerate executive recalled trying to persuade the U.S. government to help make sure Chávez did not win: "We had many meetings with the North American ambassador [to say] that he [Chávez] was crazy, that he would take us in the direction of Cuba" (Interview 34, 12).

These recollections reflect the widespread opposition to Chávez among business leaders. Even after Chávez tried to "temper the fear of companies" at the annual meeting of FEDECAMARAS, Venezuela's peak business association, a poll indicated that only 10 percent of delegates thought they might vote for Chávez (Carmona Estanga 1998). Pedro Carmona Estanga, a leader of FEDECAMARAS whom military leaders would later install as president during a failed coup attempt against Chávez in 2002, ironically decried Chávez for "'stamping out' the existing order, and calling for a 'sovereign' for which neither the constitution, nor the laws apply." In contrast, he praised the other presidential candidates for advocating political reforms "within a democratic framework and understanding" (Carmona Estanga 1998).

Yet during the 1998 campaign and after, there were reports that some business executives had, in fact, assisted Chávez. The idea that business may have assisted Chávez inspired at least two journalists to investigate the matter and to identify by name a host of individual business elites who were thought to have given money or to have made significant in-kind donations to the campaign (Santodomingo 1999; Zapata 2000). The possibility that some individual business elites assisted Chávez became even more intriguing when I learned that Venezuela's community elite had changed its political behavior in 1998. According to one of Venezuela's leading business consultants, it was common for Venezuela's business elite to "individually support their own candidate" before 1998. In the election of 1998, however, he thought that businesspeople had not been as eager to assist individual candidates. He recalled that, instead, many had pooled their resources and financed a general campaign to "try to explain to Venezuelans what type of change we needed in the country" (Interview 46, 4). This made it even more surprising that some individual business executives may, in fact, have assisted Chávez. Two questions thus presented themselves: Who were the outliers among Venezuela's business elite, and why did they assist Chávez?

Analyzing the political calculus of the "elite outliers"—those individual business executives who reportedly assisted Chávez—reveals that very few had economic interests that predisposed them to favor Chávez's protectionist economic policies. Instead, it demonstrates that the majority of them actually had economic interests that predisposed them to pursue access to the state even if it meant overlooking the policies Chávez advocated; most were dependent on direct cash transfers from the state. Because of their economic dependence on the state, they were inclined to support whichever leading presidential contender gave them the best chance of securing some of the state's resources on which they depended. Their calculations were, therefore, likely to be access based rather than policy based. Furthermore, several access-based reasons for these elites to assist Chávez emerge when we consider why only some but not all state-dependent elites assisted Chávez. The eite outliers were more likely to have acute reasons to fear losing access after the election than to have reasons to trust Chávez. Indeed, only a minority of state-dependent elite outliers had a personal connection with Chávez that might have given them a reason to trust him. Interviews with some outliers as well as with non-outlier business elites illustrate how the political prominence of business generated these acute fears of losing access. They thereby reveal how the political prominence of business interacted with the economic dependence of Venezuela's business community to shape the political calculus of business executives in Venezuela's two-party democracy. They elucidate, in short, how the dependent prominence of business influenced the calculus that elite outliers made to assist Chávez.

The Elite Outliers

It is impossible to know for sure who assisted Chávez in the 1998 presidential election. Venezuela's election laws require campaigns to submit records to the Consejo Nacional Electoral (CNE, or National Electoral Council), but they do not require campaigns to report the names of donors (Alvarez 1995). Thus, the records that the CNE has on file for the Chávez campaign contain donation amounts and dates of deposits into campaign accounts, but, with one exception, they do not identify the sources of the funds by name (Sánchez Molina 2000). To verify some of these likely backers of Chávez, I took the advice of an expert on Venezuelan finance (Interview 4) and turned to those who had been involved in Chávez's campaign. Three campaign insiders were willing to speak about which business executives may have assisted Chávez during the campaign. I asked the campaign insiders who they thought the likely contributors had been. I then presented them with a list of likely Chávez backers from the business community that I had drawn from newspaper reports ("Coup and Counter-coup" 2002; "El Diario Venezdano 'La Razon' Asegura" 2002; Romero 2002), the two books by journalists (Santodomingo 1999; Zapata 2000), and a few additional academic sources (Hellinger 2003; Ortiz 2004; Sánchez Molina 2000). The three campaign insiders, all of whom were intimately involved with managing the financing strategy and media relations of the campaign, were able to confirm a list of business elites who were likely to have assisted Chávez —elite outliers. I interviewed three of these elite outliers.

The Chávez campaign insiders verified twenty-eight out of thirty-five business elites who might have assisted Chávez, saying they were likely to have made either financial donations or in-kind donations.[1] I verified all elite outliers with at least one campaign insider and all but four with at least two insiders. Unfortunately, this method of verifying elite outliers is not exhaustive. Undoubtedly, there were some less prominent Venezuelan businesspeople who may have helped out with Chávez's campaign—people whom journalists did not find noteworthy enough to report on or that Chávez's campaign insiders had forgotten. Nonetheless, the benefit of this method is that it yields a list of those business elites who stood out either because they were leading members of Venezuela's business community or because they demonstrated extraordinary commitment to Chávez's campaign. For example, the list of elite outliers includes a Venezuelan billionaire (Santodomingo 1999, 36; Zapata 2000, 69).

Policy Predispositions of Elite Outliers

We might expect the elite outliers who assisted Chávez to have economic interests aligned with the protectionist economic policies that Chávez had advocated on the campaign trail. This hypothesis stems in part from what we know about Latin America's first generation of populist presidents, who promoted unionization, regulations on business, and major social welfare initiatives (Collier and Collier 1991). Despite their populist championing of urban worker demands, such presidents received assistance from business elites who concurred with their economic agenda. Just like Chávez, these populists espoused protecting domestic producers from global market pressures. Thus, one might anticipate that there would have been a subset of business elites who were willing to assist Chávez because they had a structural predisposition to favor his protectionist policies.

This hypothesis also derives from a well-established theoretical tradition that ties the political behavior of business elites to the underlying logic of their sector-based economic interests (Frieden 1991; Gourevitch 1986; Rogowski

1989; Shafer 1997). Scholars contributing to this tradition have reasoned that policy preferences among business elites correspond to their particular asset structure and market orientation. Jeffrey Frieden, for example, argues that business elites with predominantly fixed assets (those with investments in factories and heavy machinery) have a structural predisposition to favor protectionist trade policies and oppose facile capital flows in and out of the country. This predisposition holds true, he reasons, because they have greater difficulty "cashing out" of their investments during crises.[2] Eduardo Silva (1996) further refines Frieden's thinking. He notes that fixed-asset sectors vary in their market orientation. Only those fixed-asset sectors that have historically been oriented toward the domestic market and have little chance of expanding to include foreign markets, he argues, are likely to oppose neoliberal reforms and favor protectionist economic policies.[3] According to these scholars, we might expect the elite outliers to be in fixed-asset sectors with little competitive advantage in international markets. These sectors would harbor the business elites with a structural predisposition to favor protectionist policies and therefore to assist Chávez.

This hypothesis was also consistent with what we know about the types of business elites who backed Franklin Roosevelt's New Deal in the United States and those who resisted recent neoliberal reforms in Latin America. Certain businesses in the United States, such as oligopolistic firms (Domhoff 1972; Ferguson and Rogers 1986; Kolko 1963; Lindblom 1977) and/or banks (Mintz and Schwartz 1985; Mizruchi 1982) that tended to be well connected (Useem 1984), had a structural predisposition to favor Roosevelt's liberal economic policies. Studies of recent efforts to introduce neoliberal reforms throughout Latin America implicitly acknowledge that some sectors of business have a structural predisposition to oppose neoliberal reforms. They reveal that these reforms could succeed only where reformers neutralized businesses unlikely to benefit from them (Shadlen 2004) and forged a political alliance with businesses that would have a structural advantage once reforms were in place (Conaghan and Malloy 1994; Pastor and Wise 1994; Schamis 2002; Silva 1996; Thacker 2000).

We might therefore anticipate that the elite outliers would have opposed neoliberal policies, as Chávez did. Chávez was "the only candidate to attack the market economics" that had gained traction in Venezuela during the 1990s ("Venezuela: It's All Chávez" 1998). Despite hosting the region's most vigorous anti-neoliberal backlash, including food riots, a general strike, and proceedings to impeach a democratically elected president (Carlos Andrés Pérez), Venezuela had undertaken an aggressive stabilization program and made a number of structural adjustments to its economy during the 1990s (Corrales 2002; Naím 1993). It also sought to stabilize the economy by deregulating a complex system of price controls, interest rates, and currency exchange rates. It structurally adjusted the economy by privatizing major companies, including the telephone company, two national airlines, and the steel industry, as well as by opening up the oil industry to private foreign investment (Ellner 2008, 107). But Chávez "condemned the free market" (Gutkin 1998) and called for "a reversal of some market-opening reforms" (Cooper and Madigan 1998). More specifically, he "called for a halt to privatization of state assets . . . until the country has some assurance that the revenues from the sales of assets are going to the national budget rather than the personal accounts that corrupt officials have in Miami" (Schemo 1998). Although he declared his "respect for private property" (Gutkin 1998) and stopped calling for a moratorium on foreign debt payments two months before the election, Chávez kept up his harsh criticism of neoliberalism, labeling it "savage" (Peña 1998).

We might expect that elite outliers would not only oppose neoliberal policies but also favor the protectionist, state-interventionist economic policies that Chávez advocated. Chávez promised to "humanize Venezuela's economy by investing heavily in housing, education, and health care, as well as promoting huge private investment in railroads, ports, and tourist facilities" (Gutkin 1998). He called for social policies such as increasing workers' wages "rationally and judiciously," even in the final months of the campaign (Peña 1998). He "defended state intervention in the economy, state control of the oil industry, and other basic industries" (Ellner 2008, 105). He championed the use of trade barriers to protect producers from foreign competition. International journalists characterized Chávez ominously, saying that he "raised the specter of protectionist barriers to foreign trade" (Schemo 1998) and used "populist discourse" to promise "a nationalist economic policy modeled more on North Korea than on the free market" (LaFranchi 1998). Nonetheless, as others have rightly pointed out (Ellner 2008, 58, 105–6), Chávez advocated protectionist policies similar to those that the two dominant parties in Venezuela had embraced for three decades before the 1990s. As such, we might expect his policy agenda to have earned the support of businesspeople predisposed to favor protectionism.

However, only a small minority of the elite outliers, in fact, had a predisposition to favor Chávez for his protectionist policies. Table 5.1 presents the expected policy preferences of those who assisted Chávez, based on their primary and secondary economic (sector-based) interests. It demonstrates that only seven of the twenty-eight elite outliers had either primary or secondary economic interests in sectors we would expect to favor protectionist policies. Six of those in fixed-asset noncompetitive sectors had interests in agro-industry: five were agro-industrialists at the time, and an additional elite outlier had formerly been an agro-industrialist. Agro-industrialists were protectionists because their investments were primarily fixed assets and their products were primarily oriented toward the domestic market, with little potential to compete internationally.[4] The one elite outlier without an interest in agro-industry had interests in the aviation industry. But the aviation industry, like agro-industry, is a fixed-asset sector that depends on government protections.

These outliers would have been among the protectionist businesses, particularly those hurt by the neoliberal program of the 1990s that Chávez won over (Gómez 1998). The concentration of outliers in agro-industry is also consistent with the claims of someone inside the National Confederation of Agricultural Producers, FEDEAGRO, that FEDEAGRO had diverted about $2 million in public funds to the Chávez campaign (Sánchez Molina 2000, 105). One of the outliers, a businessman who characterized himself as "an important factor" in helping elect Chávez, said that he identified with Chávez's protectionism. He explained, "We supported Chávez not because he was going to win, but rather because he understood our platform. . . . We identified Salas Römer as a representative of the neoliberalism . . . we were against. We were anti-neoliberal" (Interview 38, 2).

Nevertheless, having protectionist economic interests was not a necessary condition to become an elite outlier in 1998. In fact, the majority of elite outliers that I identified did not have protectionist economic interests. As table 5.1 illustrates, a mere 25 percent of elite outliers had protectionist policy predispositions (those in fixed-asset, noncompetitive sectors). Moreover, the majority of elite outliers had economic interests that would have predisposed them to favor policies at odds with Chávez's protectionist, anti-neoliberal platform. Table 5.1 shows that most of the elite outliers had economic interests that should have made them favor neoliberal economic policies. Notably, 57 percent

TABLE 5.1. Economic interests of elite outliers by policy predisposition

	Asset structure and market orientation		
Policy predispositions	Liquid asset sectors	Fixed asset, potentially competitive sectors	Fixed asset, noncompetitive sectors
Primary policy predisposition			
Protectionist			Aviation (1) Agro-industry (5)
Nonprotectionist	Financial services[a] (12)	Manufacturing: Cement (1) Manufacturing: Food Processing (1) Construction (1) Telecommunications/ Media (5) Tourism (1)	
Number of elite outliers	12	9	6
Percentage of total outliers	43%	32%	21%
Secondary policy predisposition			
Protectionist			Agro-industry (1)
Nonprotectionist	Financial services (4)	Manufacturing: Food Processing (1) Manufacturing: Paper (1) Construction (2) Telecommunications/ Media (4)	
Number of elite outliers	4	8	1
Percentage of total outliers	14%	29%	4%
Summary of both primary and secondary policy predispositions			
Number of elite outliers[b]	16	13	7
Percentage of total outliers	57%	46%	25%

Sources: See appendix D. This is a modified version of a table originally published in Gates 2007.

[a] The numbers in parentheses refer to the number of elite outliers.

[b] The total number of elite outliers is twenty-eight. Some outliers had multiple policy predispositions. One individual had only secondary business interests. This individual built a career at a bank but then moved into government in the early 1990s.

of elite outliers had either primary or secondary interests in the financial sector, interests characterized by liquid assets.

Even the four elite outliers who had economic interests in the manufacturing sector were in the few manufacturing industries that were *not* predisposed to favor protectionist policies. Most Venezuelan manufacturers, like agro-industrialists, historically struggled in the face of seemingly insurmountable competition from foreign products. Many flourished only after the government placed high tariffs on imports (Bitar and Troncoso 1990; Jongkind 1993; Naím and Francés 1995; Thorp and Durand 1997), and they thus found themselves struggling after neoliberal reforms were introduced in the 1990s (Seara 1998). Yet the elite outliers who were manufacturers were not in these manufacturing industries, as we might have expected. Rather, they were in the few manufacturing sectors that flourished after Venezuela introduced neoliberal economic reforms (Jongkind 1993, 81–82; Keller 1997, 348).[5] They were in the internationally competitive manufacturing sectors (i.e., the fixed-asset, potentially competitive sectors).[6]

Moreover, the nine elite outliers who had economic interests in the telecommunications and media sector (five with primary interests and four with secondary interests) were also not predisposed to favor Chávez's protectionist economic policies. These elite outliers included several executives of television networks that provided positive coverage of Chávez during the 1998 campaign (Zapata 2000, 130). In fact, one was the head of a large Latin American media conglomerate (Colitt 1997, 1998) as well as the controlling owner of a leading Caracas daily newspaper that published the first public opinion polls indicating Chávez's ascent (Santodomingo 1999, 34). The telecommunications sector, like manufacturing, is a fixed-asset sector that includes a diverse set of industries, including the telephone industry, major radio and television networks, and cable providers. But unlike manufacturing, these sectors shared an interest in privatizing and deregulating the industry.[7]

Needless to say, it is surprising that so many elite outliers had economic interests at odds with Chávez's professed protectionist, anti-neoliberal policy positions. This suggests that the underlying logic of elite outliers was not, in fact, to assist candidates aligned with their policy predispositions. We must therefore consider an alternative political calculus of business elites with regard to the presidential race of 1998.

The State-dependent Elite Outliers
and Their Pursuit of Access

As noted in chapter 2, some businesses have economic interests that shift their political calculus away from their structurally determined economic policy inclinations. Research shows that businesses that depend on providing a service or a product for the state, which would include defense or infrastructure contractors, have this sort of economic interest. These state-dependent businesses are more likely to finance incumbents regardless of their party affiliation, even if challengers to the incumbents advocate economic policies more in line with their sector-based interests (Gopian, Smith, and Smith 1984; Grier, Munger, and Roberts 1994; Handler and Mulkern 1982). In other words, their economic interests divert their calculus toward pursuing access to the state even when it means supporting a candidate who does not advocate their preferred policies. We can say, then, that state-dependent businesses have a structural predisposition to pursue access to the state rather than to make sure the government adopts certain economic policies. That is, they have a structural preference to assist candidates most likely to grant them access to the state.

A former Venezuelan business executive described how economic dependence on the state drove elite outliers to assist Chávez. He acknowledged that there were probably some businesspeople who "identified" with Chávez's political agenda and who, therefore, favored a political style he framed in derogatory terms as "political clientelism." But he also clarified that, "practically speaking, there were very few of these." Instead, he thought the more common reason businesspeople assisted Chávez was because their businesses depended on "being close" to the state. He explained that "there were some businessmen who, because of their particular economic activity, would want to be close to the government, whatever its type" (Interview 48, 4). These businesspeople, he thought, were preoccupied with ensuring that they had access to the state, regardless of policy positions, party affiliations, or the political style of the government's political leaders.

In general, the elite outliers were structurally predisposed to pursue access to the state. The vast majority of elite outliers, twenty-one of the twenty-eight (75 percent) had primary business interests in state-dependent sectors. In 1998, Venezuela's state-dependent economic sectors included construction and cement manufacturing, which depended on building contracts from the state; as well as banks, which depended on contracts to serve as the intermediaries for government deposits; and the media, which depended on lucrative government advertisement contracts.[8] These economic interests would have predisposed elite outliers to overlook the policy preferences of candidates and instead to support the candidate they believed would be most likely to grant them access to the state.

But why would these state-dependent businesspeople believe they had to assist Chávez in order to secure their access to the state? After all, businesses in a wide range of economic sectors were dependent on the state in Venezuela. Nonetheless, not all state-dependent elites assisted Chávez, even though he became the front-runner in the final months of the campaign season. What reasons did the small coterie of state-dependent elite outliers have to assist Chávez? Or, to put it in other terms, *how* did economic dependence on the state translate into a willingness to make such an unlikely alliance with Chávez?

The Access-based Reasoning
of State-dependent Elite Outliers

We might expect business elites who want access to the state to be particularly attracted to candidates with whom they have a personal connection, either directly or through a close friend. Such a connection would give them a reason to trust a particular candidate, even if he or she advocated policies they did not support. One of the elite outliers who had such a connection detailed the importance of gaining access when he explained why he assisted Chávez. He described his relationship with Chávez at the time as "very close," having "had various meetings with [Chávez] about politics" during the campaign. He admitted that he, like those in the private sector more generally, had many policy differences with Chávez, but he argued that such policy differences could be overcome as long as fluid communication could be established with Chávez. As he put it, "I had an attitude which many people criticized; I believed that the private sector and Chávez should come to an understanding" (Interview 17, 3).

But surprisingly few of the state-dependent elite outliers had a personal connection with Chávez.[9] Table 5.2 presents the access-based reasons that state-dependent elite outliers might have had for assisting Chávez. As the table illustrates, some state-dependent elite outliers had more than one reason. The top

TABLE 5.2. State-dependent elite outliers by their access-based reasoning to assist Chávez

	Reason to trust Chávez[a]	Reason to fear political reprisal[b]	Reason to fear prospective businocrats[c]	Number of outliers
			X	9
		X	X	6
	X			2
		X		2
	X		X	1
	X	X		1
Column sum	4	9	16	21
Percentage of total	19.0%	42.9%	76.2%	100%

Sources: See appendix D.

[a] Coded as having a reason to trust Chávez if they had a personal connection to Chávez.

[b] Coded as having a reason to fear political reprisal if they had conspicuous ties to political competitor.

[c] Coded as having a reason to fear prospective businocrats if they were business competitors of prospective businocrats.

row displays the various access-based reasons elite outliers had to assist Chávez. The bottom two rows summarize the total number and percentage of state-dependent elite outliers who had that access-based reason to assist Chávez. The table reveals that only four (19.0 percent) of the state-dependent elite outliers had a personal connection with Chávez and, therefore, a particular reason to trust him. Instead, most elite outliers had one of the other two access-based reasons to assist Chávez. These two other reasons were connected to the various ways that business became visible, or prominent, in Venezuelan politics.[10]

Fear of Losing Access Due to Political Reprisals

Many of the elite outliers had acute fears of facing political reprisals and therefore losing access to the state if they did not assist the candidate poised to win. By mid-1998, that candidate was Chávez. I traced these acute fears to the conspicuousness of the relations that some elite outliers had with particular political leaders.

Michael Coppedge first described one of the common relations between Venezuelan business elites and political elites as "reverse clientelism." Like a patron-client relation, these relationships typically constituted an asymmetrical face-to-face relationship between two individuals. Patron-client exchanges involve a transfer of material favors or patronage for political support (typically votes). However, in Venezuela these *reverse* patron-client exchanges involved an exchange of political favors for material support or patronage of the politician (Coppedge 2000, 118). He explains that business patrons in Venezuela, much like campaign financiers in the United States, "could expect privileged access on general policy questions; small regulatory favors such as import licenses and tax breaks; diplomatic appointments; exclusive bids on lucrative state contracts; and sometimes the ability to designate trusted associates to fill a few seats in Congress or a powerful cabinet post, such as Finance Minister" (Coppedge 1999, 22).

However, business patronage could be a double-edged sword. Business patrons who appeared to obtain a visible or conspicuous benefit, such as a lucrative contract or a political appointment, had reason to believe that they might be the target of political reprisals if candidates other than their political clients were to win the election. Such business patrons feared that rivals of their political clients might find it attractive to prevent their access to the state. Worse, they feared that rivals of their political clients might find it politically convenient to pursue corruption allegations against them. As earlier chapters describe, corruption allegations implicating business actors, or business corruption, had become a central element of political life in Venezuela by the 1990s. Politicians who made corruption allegations against the business patrons of their political rivals could kill two birds with one stone. They could appear tough on corruption even as they conveniently undermined the actual or suspected financial backers of their political rivals. Thus, these fears of political reprisals shaped the political calculus of state-dependent elite outliers in 1998.

According to table 5.2, 42.9 percent of state-dependent elite outliers had a reason to fear political reprisal if they did not assist Chávez. They had become identified publicly as patrons of Luis Alfaro Ucero, the aging Acción Democrática leader who was one of Chávez's challengers. These elite outliers championed Alfaro Ucero for president in the early days of the 1998 campaign season, when other candidates seemed more likely to ultimately triumph at the polls.[11] They also appeared to have benefited conspicuously from Alfaro Ucero or the protection of the party under his leadership.[12] Three outliers, for example, had significant business ties to troubled banks that nearly failed during the 1994 bank crisis but that survived thanks in part to Alfaro Ucero's intervention (Zapata 2000, 101). Two others may have felt indebted to Acción Democrática for protecting them against corruption charges.[13] Another had been promoted to a coveted leadership position in a Venezuelan business association after Alfaro Ucero championed him for the position (Zapata 2000, 101). Thus, when polls indicated that Alfaro Ucero was unlikely to win, they might have feared they would lose access to the state if they did not cultivate a relationship with the likely winner. The unexpectedness of Alfaro Ucero's candidacy undoubtedly compounded their anxiety. Alfaro Ucero became a candidate only after plummeting oil prices in 1998 knocked out the leading contender for Acción Democrática's presidential candidate: the head of Venezuela's state oil agency, Petróleos de Venezuela, S.A., or PDVSA (Hellinger 2003, 40).[14] These business elites, therefore, had to scramble to demonstrate support for other candidates, first switching their support to former beauty queen Irene Sáez when she led in the polls and then to Chávez when he became the front-runner (Santodomingo 1999, 47; Zapata 2000, 22, 100).[15]

That elite outliers might have assisted Chávez for these reasons seems plausible given what interviews with non-outlier business elites revealed. They, too, exhibited an acute sensitivity to the charge of benefiting unfairly from an exchange of financial support for a political favor (i.e., they were sensitive to being viewed as a business patron of a political leader). They spoke of their fears that others might misconstrue their relationship with state officials as being too close. For example, in one interview, a non-outlier elite described a time when he had fears that paralleled those that some elite outliers seemed to have. This businessman remembered being acutely fearful that future administrations would exclude him from access to the state in 1989 because he appeared "too close" to political leaders in earlier administrations. He recalled that, during the 1980s, he had done "a lot of work in the previous government, getting close to government. . . . I had the political party, the party hacks, the political actors all behind me." He added, "By then, we were really friendly with [President] Lusinchi." Furthermore, he became "best friends" with a senator who was an important leader of Lusinchi's party. Naturally, the senator had "wanted there to be big investments in that area [his home state]," and this businessman had obliged. Then, "right at the end of the [presidential] period, it becomes clear that [Carlos Andrés] Pérez is going to come in and I thought, oh no, now we're really going to be in trouble . . . the other side is going to come in." The party leaders he had backed, outgoing President Lusinchi and the friendly senator, happened to be the longtime political enemies of Pérez within Pérez's own party. He recalled making every attempt to offset the chances that Pérez would exclude him from access to the state. "So I thought I'd have to get to know him [Pérez]. . . . I started going to see him, [I] visited and visited," even though he thought Pérez was "arrogant and unpleasant" (Interview 42, 15–16, 30). In other words, he, like the 1998 elite outliers, cultivated a relationship with the likely presidential winner to hedge his bets against the risk that the likely winner would eliminate his access to the state.

It is also plausible that elite outliers feared political reprisals if they believed others were likely to view them as being too close to a political leader, given that the non-outlier elites I interviewed took pains to distance themselves from "the ones who really got into the nitty gritty" of courting political leaders (Interview 43, 24). For example, an executive at a Venezuelan conglomerate admitted that "we have direct relations with ministries and a long history with various governments and various agencies of the government because you need clear public policy in order to develop your sector, but this doesn't mean that I am a *compadre* or [intimate] friend of that person. I don't believe in this" (Interview 28, 1). He quipped, "It's one thing to be political, to do politics; it's another to have representation" (Interview 28, 4). The president of a large commercial conglomerate similarly acknowledged that his firm had tended to express its interests "through direct contacts" but added "I mean . . . we are here and you [the government bureaucrat] are there; we don't mix things" (Interview 40, 1). In straining to distinguish their relationships to the state from those they considered inappropriate, these business elites conveyed their anxiety that their own contacts not be interpreted as too close and their awareness that such an interpretation would open them to suspicions of being corrupt. Clearly, some forms of visible relationships with the state or particular political leaders, in other words, some forms of political prominence, could be dangerous for Venezuela's business elites.

Such fears of political reprisals are also plausible given how easily relationships to political leaders could be misconstrued. There seemed to be a fine line between inoffensive or appropriate relationships with the state and relationships that were too close and therefore might put a business executive at risk of political reprisal. A number of business elites for instance maligned businesses that they viewed as too close to government. One used the phrase "doing business with the government" to describe such an unethical relationship to state actors (Interview 49, 4–5). A longtime business consultant tried to explain what "doing business with government" was and how it differed from a working relationship with government officials (Interview 46, 2). He began by noting that "in a country with such a large state, it is difficult to avoid a relationship with the state." Even Venezuela's leading food conglomerate, he contended, could not avoid a relationship since "almost all agricultural products are financed by the state . . . and the company produces products for mass consumption . . . products with [state] controlled prices." But, as he explained, the practice of "I'll do business with you, I'll give you a commission, and I'll support you politically" (Interview 46, 2) was what he argued was considered inappropriate. He asserted that "establishing a working relationship with the state is very different from doing business with the state in exchange for political favors." When pressed, the business consultant acknowledged that most of those who avoided being too close to the government made campaign contributions. He also acknowledged that even the conglomerate that he thought exemplified a proper relationship with the government "may even have contracts with the government." "But," he clarified, "they aren't contracts in exchange for political favors, based on political exchanges or commissions" (Interview 46, 2).

In other words, according to the business consultant, having informal direct relationships with government officials or even financing campaigns was not necessarily an affront to ethics. Neither was having a government contract. Rather, it was an explicit exchange of political support for an economic benefit granted by the state, such as a contract or authorization, that constituted having too close a relationship to the state. This is the type of connection that might put that business and its executives in danger of being politically identified and subsequently excluded from state access or, worse, being the target of corruption charges. But such a political exchange would be nearly impossible to verify. Even if Venezuelan laws required electoral campaigns to be transparent about their financial backers, outside observers could not verify such a political exchange. In such a context, we might expect businesspeople to fear that conspicuous profit or evasion from prosecution in combination with apparent vocal or financial support for a candidate would be taken by others as a sign that they had benefited from a suspicious political exchange.

Some elite outliers did indeed have reason to be acutely fearful of being targeted for political reprisals and thereby losing access to the state unless they established a relationship with the likely winner in 1998, even if that likely winner was someone like Chávez. Some forms of business's political prominence, therefore, may generate an unexpected political calculus to assist an antineoliberal candidate.

Fears of Losing Access
Due to Businocrats

Most state-dependent elite outliers had yet another reason to assist Chávez. They had reasons to fear losing access to the state specifically if Chávez's leading opponent, Salas Römer, won the election. As Salas Römer's campaign gained momentum in 1998, the media reported on a number of current and former business executives who might obtain cabinet-level positions in a Salas Römer administration (Santodomingo 1999; Zapata 2000, 22). Like his predecessor, it seemed probable that Salas Römer would appoint businocrats, or individuals with significant business experience, to his cabinet. But these prospective businocrats raised a red flag for some elite outliers because a large number of them were the business competitors of elite outliers. Thus, such elite outliers had reason to fear that, if given power, these prospective businocrats would exclude them from access to the state.

As table 5.2 shows, the majority of elite outliers had reasons to fear Salas Römer's election even more than they feared Chávez's policies. For example, one of the individuals rumored to be a top candidate for finance minister in a Salas Römer administration was a well-known banker, Oscar García Mendoza (García Mendoza 1998; Santodomingo 1999, 46; Zapata 2000, 134). García Mendoza was the longtime president of one of Venezuela's premier banks, Banco Venezolana de Crédito (Santodomingo 1999, 29). As table 5.1 showed, nearly half of the elite outliers had primary business interests in the financial sector. Thus, they had reason to fear that a banker like García Mendoza would put them at a disadvantage if he were to gain power as a businocrat in a Salas Römer administration. After all, one could easily assume that he would be likely to favor his own bank.

Salas Römer's alliance with other business executives alarmed many elite outliers because they had previously battled against those same businessmen for market dominance. One such potential businocrat in a Salas Römer administration was Carlos Bernárdez Lossada, the former president of Banco de Venezuela.[16] Two elite outliers had defeated Bernárdez Lossada in a fight over the control of his bank in 1993 (Krivoy 2002, 194).[17] The takeover had cemented an alliance among most bankers against these two newly powerful bank executives (Zapata 1995, 42). Thus, when rumor spread that Salas Römer had a close association with Bernárdez Lossada, it gave the bankers who had orchestrated the takeover of his bank a powerful reason to distrust Salas Römer.

Similarly, a Salas Römer administration seemed likely to benefit media mogul Marcel Granier (Santodomingo 1999, 29), who had battled two elite outliers for control over the country's television airwaves. As noted earlier, tele-vision networks were state dependent in Venezuela because they often relied on lucrative advertising contracts with the state. They also needed the federal government's permission to operate. Granier had historically split the television market with one of the elite outliers who owned a television network. Then, in 1988, after Granier's rival harshly criticized the current administration for not doing enough to end corruption, the federal government approved a third private broadcasting network (Ortiz 2004, 80–81). In the 1990s, the head of this newer broadcasting network worked with Granier's original network rival to further marginalize his market share (Ortiz 2004, 80). Thus, these two media moguls had reason to believe that Granier might seek to undermine their current market dominance if he were to gain power via a Salas Römer victory (Ortiz 2004, 86).

It is plausible that business executives would be sufficiently fearful of prospective businocrats in a Salas Römer administration to assist an anti-neoliberal candidate, given that many of the non-outlier elites I interviewed articulated a similar distrust of past businocrats. They seemed preoccupied with the risk that businocrats would use their power to put their business competitors at a disadvantage. Some agreed that having members of the private sector in positions of government authority could "help ensure that the country was progressing in the best way" (Interview 48, 2), but they were also quick to point out that businocrats often disappointed. Businocrats were often suspected of protecting their own business interests at the expense of their competitors. No businocrat provoked more controversy than Pedro Tinoco, head of Venezuela's Central Bank, during the second administration of Carlos Andrés Pérez (1989–1993).

One industrialist pointed to Tinoco's term as president of the Central Bank (1989–1992) as exemplifying how businocrats often pursued their own interests at the expense of others. He commented,

I don't know the level of participation these conglomerates had in political decision making, but I can give you an example that I experienced. In the Central Bank they developed a credit instrument . . . called the zero coupon, which was a bond that didn't pay interest and that [commercial banks] sold at a discount to the Central Bank to recuperate their losses. . . . The interests [on these bonds] were extremely high. Fundamentally, in the estimation of most industrialists, this was a subsidy to the banking sector. This bonus was something Tinoco created as the head of the Central Bank, but he was also the president of the second-largest Venezuelan bank at the time, which was Banco Latino. In this case there was a direct relationship between the interests of a subsector of the bank against the interests of industry that was seeking loans. (Interview 25, 4)

In the opinion of this industrialist, Tinoco had designed a policy that disproportionately favored bankers. Moreover, this industrialist posited that Tinoco's policy had benefited Banco Latino in particular, the bank Tinoco had headed before becoming president of the Central Bank. A former businocrat had a similar impression of Tinoco. He recalled numerous conflicts within the cabinet in which Tinoco's leniency toward banks became apparent. He asserted, "I think he and the other bankers made a fortune" (Interview 44, 6). But another former businocrat defended Tinoco, characterizing him as a victim of the political system. He explained, "[Tinoco] played the game, he was playing the system." At the same time, he contended that Tinoco "did the best he could in the system. He wasn't just trying to make himself more powerful. No, he was actually trying to help the system. He was an idealist" (Interview 43, 24).[18] That the same businocrat could be viewed as acting as a business competitor by some and as legitimately working the system by others underscores how easily a businocrat could be misconstrued as corrupt.

It is even more plausible that elite outliers might have feared prospective businocrats, given the forceful criticism of businocrats expressed by some of the non-outlier elites. Some of these business elites categorically dismissed past businocrats as government officials who did not protect the business community, let alone the nation's interests. Instead, according to these elites, businocrats often looked out for their own business interests. For example, a former president of a sectoral business association noted that there were many businesspeople in both administrations during the 1990s who "were there defending the interests of their companies and of their sector, even though they didn't say so" (Interview 38, 4). A former leader of another sectoral business association argued that those individuals with significant business ties who were appointed to be ministers had tended to "serve their own interests more than the general interests" (Interview 25, 3). Moreover, he thought they mostly gave big business a competitive edge: "The big conglomerates had individuals in the public administration who were their civil servants. . . . The ministers of finance and development, which were the areas that were of greatest interest to business, were often men from the economic conglomerates" (Interview 25, 2). He explained, "You would have in the upper echelons of government a treasury minister from a conglomerate, but who didn't represent [the private sector]." He relayed an example of a businocrat in the 1980s who was affiliated with a large Venezuelan conglomerate, noting that this businocrat "wasn't responsive to me at all" (Interview 25, 3). He remembered another instance in the 1980s when a minister of housing pursued the particular interests of some businesses in the construction industry over those of the private sector more generally (Interview 25, 4).

These interviews with business elites illuminate the fact that businocrats were often viewed as controversial by other members of the business community. It was not that business executives necessarily thought that businocrats were corrupt or even that they intentionally undermined their competitors. But the business elites I interviewed certainly distrusted the judgment of businocrats, particularly if they had been their competitors. They worried that businocrats might be tempted to continue to act as their competitors. Given their distrust of businocrats, it seems likely that state-dependent business elites would have sought out information about the prospective businocrats in each presidential candidate's prospective cabinet as part of their evaluation of the likelihood of securing access to the state through each candidate. Furthermore, given the suspicions that businocrats might act as competitors, we might expect businesspeople to try to ensure the electoral defeat of any politician likely to promote their competitors as ministers, even if it meant supporting a candidate like Chávez, who advocated policies at odds with their economic interests and policy preferences.

State-dependent elite outliers thus had a number of access-based reasons to assist a candidate as unlikely as Chávez. These reasons were typically shaped by the prominence of business: either their own or that of others. But state-dependent outliers were not the only elite outliers with access-based reasons to assist Chávez.

	Structurally predisposed to favor protectionist policies	Reason to trust Chávez[a]	Reason to fear political reprisal[b]	Reason to fear prospective businocrats[c]	Number of outliers
	X	X			4
	X			X	1
	X		X		1
		X			1
Column sum	6	5	1	1	7
Percentage of total	85.7%	71.4%	14.3%	14.3%	100%

TABLE 5.3. Non-state-dependent elite outliers by their economic interests and access-based reasoning

Sources: See appendix D.

[a] Coded as having a reason to trust Chávez if they had a personal connection to Chávez.

[b] Coded as having a reason to fear political reprisal if they had conspicuous ties to a political competitor.

[c] Coded as having a reason to fear prospective businocrats if they were business competitors of those prospective businocrats.

The Access-based Reasoning
of Non-state-dependent Outliers

We might expect that only state-dependent elite outliers had access-based reasons to assist Chávez. However, I find that all elite outliers, not just the state-dependent ones, had such reasons. Table 5.3 presents the remaining combinations of policy predispositions and access-based reasons to assist Chávez. It reveals that even the six non-state-dependent elite outliers had reason to consider their likely access to the state in deciding whether or not to assist Chávez in 1998. They each had at least one of the access-based reasons to assist Chávez. Table 5.3 thus shows that non-state-dependent outliers who had a structural predisposition to favor Chávez's protectionist policy preferences had an additional reason to assist Chávez. Therefore, policy predispositions were neither necessary nor sufficient to induce elite outliers to assist Chávez.

According to table 5.3, four protectionist elite outliers had a personal connection to Chávez. They represented the majority of protectionists (four of the six protectionists) and equaled in number the state-dependent elite outliers who had a personal connection to him. These protectionist outliers included a major agro-industrialist who, together with a minor agro-industrialist and fellow outlier, had spearheaded the silent pro-Chávez rebellion within the otherwise pro-neoliberal business organization, FEDECAMARAS (Becker 1990; Giacalone 1999; Santodomingo 1999; Zapata 2000, 31, 96, 97, 132). Despite having been a vocal protectionist, one elite outlier, who regretfully told me he had been "a friend of Chávez" and was "guilty of [assisting] Chávez," did not underscore Chávez's protectionist policies when he explained why he had assisted Chávez. Instead, he emphasized Chávez's qualifications as a political outsider. He explained that he had assisted Chávez "because I am very anti-AD [Acción Democrática] and anti-COPEI [the other historically dominant party, the social Christian party] and I saw in Chávez a possible solution" to the country's political crisis (Interview 33, 5).

Interviews with industrialists who were protectionists but did not assist Chávez further confirmed that having protectionist economic interests was not a sufficient reason to support the anti-neoliberal candidate. An advocate of protectionism characterized the sentiment among most members of the Venezuelan Confederation of Industrialists (CONINDUSTRIA) regarding Chávez as "definitely one of rejection." He expressed disgust with fellow industrialists who had assisted Chávez, describing them as "tremendously irresponsible and crazy people" (Interview 25, 6). His sharp criticisms illustrate the fact that protectionists did not automatically support Chávez. Their support required an additional inducement, such as a personal connection to Chávez, which would lead them to believe they also had a strong chance of securing access to the state through him.

Even the business association we would expect to be the most protectionist —the association representing small and medium-sized industrialists (Federación de Cámaras y Asociaciones de Artesanos, Micros, Pequeños y Medianos Industrias y Empresas de Venezuela, or FEDEINDUSTRIA)—issued a thinly veiled warning against a Chávez victory just twenty days before the election. It declared, "Once again, the messianic and populist visions stimulate the illusion that protectionism . . . can resolve complex problems" ("Fedeindustria" 1998).

Furthermore, several non-state-dependent elite outliers had reasons to fear losing access if they did not assist Chávez. For example, although one elite outlier was a minor agro-industrialist who might have favored Chávez's protectionist policies, he also had a strategic reason to assist Chávez because others might associate him with Alfaro Ucero. Similarly, another probably would have favored Chávez's protectionist policies because of his business's need for protection from foreign competitors. But he also had a reason to fear losing access if Salas Römer won the election because of the businocrats that Salas Römer was likely to put in place.[19] The lone case in which a personal connection in the absence of any other inducement was sufficient to swing an outlier's vote to Chávez further illustrates the potency of access to the state in the political calculus of Venezuela's business elite. A business executive from the hospitality industry was neither in a sector we would expect to favor protectionist policies nor dependent on the state. Nevertheless, he did have a personal connection to Chávez.

The fact that non-state-dependent elite outliers also had access-based reasons to assist Chávez indicates that pursing access to the state was important to more businesses than just those that were state dependent. This suggests that even businesspeople who did not directly depend on the government might find themselves at a disadvantage if they lacked access to the state. It suggests, then, that we might expect all businesspeople in Venezuela to consider first and foremost which candidate is most likely to give them access to the state and, therefore, to be particularly attuned to signs that candidates might either grant them or exclude them from access. This finding is broadly consistent with the characterization of Venezuelan business as more generally oriented toward "courting the state" (Naím and Francés 1995). It also underscores the importance of intra-elite conflict over state access in Venezuelan politics.

The experts and non-outlier business executives I interviewed concurred with this argument, saying that elite outliers probably assisted Chávez because they prioritized access to the state over policy proscriptions. An expert on campaign finance surmised that, near the end of election cycles, most of Venezuela's top business elites tended to "bet" on the candidate they thought most likely to win in order to ensure access to the state and that the 1998 elite outliers were no different (Interview 4, 1). He recounted a conversation he had had with a banker in 1998 that suggested to him that elite outliers had pursued access to the state. The banker had commented that he had given Chávez money "just in case." The banker explained that he did not believe Chávez was so radical. Moreover, he believed it would be possible to "manipulate" Chávez after the election. This conversation, he noted, mirrored other conversations he had in the course of the 1993 presidential campaign, during which a banker pleaded with him to say whether he, the expert, thought a close contender for the presidency might have a reasonable chance of winning. If so, the banker had commented, he would need to make a campaign contribution in order to ensure that he had access to the next administration, even though he had been assisting a different candidate.

In interviews, business executives confirmed that elite outliers discounted Chávez's radicalism and instead pursued access. One told me about a meeting, before the election in 1998, in which this elite outlier was so confident that he would be able to influence Chávez that he was canvassing members of Venezuela's business elite to draw up a slate of cabinet members they could propose to Chávez (Interview 43, 10). In another interview, a preeminent business consultant intoned the inner thought process of elite outliers: "Yes, sure . . . he [Chávez] goes against my ideological interests, but if I finance him, afterward I can collect on my financing and secure a favor." He added that this logic "is very common; it has always happened [in Venezuela]" (Interview 46, 8). Another conglomerate executive in Venezuela admitted having favorable impressions of Chávez "at the beginning" (Interview 40, 9). He explained, "I mean I didn't buy his message, but I never thought it would become what it has. I mean many people who voted for him were simply turned away after the election." He, like others, had been willing to look past Chávez's "message" in the hopes of gaining access, and he, like others, had an expectation that after offering assistance during the campaign, the new administration would not "turn him away."

How Dependent Prominence Produced Chávez's Unlikely Elite Allies

The calculus of Chávez's elite outliers counters one of our most widely accepted notions about the political calculus of business actors. We generally expect business executives to support the candidates who advocate economic policies that seem most likely to develop business in their economic sectors. In other words, we generally expect them to act according to the policy predispositions given by their economic interests. Nevertheless, in Venezuela, this was not the case for the group of elites that reportedly assisted Chávez in 1998. Only a minority of those elite outliers—those business elite who veered away from the general trend to oppose Chávez's candidacy—had economic interests that predisposed them to favor Chávez's protectionist policies. Instead, most elite outliers tended to have economic interests diametrically opposed to Chávez's policy positions. Policy predispositions cannot, therefore, explain most of the elite outliers.

It is an alternative political calculus that prevailed among the elite outliers—that of pursuing access to the state. We have seen that the vast majority of those who assisted Chávez had a predisposition to pursue access to the state. But even those elite outliers who were not state dependent (and therefore not otherwise predisposed to pursue access to the state) tended to have access-based reasons to assist Chávez. The calculus of Chávez's elite outliers thus reveals what may be one of the central social conflicts of oil economies: intra-elite conflict over access to the state. As such, it suggests that the pursuit of access to the state characterizes the politics of a state-dependent business class. However, it was the political prominence of business that fomented the fears of losing access, which led many elite outliers to assist Chávez. In short, it was business prominence that politically splintered rather than bonded elites. On the one hand, the political identifications of some elite outliers gave them a reason to have an acute fear of losing state access and thus a reason to assist Chávez once he became the front-runner. As non-outlier elites viewed it, business executives who successfully cultivated a relationship with political leaders could face special risks. If they became politically identified as patrons of political leaders, or perceived as *too close* to a party and its leaders, they could become a target of political reprisal.

On the other hand, many elite outliers had a particular fear of Chávez's main opponent because of the business executives this opponent was likely to promote as ministers (prospective businocrats). These outlier elites had reason to fear prospective businocrats because the businocrats were their competitors. The elite outliers had reason to suspect the businocrats would exclude them from access to the state as part of their strategy to disadvantage their business competitors. The fear that businocrats would bar certain businesses' access to the state was consonant with the potent distrust of businocrats expressed by non-outlier business elites. This distrust of businocrats counters the widely accepted idea that those bureaucrats with business experience should inspire the confidence of others in the private sector. The opposite seems to have been the case in Venezuela. Thus, the calculus elite outliers used to ensure their access to the state in 1998 reveals an unexpected and no doubt unintended consequence of business political prominence. We can say then that the politics of ensuring access to the state may be contingent on the relative prominence of a state-dependent business community.

In these ways, the political prominence of business *during* the 1998 campaign shaped the political calculus of the 1998 elite outliers. However the political prominence of business before the campaign also informed the calculus of these outliers. Specifically, the historical roots of this unexpected political calculus reach back to the 1994 bank crisis, when the political prominence of business contributed to suspicions of unfair treatment among former executives at government-seized banks. Many of these former bankers went on to become elite outliers in 1998.

6

•

POLITICALLY PROMINENT BANKERS

AND THE HISTORICALLY ROOTED

CALCULUS TO ASSIST CHÁVEZ

THE GOVERNMENT'S response to Venezuela's 1994 bank crisis shaped the political calculus of a core group of the elite outliers who reportedly assisted Chávez in 1998. As described earlier, the bank crisis was the font of numerous corruption allegations against both high-ranking government officials and bankers. It was the political prominence of business in the midst of this scandal-driven crisis, however, that fueled divisions among bankers in 1994, divisions that shaped the political calculus of bankers in 1998. We can discern this historically rooted political calculus of the elite outliers only by looking beyond the immediate interests of businesspeople and considering how these interests are framed by perceptions of state-business relations in the near past.

To see how the political calculus of the business elite is historically rooted, we must first understand how the political prominence of business during the

1994 bank crisis fueled divisions among bankers. The Caldera administration (1994–1998) appeared to break with the tradition in Venezuela of swiftly rescuing banks at risk of insolvency and not punishing their former executives. That administration's response to troubled banks, which some viewed as slow, harsh, and uneven, divided bankers. Some bankers, mostly those at troubled banks, suspected that the Caldera government had treated them unfairly. Others, mostly those not at risk of insolvency, believed that the government had done what was necessary to get the country out of financial crisis.

We must then consider how the two ways that bankers were politically prominent at the time fueled suspicions that the government's response to the 1994 bank crisis had been unfair. Some bankers had gained political prominence because they became identified as the likely patrons of political leaders during the Carlos Andrés Pérez administration (1989–1993). In fact, the banks the Caldera administration was accused of treating unfairly had been represented within the disgraced administration of President Pérez, President Caldera's longtime political rival, through a number of high-profile political appointments. Some bankers associated with troubled banks had also become identified politically as the patrons of Caldera's contenders in the 1993 presidential election. The political identification of certain bankers with Caldera's political rivals led many to speculate that Caldera's slow, harsh, and uneven response to the troubled banks had been unfair. They suspected his actions had targeted the banks of politically identified bankers for political reprisals. Regardless of their veracity, the speculations reveal how becoming politically identified in Venezuela aroused fears among business actors that the rivals of their political clients, when in power, might target them for reprisals.

Other bankers had gained political prominence within the Caldera administration. The proliferation of businocrats among the financial sector regulators (those who orchestrated the Caldera government's response to the 1994 crisis) fueled speculation that the government had treated the failing banks unfairly. In fact, those responsible for the government's response to the crisis tended to have ties to banks that emerged largely unscathed from the crisis. This circumstance led many to speculate that the Caldera administration responded to the crisis more in accordance with the interests of the banks represented inside the government than with those of the wider banking community or the public more generally. Again, regardless of their veracity, these speculations reveal how the presence of businesspeople within government aroused fears among businesses that the government was acting on behalf of their businocrat competitors.

That a visible presence of business within the political arena might divide business and arouse suspicions of the government runs counter to leading theories and affirms an underappreciated insight of Venezuelanist Javier Corrales. Leading theories of economic development posit that the ideal developmental state—one that is best able to foster economic development—is both autonomous enough (independent of any particular business interest) to act on behalf of the public's general well-being and embedded enough within the business community to inspire business cooperation (Evans 1995). But Corrales revealed that the economic reformers who encountered the greatest resistance from business in Venezuela were, ironically, those with significant prior business experience (Corrales 2002, 163–66). My analysis of bankers and the 1994 crisis affirms Corrales's argument that businesses may be particularly suspicious of the policies enacted by policy makers with significant prior business ties to their sector.

This study extends Corrales's insight to a new context, that of the political calculus of business actors, and shows how state-business interactions in the past became the crucible in which key 1998 state-business political alliances were formed. Indeed, most of the elite outliers in 1998 who were bankers had negative experiences with the 1994 bank crisis. Thus, only by considering how the calculus of business is historically rooted can we solve the puzzle of why a small portion of the business community broke from the pack to assist a staunchly anti-neoliberal candidate in 1998.

The Government's Divisive Response to the 1994 Bank Crisis

The government's response to the 1994 bank crisis divided bankers for two reasons. First, some thought the government's initial response was much slower and harsher than government responses to past bank crises. Second, some thought that the government's response was not the same for all troubled banks.

In the past, Venezuela had experienced a number of financial meltdowns that were similar to the 1994 bank crisis in that there were accusations of bankers defrauding the government or making improper loans to their friends or bank affiliates. For example, between 1961 and 1963, sixteen of the country's private banks, representing 40 percent of the country's total deposits, were failing (García Osío, Rodríguez Balza, and Salvato de Figueroa 1998, 277–316). The 1960s bank crisis, much like that of 1994, was widely attributed to fraud and bad loans to friends of the bank owners (Krivoy 2002, 36–37). Similarly, in 1978, after the failure of Banco Nacional de Descuento, then the country's largest bank, incriminating evidence surfaced, revealing that the bank had a general practice of making loans to itself and the bank's friends and affiliates (Krivoy 2002, 37). In 1985, the government seizure of a private bank, Banco de Comercio, revealed that 70 percent of the bank's loans had been made to companies controlled by shareholders of the bank. It was also revealed that bureaucrats responsible for the decision to authorize government deposits into the bank had accepted an unauthorized commission worth 2 to 5 percent of the prospective government deposits (Krivoy 2002, 38).

According to many observers of the 1994 crisis, the government had moved relatively swiftly to bail out the banks in earlier crises and had generally not prosecuted the bank executives charged with irresponsible and allegedly illegal activities. As a former president of the Central Bank in Venezuela saw it, before the 1994 crisis, Venezuela had experienced "thirty years of bailouts" (Krivoy 2002, 36). In the mid-1960s, for example, the government engaged in "a massive rescue operation" to bail out the banks (García Osío, Rodríguez Balza, and Salvato de Figueroa 1998, 288), and, despite widespread acknowledgment of fraudulent activity among bankers, "no one was punished" (Krivoy 2002, 36–37). Indeed, in this earlier wave of bank failures, the Venezuelan Central Bank granted even more financial aid relative to the country's gross domestic product than it did during the 1994 crisis (García Osío, Rodríguez Balza, and Salvato de Figueroa 1998, 288). Even in the 1985 case of Banco de Comercio, the Venezuelan government did not bring formal charges against the bank's former executives or board members (Krivoy 2002, 39).

During the 1994 bank crisis, however, the government initially seemed reluctant to bail banks out and, for the first time, aggressively prosecuted former bank executives. The president of the Central Bank recounts numerous thwarted attempts to persuade the country's interim president, Ramón Velásquez, and his finance minister (in office from mid-1993 to early 1994) and President Caldera and his finance minister (who began serving in February 1994) that Banco Latino's predicament required swift government action (Krivoy 2000). Incoming President Caldera even commented, on the very day his government closed Banco Latino, that "the Banco Latino problem is a complex situation that doesn't concern me" (quoted in Krivoy 2002, 116). After taking office, he moved slowly in nominating viable candidates for the two key institutions responsible for regulating the bank sector: the bank superintendent and the president of the depositor insurance fund (FOGADE, Venezuela's equivalent of the U.S. Federal Deposit Insurance Corporation) (García Osío, Rodríguez Balza, and Salvato de Figueroa 1998, 223).[1] The team of administrators whom Caldera appointed to manage Banco Latino after it was seized delayed the bank's reopening nearly three months, until April 5, 1994 (García Osío, Rodríguez Balza, and Salvato de Figueroa 1998, 226). In the view of experts looking back on the crisis, government officials should have considered Banco Latino, the second-largest commercial bank at the time, "too big to fail."[2] History, they note, has taught us that the ripple effect of large bank failures can be contained only with swift government bailouts.

Many others also felt that the government's response to Banco Latino seemed unusually harsh. When the interim Velásquez administration, in consultation with incoming President Caldera, finally decided on a course of action ("Banco Latino to Be Privatized" 1994), it took the drastic step of closing the bank indefinitely, rather than closing it for only a few days.[3] This action undermined, rather than inspired, depositor confidence in Venezuela's banks (Krivoy 2000). Experts note that such actions have historically exacerbated rather than curtailed financial crises, and they wonder why "none of the regulating organizations or even the business associations of the sector tried to advocate for any other strategy but an intervention that would close Banco Latino" (García Osío, Rodríguez Balza, and Salvato de Figueroa 1998, 220).

The Caldera government underlined its stern approach to Banco Latino on March 2, 1994, when it instigated corruption investigations against eighty-three former executives, managers, and board members of Banco Latino (Gates 2007, 112). In her chronicle of the 1994 bank crisis, Ruth de Krivoy, president of the Central Bank at the time, issues a scathing critique of President Caldera's prosecutions. She writes that, "instead of organizing a plan for how to handle the crisis, the government concentrated on the search for individuals to blame" (Krivoy 2002, 152). According to Krivoy, the Caldera government "blamed bankers" for the bank crisis (Krivoy 2002, 182). She bemoans the situation, stating that bankers were "treated as if they were common delinquents" (Krivoy

2002, 153) and "presented . . . like members of an organized mafia, who intentionally attract depositors with high interests rates and then redirect their money to other businesses" (Krivoy 2002, 182).

The Caldera government's response to the bank crisis was also divisive among bankers because the government treated troubled banks differently (Gates 2007, 112–13). Table 6.1 lists each bank at risk of failing according to the actions the government took in response. The banks are listed roughly in order of when their liquidity troubles began. It shows that the government treated the first bank differently than the wave of banks that began to struggle immediately thereafter. The government seized and then closed for several months the first failing bank, Banco Latino. It then provided three to six months of government aid, with very few strings attached, to help eight struggling banks after Banco Latino's crisis (García Osío, Rodríguez Balza, and Salvato de Figueroa 1998, 245).

While the public generally believed that the government's decision to extend aid to these banks during the first six months of 1994 seemed too lenient, some bankers thought the government had sabotaged the banks. They pointed to the fact that the Caldera government cast a shadow of suspicion over the bank executives left in charge of the struggling banks. The government imposed travel restrictions on these bank executives, implying to the public that they might flee the country with their money. The Caldera government also required these bank executives to make a public accounting of their personal belongings (Mann 1994b). The fact that the government eventually liquidated the eight banks that had received government aid, rather than reopening them with additional public capital, seemed like further evidence to skeptics that the government had not really wanted to help these banks (García Osío, Rodríguez Balza, and Salvato de Figueroa 1998, 235–36).

Table 6.1 also shows that in early August 1994 the government shifted its strategy for responding to troubled banks. The new strategy became apparent when the Caldera government did not simply grant aid to Banco de Venezuela. Instead, it seized and then infused Banco de Venezuela with US$249 million worth of public money to "recapitalize the bank" (Mann 1994b). In effect, then, "the shareholders of the bank lost money and control over the bank, first, and then the state absorbed the rest of the bank's losses, assumed control of the institution, insured the depositors, and kept the bank open" (García Osío, Rodríguez Balza, and Salvato de Figueroa 1998, 246). The government then sought to induce the next eight banks at risk of failing to restructure and re-

TABLE 6.1. Troubled banks by government actions and 1994 bank crisis outcome

Bank	Date govt. began or promised aid	Date govt. seized bank	Bank crisis outcome
Banco Latino	No aid	1/16/94	Closed—liquidated[a]
Maracaibo	1/25/94	6/14/94	Closed—slated to be liquidated[a]
Barinas	1/27/94	6/14/94	Closed—liquidated[a]
Construcción	1/27/94	6/14/94	Closed—liquidated[a]
FIVECA[b]	2/03/94	6/14/94	Closed—liquidated[a]
Metropolitano	2/11/94	6/14/94	Closed—liquidated[a]
La Guaira	2/16/94	6/14/94	Closed—liquidated[a]
Bancor	3/22/94[c]	6/14/94	Closed—liquidated[a]
Amazonas	3/29/94	6/14/94	Closed—liquidated[a]
Bco. Hipo. de Occidente	No aid	6/14/94	Closed—liquidated[a]
Banco Popular	No aid	6/14/94	Closed—liquidated[a]
Banco Tequendama	No aid	6/14/94	Closed—liquidated[a]
Banco de Venezuela	No aid	8/09/94	Open—public recapitalization
Consolidado	8/9/94 promised[d]	9/11/94	Open—public recapitalization
Andino	No aid	11/11/94[e]	Closed— liquidated
Progreso	8/9/94 promised[d]	12/14/94	Open—public recapitalization—closed[f]
República	8/9/94 promised[d]	12/14/94	Open – public recapitalization
Italo-Venezuela	8/9/94 promised[d]	2/01/95[g]	Closed—liquidated
Profesional	8/9/94 promised[d]	2/01/95[g]	Closed—liquidated
Principal	8/9/94 promised[d]	2/01/95[g]	Closed—liquidated
Empresarial	No aid	8/11/95	Closed—liquidated
Federal	No aid	Not seized	Open—private recapitalization[h]
Internacional/Interbank	No aid	Not seized	Open—private recapitalization[h]
Unión	No aid	Not seized	Open—private recapitalization[h]

Sources: Adapted from Krivoy 2003.

[a] Slated to be liquidated August 1994; mostly liquidated by the end of 1994. The government retained Banco Latino until it was fully liquidated in 1997 (Krivoy 2002, 207) and Banco Maricaibo until it was sold in 1998 (García Osío, Rodríguez Balza, and Salvato de Figueroa 1998, 243).

[b] FIVECA was the only affected financial institution that was not a commercial bank.

[c] On February 20, 1994, the bank asked for a loan from FOGADE but did not use it until March 22, when its attempt to persuade Banco del Caribe to save it failed (Krivoy 2002, 157–58).

[d] Aid promised by the government was contingent on the bank's compliance with a plan to recapitalize and restructure.

[e] Temporarily managed by Banco Industrial, a government-owned bank.

[f] In January 1995, the government transferred remaining assets to other government-owned banks (García Osío, Rodríguez Balza, and Salvato de Figueroa 1998, 249).

[g] Restructuring plans fell through (García Osío, Rodríguez Balza, and Salvato de Figueroa 1998, 251). Just hours after saying it would not to do so, the government seized these banks.

[h] Suffered depositor withdrawals in January 1995 but survived thanks to private infusions of additional capital. Banco Federal's own shareholders invested large sums of capital to save the bank. Banco Internacional reduced depositor withdrawals after the bank's president met with president Caldera to publicly discredit rumors that he had lost control of the bank to one of the disgraced bankers (Zapata 1995, 33). Several of Interbank's major investors injected new capital (Zapata 1997, 80–81, 97). Banco Unión survived after selling off half the business to a Colombian bank for one-fifth its value.

capitalize (Mann 1994b). It did this by promising to grant them aid if they would comply with a plan to restructure and recapitalize (Krivoy 2003). None of these banks, however, was able to realize the scheme for recapitalization. Thus, the government ended up seizing these banks, some sooner than others.[4] Nonetheless, unlike the first wave of banks that the government seized on June 14, in this subsequent wave the government generally sought to keep the big banks, like Banco de Venezuela and Consolidado, open by recapitalizing them with public money.[5]

Defenders of this policy argue that it was effective because depositors were not inconvenienced the way they had been when the first wave of troubled banks closed. They also note that once the government took over, the banks no longer faced massive withdrawals (Krivoy 2003). Nevertheless, others thought it was suspicious that the recapitalization strategy effectively concentrated financial sector power in the hands of a few government regulators with bank ties (i.e., businocrats).

Table 6.1 further illustrates why some perceived the government as veering from favoritism to total disinterest in its treatment of several other banks after August 1994. For example, the government appeared to give special treatment to Banco Andino. The government did not require it to submit to the same stringent restructuring plans as other banks facing difficulties at the same time (August 1994). Instead, the government placed Banco Andino under the control of a state-owned bank charged with helping the bank restructure. Meanwhile, the government seemed unwilling to rescue several other banks that faced similar liquidity problems in January 1995. These banks had to fend for themselves and survived thanks to private recapitalization plans. In effect, the authorities had "pressured the owners to find a partner to capitalize the bank or sell part of it immediately, avoiding state aid" (García Osío, Rodríguez Balza, and Salvato de Figueroa 1998, 252).[6]

The initially slow and seemingly harsh treatment that was part of the government's varied responses to troubled banks provoked speculation that the government had treated some banks unfairly. These suspicions were often rooted in the political prominence of bankers. Some suspected that the Caldera administration had used the 1994 bank crisis as an opportunity both to target the banks tied to bankers that were politically identified as patrons of President Caldera's former political rival and to benefit the banks linked to businocrats orchestrating the Caldera government's response to the 1994 bank crisis.

Suspicions of Political Reprisals

Some observers raised the question of whether the Caldera administration's seemingly slow, harsh, and uneven treatment of some of the troubled banks was a way to punish his political rivals.[7] Had President Caldera been waging a "particularized war" against politically identified businesses, as the Acción Democrática stalwart, Alfaro Ucero, had argued (Zapata 2000, 134)? A journalist asked if these banks were victims of political "vengeance" (Zapata 1995, 37). Might these banks have survived if their financial difficulties had not presented the attractive opportunity to undermine the business patrons of President Caldera's longtime political rival, former president Carlos Andrés Pérez (Zapata 1997, 32)? Some bankers declared publicly that they believed the Caldera administration had targeted them politically because they were patrons of Caldera's political rivals. For example, one banker proclaimed that the Caldera government had instigated "a criminal campaign against the banking community" (Zapata 1995, 37). He declared that the government's search of his home in connection with the ongoing difficulties of his two banks and a subsequent intervention in his financial conglomerate was politically motivated (Mann 1994a). In the 1993 presidential election, he had financed the left-leaning Causa Radical party (Gunson 1996) and had also used his control over numerous radio stations to critique Caldera during the campaign ("Venezuela: A Tough Task" 1993).

The failure of Banco Latino, in particular, fueled speculation that the government had targeted it for its apparent political identification with the former Pérez government. Banco Latino's conspicuous growth during the 1990s had raised eyebrows. Pérez had appointed Banco Latino's former president, Pedro Tinoco, to be president of the Central Bank. Soon thereafter, the bank won a host of state contracts to serve as the primary depositor for major state agencies. By 1994, Banco Latino had become the country's second-largest commercial bank. The accounts of the bank's more than 675,000 depositors represented nearly 10 percent of the nation's deposits (Krivoy 2003). Moreover, Banco Latino's growth stimulated the expansion of its affiliated and much larger financial group, the Latino Group.

The president of Banco Latino also speculated that the bank had been targeted for political reprisal due to his identification with another rival of President Caldera. After a U.S. federal judge cleared him of fraud, he "insisted that former president Rafael Caldera wanted to punish Banco Latino because the bank had supported Caldera's opponent in the 1993 presidential race" (Bussey 2000). In his view, Banco Latino's problems had been no worse than those of other commercial banks. It was the spreading of rumors that the bank's financial condition was tenuous that he and other managers of the bank believed had instigated a run on deposits that led to the bank's collapse in January 1994 ("Yesterday's Money" 1994).

Similarly, the head of the major conglomerate linked to Banco Latino claimed that his political ties to Pérez had created incentives for President Caldera and his appointees to act slowly in responding to Banco Latino's plight. This mogul suspected that Banco Latino's failure and the subsequent prosecution of his brother were part of a politically motivated campaign, launched perhaps by the president's son, Andrés Caldera, to undermine his conglomerate (Zapata 2000, 64). Thus, even though Banco Latino had derived its extraordinary growth from what a Central Bank president deemed "the traditional style of mixing business with politics" in Venezuela (Krivoy 2002, 3), scholars concluded that Banco Latino had become a "kind of 'leper' within the [financial] system" (García Osío, Rodríguez Balza, and Salvato de Figueroa 1998, 220) because of its "dubious reputation" as being too close to the disgraced former president Pérez. Banco Latino seemed to many to have been targeted.

The Caldera government's response to the next wave of banks that had difficulties also appeared to be political because many of these banks were politically identified with the former Pérez government. A number of these eight banks, which were eventually liquidated, had ties to former president Pérez. One bank (La Guaira) had two high-ranking appointees in the Pérez administration. Two larger banks (Barinas and Maracaibo, the latter nearly as big as Banco Latino [Krivoy 2003]) had become subsidiaries of Banco Latino during its expansionary period of the early 1990s (Zapata 1995, 51). Two smaller banks were also closely associated with Banco Latino.[8] Two additional banks (Bancor and Amazonas) were historically associated with major economic conglomerates presumed to be patrons of Pérez. The political identification of these banks with Pérez fueled speculation that they had been liquidated, at least in part, because Caldera had been unwilling to save banks that sponsored, albeit indirectly, his lifelong political rival.

It is hard to know whether President Caldera's administration had designs to punish politically identified banks like Banco Latino. Even if it did, it is hard to imagine an admission to such blatant partisan intentions at a moment of economic crisis. In many respects, however, it does not matter whether Caldera's administration actually had such designs. What matters is that the political identification of so many of the banks that the Caldera government liquidated as banks linked to Caldera's political rivals convinced many that they had been targeted. The political identification of some bankers during the 1994 bank crisis, however, is not the only form of political prominence during that period that ultimately contributed to business elites' fears of losing access if they did not assist Chávez.

Suspicions of Businocrat Competitors

The visible presence of former bankers among Caldera's financial regulators, who crafted the response to the 1994 crisis, further fueled speculation that the government had treated some of the troubled banks unfairly. Some speculated that the bank ties of government regulators gave them a motivation to respond slowly, harshly, and unevenly to banks in trouble. Adding fuel to this speculative fire, many of the banks to which Caldera's businocrats had ties experienced conspicuous growth during the Caldera administration. Although the former president of the Central Bank opined that these banks "attracted depositors because they were seen as a refuge" (Krivoy 2002, 168), she acknowledged that others did not share her assessment.[9] She recalls that "some politicians accused these banks of taking advantage of the crisis" (Krivoy 2002, 185) and benefiting from their representation within government. The journalist Juan Carlos Zapata captures these suspicions when he paraphrases a banker as concluding that "half of Venezuela's bankers buried the other" (Zapata 1995, 11). With this observation, the banker suggested that the financial sector regulators used their power to "bury" their business competitors.

These suspicions seemed legitimate because of the political identification of some of the troubled banks. Table 6.2 lists all banks that had representation within government through high-level businocrats during the 1990s. Of all thirty-five commercial banks at the time of the 1994 crisis, ten had associated businocrats. In other words, former executives or board members of these ten banks were appointed to high-ranking government positions during the three administrations of the 1990s: the Pérez, Velásquez, and Caldera administra-

TABLE 6.2. Banks with businocrat representation
by 1994 bank crisis status and administration

Bank	Administration	Number of businocrat appointees
Banks troubled in 1994		
Banco Latino	Pérez	1
La Guaira	Pérez	1 [1]
Banco de Venezuela	Pérez	1 [1]
	Caldera	2
Consolidado	Pérez	1 [1]
República	Pérez	[1]
Unión	Pérez	1
Banks not troubled in 1994		
Caribe	Velásquez	1
	Caldera	1
Mercantil	Caldera	1
Orinoco	Caldera	1 (2 nominees)
Provincial	Caldera	1

Sources: Political biographies discussed in appendix C.

Notes: Only businocrat appointees who were high-ranking government officials responsible either for regulating the financial sector or for executing economic policy more generally were coded for whether they had bank ties. Financial regulators include all those responsible for responding to the crisis in late 1993 and all related appointments made during 1994. Economic cabinet members include all former economic cabinet members during the Pérez administration and Caldera's first round of appointees for his economic cabinet. The number of economic ministers not responsible for regulating the financial sector is indicated in brackets.

tions. The ten banks are listed in table 6.2 according to whether they had trouble during 1994 or whether they survived the crisis. The second column of the table lists the president who appointed that bank's related businocrat. The final column sums the number of appointees with ties to that bank.[10] Table 6.2 reveals that the troubled banks with ties to a particular administration were more likely to be linked to the Pérez administration through businocrats. In contrast, the banks that remained out of trouble during the 1994 bank crisis and had ties to a particular administration were more likely to be linked to the Caldera administration through businocrats. This difference fueled speculation that the Caldera government's response to the 1994 crisis had been unfair.

From the beginning of the crisis, businocrats with bank ties fueled suspicions about the government response to the troubled banks. The fact that the finance minister in the interim Velásquez administration had been a longtime board member of Banco Caribe, for example, provoked speculation that this relationship made him less willing to react quickly to the Banco Latino crisis. Banco Latino's troubles first came to the attention of government financial sector regulators in late 1993, during the interim presidential administration of Velásquez. The Pérez-appointed president of the Central Bank remembered the Velásquez-appointed finance minister as particularly sluggish in responding to her call for reforms and actions to avoid catastrophic financial meltdown (Krivoy 2002, 90). According to her, he showed no interest in aiding Banco Latino or in reforming bank regulations (Krivoy 2002, 95).[11] We might expect any Pérez appointee to have faced an uphill battle to persuade the interim Velásquez administration to act more quickly. After all, President Pérez was forced to leave office in a hail of corruption allegations. But the presence of a businocrat in the finance ministry undoubtedly deepened the suspicions among business patrons of the now-disgraced President Pérez.

The bank ties of Caldera's political appointments also help explain why some observers speculated that the government had treated troubled banks unfairly. For example, President Caldera's most important initial appointment, that of finance minister (who would be the supreme authority on the bank crisis), was a businocrat tied to Banco del Orinoco.[12] Caldera's finance minister had founded an insurance agency that, by 1994, had grown and transformed into a financial conglomerate anchored by Banco del Orinoco. The fact that a former banker was so prominent in crafting the government's bank response, however, raised questions about his motives. For example, when Caldera's finance minister maligned a major Venezuelan conglomerate as having "*sexo financiero*" with the embattled Banco Latino, his attack could be, and in some cases was, construed not only as a justified attack on improper bank practices but also as an effort by a business competitor to undermine his competition (Zapata 1995, 79).[13]

Venezuela's senate immediately rejected two of Caldera's nominees (prospective businocrats) for key positions regulating the financial sector because of their bank ties: the superintendent of banks and the president of FOGADE (the depositor insurance agency). Caldera nominated former executives of his finance minister's conglomerate for both positions.[14] The senate apparently rejected these candidates because they were believed likely to act more as business competitors than as guardians of the public interest (Krivoy 2002, 145). After having to rescind these nominations, Caldera nominated individuals who did not have such evident ties to private financial institutions to fill these key posts.

The business ties of another key Caldera financial regulator sparked so much controversy that the regulator had to resign. Such was the case for Gustavo Roosen, Caldera's point man on the bank crisis.[15] Although Roosen had been appointed by Pérez to head the state oil company (PDVSA), he had had a long-standing relationship with Banco Provincial and its conglomerate, Grupo Polar. Federal legislators from nearly every leading political party, including President Caldera's own party, argued that the inclusion of Roosen in the Financial Emergency Committee (Junta de Emergencia Financiera, or JEF) "could be misunderstood by others in the financial sector, given his association with a banking conglomerate" (C.S. 1994b). They expressed concern that his participation in formulating the plan to seize eleven banks in June 1994 would undermine the good intentions of the new JEF. As the president of the Central Bank remembered it, "Some politicians and bankers were worried, thinking that the prior ties Roosen had with the owners of Banco Provincial would mean that this bank would end up taking the best part of the failed banks[,] which might produce a dangerous monopoly. The [conspicuous] growth of Banco Provincial at the time was, for them, a sign of danger" (Krivoy 2002, 168). Roosen resigned in the wake of these speculations.

A former banker whom Caldera's finance minister recruited to help with managing the bank crisis also generated considerable controversy (Zapata 1997, 42–49). This banker, Jacques Vera, was, at the time of his appointment, the board president of an investment bank (Fivenez Sociedad Financiera or Fivenez Financial Society), which is not listed in table 6.2 because it was not a commercial bank). Caldera's finance minister initially recruited Vera to be on Banco Latino's intervention team. Vera later became the president of Banco de Venezuela, once one of Venezuela's premier banks, after the state seized it and recapitalized it as a state-owned bank (Krivoy 2002, 153). But Vera became the target of banker ire when he harshly criticized his fellow bankers. He infamously declared that Venezuela had "too many banks, but too few bankers" (quoted in Zapata 1995, 15). The phrase became a rallying cry for those who denounced the unethical practices of bankers. Some bankers suspected that Vera spread the rumors of imminent bank failures that led to a rush of withdrawals in many banks during 1994 (Zapata 1995, 15).

In April 1994, Caldera made perhaps his most controversial appointment during the bank crisis.[16] He appointed a former bank executive and investor,

Carlos Bernárdez Lossada, as a minister of state and president of the Venezuelan Investment Fund (Fondo de Inversiones de Venezuela, or FIV). Some suspected Bernárdez Lossada's own business interests had influenced the government's subsequent shift in response to troubled banks (Mann 1994a). Bernárdez Lossada was widely perceived as having an ax to grind against those bankers who, through a hostile takeover, had ousted him from control over Banco de Venezuela in the early 1990s.[17] He is one of two Caldera appointees listed on table 6.2 who had ties to a troubled bank, Banco de Venezuela. Thus, it seemed suspicious to some observers that the government treated Banco de Venezuela differently than all other banks up until that point. As table 6.1 shows, the government recapitalized Banco de Venezuela after it seized it. That action enabled Bernárdez Lossada to regain control over the bank he had once owned.

Similarly, it seemed suspicious to some observers that the government shifted its strategy from providing aid through the government's depositor insurance fund (FOGADE) with few strings attached to one in which the government promised aid contingent on plans to restructure and privately recapitalize banks. This shift in policy came when the Caldera government had to address the problems of several troubled banks run by individuals who had helped oust Bernárdez Lossada from Banco de Venezuela in the early 1990s.[18] To add insult to injury, in the eyes of the former executives and owners of these banks, Bernárdez Lossada then appointed a close friend, Vera, to be the president of one of these banks, Banco Consolidado. Thus, even though depositors at Banco Consolidado regained confidence and stopped withdrawing money after the government seized it (García Osío, Rodríguez Balza, and Salvato de Figueroa 1998, 247), the former owners of the bank persisted in accusing Vera of undermining the bank (Zapata 1995, 44).

With the government seizures and public recapitalizations of Banco Progreso and Banco República on December 14, 1994, the Venezuelan government effectively controlled the financial conglomerate of the person who had ousted Bernárdez Lossada from Banco de Venezuela (Fidler 1994).[19] Again, Bernárdez Lossada appointed a former Banco de Venezuela executive (the only other Caldera appointee listed on table 6.2 who was tied to a troubled bank) as president of one of the newly seized and newly state-owned banks, Banco República (Zapata 1997, 60–61). Two of the banks that the government seized on February 1, 1995, were also banks linked to those who had orchestrated the hostile takeover of Bernárdez Lossada's bank. After Banco República's seizure, the Venezuelan government controlled 70 percent of the banking sector, and nearly all of this banking activity was directly or indirectly in Bernárdez Lossada's control (Fidler 1994).

The Caldera government's policy also seemed biased against the bankers who had ousted Bernárdez Lossada because the government aggressively prosecuted them (Santodomingo 1999, 47). The government pressed criminal charges against the two major investors who had been instrumental in ousting Bernárdez Lossada and who had been major investors in six of the banks seized since August 1994. The government pressed charges against one for his actions at Banco Consolidado before it was seized by the government and against the other for his actions at Banco Progreso before it was seized. Both bankers fled the country. One of them, Orlando Castro, was eventually convicted of fraud in a New York court of law and sent to prison.[20]

Caldera's businocrat financial regulators fueled suspicions that they had sought to undermine their business competitors. Experts argue that "the problems of complicity and conflicts of interests that were so common . . . produced a high economic and social cost . . . in the 1994–5 crisis." They argue further that this complicity contrasts with the government's response to the 1960s bank crisis, in which "the lack of interested relationship between regulating agents and financial authorities . . . enabled them to avoid the problems" that erupted in the 1994 bank crisis (García Osío, Rodríguez Balza, and Salvato de Figueroa 1998, 316). Thus, many executives and investors of troubled banks and their sympathizers emerged from the 1994 bank crisis convinced that their losses had been more severe because the Caldera government had targeted them for political reprisals or because Caldera businocrats with bank ties targeted them to advance their own business interests. As we will see, these deep and historically rooted enmities may have influenced the subsequent political calculus of bankers who became elite outliers in 1998.

Salas Römer's Allies as Advocates of Caldera's Bank Crisis Response

Chávez's chief opponent in 1998, Henrique Salas Römer, counted among his business allies three former policymakers who had been instrumental in designing the government's response to the 1994 bank crisis (Zapata 2000, 133–34). These included Gustavo Roosen, the president's point person on the bank crisis; Jacques Vera, a key member of the team administering seized banks; and Carlos Bernárdez Lossada, the person who instigated the controversial shift in policy from seizing and liquidating to seizing and recapitalizing some of the troubled banks.[21] There were also rumors that a Salas Römer administration might include two businesspeople who had vigorously defended the government's 1994 bank crisis policy: the banker Oscar García Mendoza and the media mogul Marcel Granier (García Mendoza 1998; Santodomingo 1999, 46; Zapata 2000, 128, 133, 134). Both García Mendoza and Granier had angered some elite outliers by publicly denouncing them for corruption. Granier, a vigilant critic of corruption, had used his media outlets as a platform to berate bank executives and principal stakeholders in troubled banks (Zapata 1995, 36). García Mendoza had criticized bank executives and board members during the crisis in opinion pieces published in national newspapers.

A book-length compilation of Oscar García Mendoza's public statements (García Mendoza 1995) provides ample evidence of his searing critique of the banking sector's practices throughout the 1990s. He warned that "the banking sector was granting themselves fraudulent loans" (quoted in García Mendoza 1995, 111–12) and denounced the corrupt practices of many bankers (Kilby 1997). For example, García Mendoza denounced the head of the failed Banco Consolidado for having "employed 45 personal security guards" and for having an office full of artwork that "would put J.P. Morgan to shame." He decried another banker's purchase of a series of huge, overpriced ranches. He demonstrated his support for the Caldera government's handling of the 1994 bank crisis by withdrawing his membership from the bankers association, which had criticized it. He denounced those at the helm of the business association, arguing that they had evaded their responsibility to depositors (quoted in García Mendoza 1995, 207–9).

Some Venezuelan bankers were suspicious of García Mendoza's motives during the bank crisis. For example, it seemed suspect that Garcia Mendoza's bank had grown in the midst of the bank crisis (Zapata 2000, 64). They criticized García Mendoza's lack of constructive assistance in the bank crisis and viewed his criticism as an incendiary diatribe (Zapata 1995, 16). Caldera's own finance minister fueled suspicions that García Mendoza had actually been the source of some of the rumors that certain banks were in trouble, an act that was reviled by many bankers as the reason depositors withdrew their money en masse.[22]

Elite Outliers' Negative Experiences
in the 1994 Bank Crisis

We might expect that businesspeople who had had negative experiences in the 1994 bank crisis would be fearful of candidates likely to reappoint the 1994 financial regulators to high-level government positions. A government likely to elevate these former financial regulators to prominent political positions could threaten their access to the state, a fate these state-dependent businesspeople could not afford. Thus, when Chávez's leading opponent in the presidential elections of 1998, Salas Römer, became publicly linked to some of these former businocrats, those who were suspicious of the government's response to the bank crisis had reason to fear a Salas Römer victory. As noted elsewhere (Gates 2007, 113, 117, 121), most of the state-dependent elite outliers were bankers who had had negative experiences with the 1994 bank crisis and thus had a potent reason to fear the return of the 1994 financial regulators.

Table 6.3 demonstrates that many in the large group of elite outliers who were in the financial sector had had negative experiences with the 1994 bank crisis. As the previous chapter indicated, more than half of the elite outliers (sixteen of twenty-eight) had economic interests in the state-dependent financial services sector. Table 6.3 categorizes all elite outliers who had significant business ties to commercial banks (fourteen) at the time of the 1994 crisis according to how their banks fared during the crisis.[23] I counted an elite outlier as having a significant business tie to a bank if, in the year immediately preceding the bank crisis, he or she was a board member, senior executive officer such as president, or a principal shareholder. For example, one elite outlier was the head of a financial conglomerate that controlled more than forty companies, including several major commercial banks. Of the fourteen elite outliers with significant business ties to banks, eleven (or 79 percent) had ties to banks that were at risk of failing, that is, they were troubled during the bank crisis. As table 6.3 shows, most of these businesspeople (eight of eleven, or 57 percent) had ties to banks that ended up failing and being seized by the state.

Even those elite outliers tied to banks that survived the crisis had had negative experiences in the 1994 bank crisis. Three were high-ranking officials (two presidents and one principal shareholder) at banks that, despite experiencing problems during the crisis, nonetheless survived without government aid. Moreover, several of the other elite outliers whose primary business ties were

TABLE 6.3. Elite outliers with business ties to commercial banks by 1994 bank crisis status

	Number	Percentage
Those with business ties to seized banks	8	57
Those with business ties to banks not seized	6	43
Those with business ties to troubled banks that nearly failed	3	21
Those with personal ties to executives at seized banks or troubled banks that nearly failed	3	21
Total	14	100

Sources: See appendix D for elite outlier sources.

Notes: Categories are mutually exclusive. One elite outlier had significant business ties to both a seized and a surviving bank but was included only in the category of those having ties to seized banks.

to surviving banks had close personal connections to executives at troubled banks. For example, the president of one of Venezuela's premier banks at the time revealed his close relationship to an executive from a troubled bank when he attempted to help save the bank (Zapata 1995, 37). Similarly, in the view of journalist Zapata, two elite outliers were probably sympathetic to the president of a bank that nearly failed because they were his business partners in other ventures (Zapata 1997, 82–84). These personal ties to executives from troubled banks indicate why even elite outliers whose banks survived the crisis might have been sympathetic to the plight and complaints of those who suffered much greater losses.

Additionally, a high proportion of banks in trouble during the 1994 Venezuelan bank crisis produced elite outliers. At the time of the bank crisis, there were thirty-five commercial banks in Venezuela. Twenty of these thirty-five banks were troubled (at risk of failing). Seventeen of these banks actually failed and were seized by the government.[24] Table 6.4 displays the percentage of banks that produced an elite outlier according to the bank's status during the bank crisis. The banks that failed and that the government subsequently seized were much more likely to produce an elite outlier than those that survived. Twelve (71 percent) of these seized banks produced an elite outlier.[25] In contrast, only six (33 percent) of the banks that survived (i.e., were not seized) produced elite

TABLE 6.4. Banks by 1994 bank crisis status and connection to elite outlier

Bank crisis status	Number of banks	Percentage with elite outlier connection
Seized	17	71% (12)
Not seized	18	33% (6)
Total	35	51% (18)

Sources: See appendix D for elite outlier sources. List of all commercial banks excluding government, foreign, and domestic banks established after 1992 from Krivoy 2000, 51.

Note: Banks were defined as having a connection with an elite outlier if there was at least one elite outlier who had a significant business relationship to that bank, such as being its president, a board member, or a primary stakeholder.

outliers. Moreover, the percentage of all troubled banks (i.e., all those *at risk* of failing) that produced an elite outlier is even higher than the percentage of just the seized banks that produced an elite outlier (not shown on table 6.4). There were three banks that are included in the number of banks that survived but nearly failed. The presidents of two of these banks and the primary stakeholder of the third became elite outliers in the 1998 presidential election. Thus, fifteen (or 75 percent) of the twenty troubled banks that faced a serious risk of failing produced an elite outlier. There were officials at three additional banks that survived the crisis who had close ties to those at the helm of less fortunate banks and who were sympathetic to the criticisms of the government's handling of the crisis.[26] Clearly, then, suffering losses in the 1994 bank crisis or having personal connections to those who did was a defining experience for a large group of elite outliers. It was this experience that gave them a reason to fear losing access to the state if Salas Römer won the 1998 presidential election.

How the Bank Crisis Contributed
to Chávez's Electoral Victory

The political calculus of business actors choosing to assist Chávez was historically rooted in the enmities that the government's handling of the 1994 bank crisis unleashed among bankers. The suspicions of unfair treatment in 1994, which divided bankers, also divided the elite in their political calculus during the 1998 presidential election. We can thus see the importance of using a wider historical lens to see the political impact of a business community that is both economically dependent and politically prominent. It is insufficient to consider only the immediate sector-based economic interests of elite; we must also consider how the visible presence of business within government (political prominence), in the past as well as in prospective administrations, informs the calculus of businesspeople about which candidates to support. It is only when we step back from the short-term view of the months leading up to the 1998 election that the calculus of the core group of elite outliers comes into sharper focus. It is from this long-range view that one of the key political imprints of the long and escalating political prominence of business in Venezuela's two-party democratic era becomes apparent: a political calculus of business elites informed by heated conflict over access to the state.

Furthermore, there are two mechanisms whereby the political prominence of business shaped the political calculus of business actors in Venezuela. Both the political identification of failed banks as business patrons of rival politicians and the prevalence of former bankers among financial regulators in 1994 led many bankers, especially those at troubled banks, to suspect that the Caldera government's response in 1994 had been unfair. This constitutes an example of how the political prominence of businesspeople can aggravate the structural tendency of economically dependent business elites to compete for access to the state. This tendency intensified divisions among business elites within the financial sector and fueled suspicions about government actors. This is how business's political prominence can provoke intra-elite conflict and produce elite allies for unlikely candidates like Chávez.

◆

CONCLUSION

Theoretical Implications of Chávez's Election

THIS book has presented new evidence regarding Venezuela's political environment during the country's forty years of two-party democracy (1959–1998). Using this new evidence, I have sought to explain why it was Chávez who emerged as the victor in the 1998 presidential elections. My explanation rests on solving two puzzles that his victory poses: a voter puzzle and a business assistance puzzle. Business opposition should have made it particularly unlikely that a staunchly anti-neoliberal candidate like Chávez would emerge the victor. Business opposition should have made it more difficult for Chávez to defeat so many other presidential candidates who similarly attacked corruption and campaigned as political outsiders. Given his political views, business opposition should have made it more difficult for him to obtain voter support and to garner any assistance from business elites. Yet Chávez overcame each of these challenges.

As I have shown, Chávez won widespread voter support, despite business opposition, because he attracted voters who were anti-business. These anti-business voters were, therefore, less likely to be dissuaded by any fears that business opposition may have evoked. With this finding, I uncover a previously overlooked but vital public opinion that contributed to Chávez's surprising victory in 1998. My analysis even suggests that business's vocal opposition to Chávez may have helped Chávez win support from anti-business voters. I do not dispute that Chávez's fiery rhetoric may have fostered anti-business sentiment, but my evidence indicates that Venezuelans had lost confidence in business well before 1998 because of the long and escalating public association of businesspeople with both corruption and Venezuela's discredited political establishment. My finding—that both anti-corruption and anti-political establishment sentiment predicts anti-business sentiment in 1998—further affirms that widespread anti-business sentiment across all social classes was not merely the result of Chávez's rhetorical overtures to popular sectors in 1998.

This study also reveals why Chávez obtained assistance from a nucleus of outlier business elites. These elites calculated that their chances of gaining access to the upper echelons of the state were better with Chávez than with his leading opponent. Their access-based rationales for assisting Chávez stem from the political prominence of Venezuela's largely state-dependent business community. Most elite outliers feared losing access to the state either because they had been a conspicuous patron of a political leader and feared political reprisals or because they were the competitors of a prospective businocrat in the administration that Chávez's leading opponent would establish. But the calculus of a core group of the elite outliers becomes clear only when placed in the historical context of the scandal-ridden bank crisis of 1994. The analysis illustrates how the prominence of former bankers among those appointed to design the government's response to the bank crisis did not necessarily reassure bankers, as we might expect. Instead, their presence divided bankers over whether the government had responded fairly to troubled banks. Even the mere possibility that an otherwise pro-business candidate might reappoint these financial regulators to government led those who believed the policies of 1994 had been unfair to fear loss of access and thus to assist Chávez. The analysis illustrates how the political prominence of business in an economy where so much of the business community depends on the state can produce elite allies for unlikely candidates like Chávez.

My argument thus demands that we rethink state-business relations in Venezuela and re-specify how corruption, social polarization, and Venezuela's political institutions shaped the outcome of the 1998 presidential elections. It has implications for how we interpret the connection between oil wealth and politics and calls for a shift in the analytic focus of those seeking to understand the anti-neoliberal political trend.

Rethinking State-business Relations in Venezuela

To account for how Chávez overcame business opposition to win the 1998 presidential election, we must rethink Venezuela's state-business relations in a number of ways. We must take more seriously the facets of state-business relations that could have undermined the public's sympathy for not only the political establishment but for the business community as well. We must focus on those points in the political process where business could have influence, such as during presidential election campaigns, and not just when business seeks authorizations and contracts from the state.

Although scholars acknowledge that business involvement with corruption was probably widespread (Coppedge 2000; Francés 1989; Naím and Francés 1995; Pérez Perdomo 1991, 1999) and that business had privileged access to decision making in Venezuela's two-party political system (Coppedge 2000; Crisp 2000; Gómez 1989; López Maya, Gómez Calcaño, and Maingón 1989), they have not contemplated how these facets of state-business relations might have reduced the public's sympathy for business. Instead, scholars tend to characterize business in ways that seem at odds with the rising anti-business sentiment described in this book. For instance, scholars tend to characterize Venezuela's business community as being vulnerable to the whims of state bureaucrats wielding discretionary authority over the state's vast resources (Francés 1989; Naím 1984) or as the unwilling handmaidens of power-hungry political party bosses engaged in internecine power struggles. Michael Coppedge captures the latter perspective well when he describes the decision of businesspeople to finance a politician as "not so much a direct purchase of immediate influence as a hedge against the risk of future exclusion. Acting as the patron of a rising party leader was simply a way to reduce the uncertainty in a very risky and political business environment" (Coppedge 1999, 22).

While these portrayals may indeed be largely accurate, this study shows that the Venezuelan public did not share such an innocent interpretation of business. Moreover, it shows that the public's antipathy toward business helped Chávez win the presidential election and may, therefore, have been important in the rise of political movements that re-politicized class throughout the 1990s. As such, there is a need to contemplate new dimensions of state-business relations that could explain the rise of anti-business sentiment. I have presented new evidence that does just that. My research indicates that the involvement of business with alleged instances of corruption and with the political establishment became increasingly visible to the public. Corruption scandals implicating business mushroomed, and the number of former business leaders in high-level government appointments and congressional positions increased during the 1990s. It is the growing visibility of these less flattering (in the case of corruption scandals) and more conspicuous (in the case of business political prominence within the government) aspects of state-business relations that were key elements behind the rise of anti-business sentiment. As such, it is these facets of state-business relations that may be vital for explaining why voters chose Chávez over the other anti-establishment, anti-corruption candidates in 1998.

Furthermore, while scholars have amply documented the ways that business "court[ed] the state" (Naím and Francés 1995), and some have pointed out that business executives frequently financed campaigns (Coppedge 2000), they have largely shied away from examining how this state-centric orientation shaped the political calculations of business elites during presidential campaigns. Instead, scholars have focused on how this orientation framed (or is framed by) interactions at moments when business actors want something from the state and are therefore less influential. It is in these interactions that we see business actors subject to an omnipotent and unpredictable state, akin to an absent-minded and undisciplined parent (Francés 1989; Naím 1984).

In this study, I have explored how this state-centric orientation of Venezuela's business community framed the political calculus of the elite outliers who assisted Chávez in 1998. Consistent with other studies of contributions made to the campaigns of left-leaning candidates (Grier, Munger, and Roberts 1994; Samuels 2001), my findings show that the elite outliers tended to be dependent on the state. It is this state dependence that I contend was the reason they courted the state and therefore assisted candidates who might secure their access to the state upon gaining a victory at the polls. I even find that this access-based reasoning was prevalent among the minority of elite outliers who were not directly dependent on the state. This latter finding suggests that the well-established state dependence of so many Venezuelan business people (Baptista 1997; Briceño-León 1990) may have defined the terms by which businesspeople more generally related to the state.

This study also demonstrates that the political prominence of business was critical in persuading some important business elites to break with the business community's broad consensus on the 1998 elections and assist a political leader who seemed otherwise unsympathetic to their interests. This study thus shows the value of extending Javier Corrales's insight (1997; 2002, 163–66) beyond the business community's reactions to policymakers and to its members' political calculus regarding which presidential candidates to support. This is the reason why we need to refocus our analysis on the business interests with which particular political administrations become identified.

My research thus illuminates why we must look at more than the business community's state dependence if we hope to understand the outcome of the 1998 presidential election in Venezuela. This seemingly innocuous, and/or subordinate, relationship between business and the state sheds little light on the rise of anti-business sentiment. Although the state dependence of business is the most likely source of the state-centered orientation of most business in Venezuela, it cannot fully explain why only some state-dependent business elites decided to assist Chávez. To explain both anti-business sentiment and the calculus of those elite outliers who assisted Chávez, we must take into account how business interests became visible, or prominent, within Venezuela's political establishment. In short, we must consider the private sector's dependent prominence—its political prominence in conjunction with its economic dependence on the state—to solve both the voter puzzle and the business assistance puzzle posed by Chávez's unlikely election.

Re-specifying Existing Theses on Chávez's Election

By solving these two puzzles, I re-specify some aspects of each of the three main arguments others have put forward to account for Chávez's election in 1998. Nonetheless, my argument also goes beyond these insights in order to explain how Chávez overcame business opposition to win the election.

I do not dispute the contention of the corruption thesis—that Venezuelans were preoccupied with corruption and that their frustration with corruption helped pave the way for Chávez. Indeed, my analysis of public opinion at the time confirms that those concerned with corruption favored Chávez in 1998. However, there is another way that Venezuela's political culture, rife as it is with corruption scandals, facilitated Chávez's victory: it undermined public confidence in business more generally. The rising tide of corruption scandals implicating business identified business, whether guilty or not, as an agent of the ongoing private diversion of public funds. This argument advances the project, outlined in the early 1990s (Morris 1991), to examine more critically how and when corruption affects political stability. I advance this effort by illustrating that corruption's political impact may have more to do with the type of actors implicated in corruption scandals than the actual level of perceived corruption.

My argument re-specifies how the nation's deepening social polarization in 1998 generated sympathy for a left-leaning anti-neoliberal candidate like Chávez. My findings affirm the expectation of the social polarization thesis that those from lower social strata in society and those with a stark and dim view of the nation's economic circumstances were more likely to choose Chávez in 1998. But I find that, contrary to the social polarization argument, having anti-neoliberal policy convictions did not distinguish those who intended to choose Chávez. Those who favored Chávez were not more likely to oppose neoliberal reforms like privatization, nor were they more supportive of state interventionism. Instead, it was anti-business sentiment, independent of class status, that was decisive in helping Chávez win in 1998. In other words, it was not just the lower strata of society that was anti-business. Thus, my research points to the importance of factors other than social polarization in explaining the success of figures, like Chávez, who politicized class during the 1990s. It points instead to the importance of trends such as the escalating number of corruption scandals that implicated business actors and the growing prominence of business within Venezuela's political establishment. Both, I have argued, could explain the widespread antipathy toward business that was so pivotal in helping Chávez win.

It is also important to recognize that the political institutions of Venezuela's two-party political establishment paved the way for Chávez. The analysis here confirms what others have also shown: that one of the most powerful predictors of an intention to vote for Chávez was the level of satisfaction individuals had with the existing democracy or political establishment. However, I diverge from the failed institutions thesis in my explanation of why the institutions failed. While the exclusion of many emerging social groups undoubtedly fueled anti-establishment sentiment, it was the *inclusion* of business actors in prominent positions, such as in the cabinet and federal legislature, that tainted this anti-establishment sentiment with antagonism toward business. This practice made visible, or public, the privileged access that business had to Venezuela's policymaking process. It thereby helped to focus the frustrations of those who were excluded from the establishment on one of the few seemingly privileged societal groups: business. It stimulated the anti-business sentiment, without which it is hard to explain how Chávez overcame voter fears of an anti-neoliberal candidate vehemently opposed by business.

This study also uncovers an additional liability of the *inclusion* of business in Venezuela's two-party political establishment. It shows how the political prominence of business within the political establishment informed the political calculus of elite outliers who threw their support to Chávez. My modifications to and adaptations of the three main theories about how Chávez triumphed in 1998 have implications for one of the most widely accepted views on politics in Venezuela more generally.

Rethinking Politics in Oil Economies

The argument I make here cautions against the facile interpretation that Venezuela's oil wealth determines politics in Venezuela. Such an interpretation is widely proffered by pundits, most often when they decry the political pitfalls of the so-called Venezuelan "petro-state" (Cohen 2007; Friedman 2006; Naím 2003).[1] This is not surprising given that these interpretations are in line with those of scholars who contend that oil increases the likelihood of authoritarianism (Jensen and Wantchekon 2004; Ross 2001) and civil war (Fearon 2005; Humphreys 2005; Le Billon 2001a, 2001b; Snyder 2006; Wick and Bulte 2006).[2] This is also not surprising given that they are in line with some of the most celebrated scholarship on Venezuela's political economy (Dunning 2008; España 1989; Karl 1997; Karl and Gary 2004; Naím and Piñango 1984; Rey 1998; Urbaneja 1992). These scholars, for example, share the view that oil wealth explains why Venezuela represented an exception from the rule of authoritarianism in its region and in most countries with oil wealth.[3] For most, the state's access to wealth derived from oil, regardless of how it obtained this wealth, facilitated Venezuelan democracy.[4] The state's enormous resources, they reason, made it easier for democratic political leaders to satisfy societal demands across the social spectrum.[5]

Using similar logic, many of these same scholars have argued that the decline in oil prices was the main cause for Venezuelans' loss of confidence in their two-party political establishment (Dunning 2008, 166–83; Karl 1997).[6] They reason, based on extensive research, that a drop in oil prices drastically reduces state capacity in societies with oil wealth. This research has revealed that the ability to readily procure resources (also referred to as rents) from "external" sources frees these so-called "rentier" states from taxing their domestic constituents, be they citizens or business elites (Beblawi 1987; Chaudhry 1989, 1997; Delacroix 1980; Mahdavy 1970).[7] Thus, scholars have found that such states eventually tend to depend nearly exclusively on income from the oil industry. Often extrapolating from the Venezuelan case (Karl 1997), scholars have reasoned that political regimes in nations with oil wealth are necessarily vulnerable to eroding public support when oil prices drop because these states are more likely to face fiscal crises (Hunter 1986; Sick 1998). The fiscal crises created by oil price declines tend, therefore, to disrupt the rentier state's ability to respond to the many, often competing, societal demands at the same time that governments may need to raise resources through the ever-unpopular measure of taxation.

Even though Venezuela's oil wealth may very well have produced a rentier state vulnerable to eroding public support during periods when oil prices declined, it did not necessarily predetermine the victory of Venezuela's anti-neoliberal candidate in 1998. As noted earlier in this study, Chávez was not the only anti-establishment candidate. Moreover, business opposition made the victory of Chávez, the one staunch anti-neoliberal candidate, unlikely. Instead, explaining why Chávez defeated the other anti-establishment candidates demands that we consider the features of state-business relations that might have undermined public support for business and provoked some outlier business elites to assist Chávez. Furthermore, the political prominence of Venezuela's state-dependent business community can help solve both the voter and business assistance puzzles. Thus, if oil did structurally determine the Chávez victory, it would have structurally determined not only state-society relations in broad terms but also, more specifically, this dual facet of state-business relations in Venezuela (its dependent prominence). While oil could very well have determined the economic dependence of Venezuela's business community, it is less plausible that it could have determined the political prominence of business in Venezuela's two-party democracy.

As I have argued elsewhere (Gates 2007, 107), the state dependence of Venezuela's business community probably originated in oil wealth and, more specifically, in the emergence of Venezuela as a rentier state. Studies of rentier states reveal that they tend to *construct* a state-dependent business community for several reasons (Karl 1997; Shafer 1994).[8] For example, this research shows that rentier states tend to unintentionally undermine the competitiveness of domestic agricultural and industrial products. This situation develops because these states have political incentives to use the free flow of foreign currency earned by exporting oil to overvalue the domestic currency.[9] This "irrationally optimistic" policy (Ross 1999, 312) enables domestic consumers to buy imports for less. It thereby enables the political leaders of rentier states to achieve the political goal of building a popular base of support. However, these studies demonstrate that this policy tends to weaken the private sector because it intensifies the competition that domestic producers encounter from imports.

These studies also find that the loss of competitiveness experienced by domestic private sector producers in turn creates powerful incentives for business elites to seek both protection from imports as well as subsidies in various forms. Some have shown that these demands intensify as firms become increasingly concentrated in large corporations oriented toward servicing the country's dominant (oil) industry (Shafer 1994, 39–42). Finally, the rentier state tends to oblige these often competing business demands, especially during oil booms (Karl 1997, 57), in part because its political leaders have incentives to do so. The political leaders of rentier states have an interest in constructing a loyal business constituency. Thus, it is the convergence of these processes, all of them unleashed by oil wealth, that seems to produce the "paradox of plenty" (Karl 1997): an anemic and largely state-dependent private sector.

This insight—that oil-based rentier states tend to produce state-dependent business communities—may be critical for understanding the political dynamics in oil-rich nations precisely because it specifies one of their central social conflicts: that of competition among elites for access to state resources. After all, access-based reasoning was prevalent even among those elite outliers who did not depend directly on the state. This finding illustrates a way that the state dependence of so many businesses in oil-rich nations defines the terms by which businesses more generally relate to the state, regardless of whether or not they depend on the state.

Nevertheless, the political prominence of Venezuela's business community, unlike its state dependence, cannot be interpreted as a necessary by-product of oil wealth and/or its closely associated rentier state. In other words, it is unlikely that Venezuela's oil wealth predetermined Venezuela's politically prominent business community and the intra-elite conflict it provoked in the decade preceding Chávez's election in 1998. Such an interpretation is consistent with those of scholars (e.g., Hellinger 2000) who dispute the view that oil wealth determines politics and who identify the conditions under which oil wealth has certain political effects (Dunning 2008). Studies show, for example, that not all oil economies facing similar fiscal constraints experience the precipitous loss of public support for the existing political establishment or the surprising elite outlier behavior that we observe in Venezuela (Herb 2005; Okruhlik 1999; Smith 2004, 2006). Studies of these seeming anomalies indicate that the reliance of federal governments on resource-derived rents so prevalent among oil-rich nations (that is, the prevalence of rentier states among oil-rich nations) may very well determine the main contours of social conflicts in such societies. They reveal, however, that rentier states do not necessarily determine how (or whether) key societal actors, such as business, resolve these conflicts (Chaudhry 1997; Gause 1994; Herb 1999).[10] The task, then, is to move beyond a structural analysis of oil economy politics that relies on the "extrapolation of interests from revenue bases" and toward "an appreciation of the historical and institutional evolution of leading social actors" in oil economies (Moore 2002, 35).

My findings suggest that the success of anti-neoliberal candidates in democratic oil states may hinge on how the business community was incorporated into the democratic political process. Recent research affirms this view. Some scholars identify variation in how states incorporate business into the political arena at the moment of state formation as an important reason for divergent political dynamics in oil economies (Chaudhry 1997; Moore 2002, 53). For example, Peter Moore shows that the historical construction of state-business relations affected both business and popular support of several Middle East oil states facing fiscal crises. He finds that a well-organized business community, formed independently (i.e., not by the state) prior to oil development, facilitated intra-elite consensus and therefore a coordinated business response to Kuwait's fiscal crisis (Moore 2002).[11] Alternately, dense family-based network ties between business and ruling elites in Qatar facilitated intra-elite consensus among business elites in favor of fiscal restraints and thus made possible the regime's survival during its fiscal crisis. In contrast, the Jordanian government struggled to contain intra-elite conflict, resulting in Jordan's "policy drift" as the regime struggled to manage competing demands from business (Moore 2004, 174).

Similarly, Moore traces the increasing intolerance of Bahrain's political leadership during its fiscal crisis to the fact that both Bahrain's business and ruling political elites were predominantly Sunni. This tie between political and business elites, one made visible through a shared ethnoreligious identity, fueled suspicions among the Shi'i majority in Bahrain that the political elites were biased against the minority Shi'i business elites. These suspicions sparked class-based politicization (Moore 2002, 52).[12] Moore's brief description of Bahrain is consistent with my own argument that the visibility of ties between economic and political elites (i.e., the political prominence of business) may be an unexpected cause for what otherwise appears as spontaneous bottom-up pressure for political change.

While these studies demonstrate the importance of variation in how business is incorporated into the formal political process for the likely stability of oil regimes, they do not speak directly to the question addressed in this book. They do not, that is, speak to the question of what explains not just regime instability but a dramatic policy shift, such as experienced in Venezuela, within an oil democracy. As such, they do not demonstrate whether the way that business actors become incorporated into the political process, and therefore embedded within the principal political institutions, affects the likelihood that anti-neoliberal candidates will succeed. Nonetheless, my findings, together with these other studies, suggest that future research on politics in oil economies should explore this relationship. In particular, these findings suggest the value of investigating the political effects of a politically prominent business community.

This book, along with the endeavor described above, advances a broader intellectual agenda of re-invigorating theories of the state that are structurally rooted but historically contingent (Paige 1999; Prechel 1990, 2003). Such approaches demand that we move beyond the absolutist theories of the state, be they of the petro-state (such as those described above), the welfare state, or the developmental state, despite their appealing parsimony. Instead, historically contingent approaches demand empirically grounded investigations of the conditions that alter the balance of state-society power relations, such that they have consequences for policies or political regimes. Such historically contingent approaches, as initially articulated by Nicos Poulantzas (1976), train our focus on the structural origins of social conflicts without presuming their likely resolution. We can best see the advantage of such historically contingent approaches in revisions of generalist theories of the state that accommodate the political realities in contexts outside of advanced industrial societies (Davis 1993, 2004; Gates 2009). While some may be dismayed at the loss of parsimony in historically contingent theories of the state, I would argue that this loss is compensated by the promise of theories that more faithfully specify the structural contours that limit as well as create opportunities for those who, like Chávez, advocate social change.

Rethinking Anti-neoliberal Politics in Latin America

My argument directs those interested in the current anti-neoliberal political trend to shift their analytic focus. The analysis herein demonstrates that public opinion about business elites may be a critical but previously untested sentiment that affects voters' willingness to support an anti-neoliberal candidate. Most studies of anti-neoliberal electoral success presume that the sentiment most crucial to their victory is opposition to neoliberal economic policies. This study of a least-likely case of anti-neoliberal success suggests otherwise. In this case, the key differentiating factor between Chávez and the other contenders was that he was able to attract voters skeptical of business regardless of their opinion of neoliberal economic policies. This study further identifies a broader political context likely to produce such anti-business sentiment: a political culture in which corruption scandals widely implicate business and a political establishment in which business is prominent.

This study's detailed analysis of how Chávez obtained assistance from elite outliers offers a theoretically grounded understanding of the conditions under which business elites support anti-neoliberal candidates. The analysis reveals that a political establishment in which business is prominent (through conspicuous patronage of politicians and businocrats) may very well intensify competition among state-dependent elites for state resources. Competition among business elites for preferred access to the state mobilized economically dependent business elites to assist an anti-neoliberal candidate whom they would otherwise oppose. It thereby shows that business assistance for anti-neoliberal candidates like Chávez may be related to both the structure of the economy and the form of state-business relations. It further implies that anti-neoliberal candidates like Chávez may be more likely to emerge in economies that foster a dependent business community and in which business prominence makes fears of losing access to the state more widespread and divisive.

The Venezuelan case thus directs us to move beyond interpreting the success of anti-neoliberal presidential candidates as a by-product of popular frustrations with rigid and corrupt political institutions. It directs us to see that such success may not have been structurally determined by neoliberal globalization and the devastating social inequities it provokes or even the achievement of charisma and deft rhetoric. Instead, the Venezuelan case directs those interested in explaining the success of anti-neoliberal presidential candidates to focus on an unlikely set of actors: business elites.

By refocusing the analysis on the relationship between the anti-neoliberal candidate and business elites, we can relocate the role that political institutions, strategic agency, and structural constraints play in bringing about anti-neoliberal presidential success. The contribution of political institutions to Chávez's popular support is thus to be found not so much in their exclusivity as in the prominence they granted business elites. The role of strategy (or agency) in bringing Chávez to power lies not so much in the candidate's rhetorical strategy but rather in the choice of some business elites to assist Chávez. The structural underpinnings of anti-neoliberal politics exist not so much in the structure of social inequality as in the structure of business elites.

The Venezuelan case thereby affirms that we cannot understand Latin America's politics without incorporating business politics (Schneider 2004). Unlike those who demonstrate how neoliberal businesses mobilized to secure neoliberal policies (Schamis 2002; Thacker 2000; Williams 2001) or how protectionist businesses opposed them (Shadlen 2004), this study establishes a counterintuitive role for business in the region's politics. It shows that members of the business community, even some who were predisposed to favor neoliberal policies, facilitated the rise of the region's first anti-neoliberal president. It reveals how the political prominence of business, in a context where business largely depends on the state, may increase the likelihood of anti-neoliberal electoral victory. The visible presence of business executives in government may both erode popular confidence in the business community's collective opinion and generate incentives for business elites to assist candidates they would otherwise oppose.

APPENDIX A.

INTERVIEWS CONDUCTED

ID #	Professional experience	Date of interview
1	University professor	11/20/2005
2	University professor	11/20/2005
3	Chávez campaign insider, 1998	11/21/2005, 12/6/2005
4	Expert on Venezuelan campaign finance (by e-mail)	11/30/2005
5	Chávez campaign insider, 1998	12/5/2005
6	Chávez campaign insider, 1998	12/6/2005
7	Expert on corruption	12/6/2005
8	Expert on Venezuelan politics	12/6/2005
9	Expert on corruption	3/28/2006
10	Expert on corruption, former anti-corruption bureaucrat	3/30/2006
11	Expert on corruption	4/5/2006
12	Expert on corruption	4/6/2006
13	Former anti-corruption bureaucrat	4/21/2006
14	Former anti-corruption legislator	4/24/2006
15	Former anti-corruption bureaucrat	4/25/2006
16	Former legislator	4/27/2006
17	Former president of FEDECAMARAS	5/2/2006
18	Former anti-corruption legislator	5/3/2006
19	Former president of FEDECAMARAS	5/8/2006
20	Former president of FEDECAMARAS	5/9/2006
21	Conglomerate executive	5/12/2006
22	Former president of FEDECAMARAS	5/19/2006
23	Former president of FEDECAMARAS	5/22/2006
24	Former president of a sectoral business association	5/23/2006
25	Former president of a sectoral business association	5/25/2006

ID #	Professional experience	Date of interview
26	Former anti-corruption legislator	5/26/2006
27	Conglomerate executive, former president of a sectoral business association	5/29/2006
28	Conglomerate executive, former president of business association	5/29/2006
29	Business executive	6/1/2006
30	Former president of a sectoral business association	6/1/2006
31	Conglomerate associate, business association policy analyst	6/2/2006
32	Expert on Venezuelan state-business relations	6/7/2006
33	Former president of a business association	6/9/2006
34	Conglomerate executive, former president of a sectoral business association	6/13/2006
35	Former conglomerate executive, former businocrat	6/13/2006
36	Expert on Venezuelan state-business relations, former economic minister	6/14/2006
37	Former president of a sectoral business association	6/14/2006
38	Business consultant, former president of a sectoral business association	6/15/2006
39	Former conglomerate executive, former businocrat	6/15/2006
40	Conglomerate executive, former president of a sectoral business association	6/20/2006
41	Former president of business association	6/20/2006
42	Conglomerate executive	6/20/2006
43	Former conglomerate executive, former businocrat	6/22/2006
44	Former businocrat	6/22/2006
45	Conglomerate associate, business association policy analyst	6/23/2006
46	Business consultant	6/23/2006
47	Conglomerate associate, business association policy analyst	6/23/2006
48	Former business executive, former businocrat	7/4/2006
49	Former business executive, former businocrat	7/5/2006
50	Former economic minister	7/6/2006

APPENDIX B.

CORRUPTION SCANDALS

This study examines two samples of corruption scandals. The team of Venezuelan researchers that identified the first sample, the 246 corruption scandals for the period from 1959 to 1992 (Capriles Méndez 1990a, 1990b, 1992), defined corruption as alleged actions that violate Venezuela's anti-corruption laws, known collectively as the Law to Safeguard the National Treasure and Inheritance after 1982 (*ley de salvaguarda del patrimonio público*). This law identifies violations and punishment guidelines for "the illegitimate transfer of that which is public to the private sphere" (Pérez Perdomo 1992, 2). To identify these 246 corruption scandals, the Capriles team first looked at news reports. It then drew on government reports and interviews to flesh out the specific allegations, identify who was allegedly involved, and detail what happened with the corruption investigations and prosecutions. In the first volume of the published study, the researchers made an initial list of cases from both weekly news sources and the reports from the congressional office responsible for investigating potential budgetary abuses (the Contraloría General, roughly equivalent to the Office of Management and Budget in the United States). They then followed the cases in the daily newspapers and conducted interviews with those who could remember the case or who were involved in the case and were willing to speak. This additional investigative research made it possible for them to select those cases that were most talked about and therefore, by definition, constituted corruption scandals. In the two published volumes of research covering the period from 1979 to 1992, they first compiled a list of all cases that were denounced in the daily press and then included all those for which they could compile a complete history. This selection process ensured that they included only those cases of corruption allegations that media attention revealed to the public.

The corruption scandals included in this sample ranged widely in the number of actors involved, scale of alleged corruption, and level of government official involved. Some scandals involved a single government official committing fraud, others involved multiple actors and government agencies in elaborate

schemes of collusion. The sample included cases implicating government officials at all levels of government and involving small as well as large amounts of
government resources. For example, the compendium includes a case involving
a low-level bureaucrat, which was the first case that resulted in an actual conviction, along with a case in which a former president was cleared of wrongdoing.

To construct a second sample of corruption scandals for the remaining years
of the two-party democratic era (1992–1998), I used similar criteria in that I
sought to identify cases of alleged corruption that were discussed in the press but
that involved only formal allegations. I followed a methodology others have used
to study corruption as reported by the media (Morris 1991) and drew a random
sample of fifty dates in each year from 1992 to 1998. I worked with a research as-
sistant to review the front page of *El Universal*, one of Venezuela's leading newspapers, and the first page of its politics section on each of the selected dates. We
then identified any article that related to corruption. I selected *El Universal*, in
part, because it was one of Venezuela's more conservative newspapers during
the relevant period, making it less likely to report corruption implicating business. Furthermore, it was not one of the newspapers that had been at the fore-
front of reporting corruption. Thus, it was more likely than its competitors to
provide a conservative estimate of corruption scandals, particularly of those implicating business. I prepared a summary of each case of corruption based on the
information in the newspaper article. Like Capriles, I counted only those corruption scandals that had involved formal denunciations by some authority and ig-
nored speculative informal denunciations. Again following the practice of
Capriles's team, I did not confine the sample to the very few instances where
those charged with corruption were actually convicted.

Each corruption scandal in both samples was then coded as to whether it implicated business. Scandals were coded as implicating business actors if they involved a formal corruption allegation against a business actor. Business actors
included managers, executives, or board members of a business.

APPENDIX C.

POLITICAL BIOGRAPHIES

To examine the degree to which business was prominent in Venezuela's two-party democracy (1959–1998), I collected biographical data on two sets of political leaders: cabinet ministers responsible for economic policy and congressional leaders who had some business experience.

The sample of economic ministers included all those who held that position in a subset of ministries responsible for economic policy during the period of Venezuela's two-party democracy. They included the following six ministries that were in existence throughout the entire period of two-party dominance: (1) Agriculture and Animal Breeding, (2) the Central Bank, (3) Public Works (1959–1977)/Urban Development (1977–1998), (4) Development, (5) Finance, and (6) Mining and Hydrocarbons. The data set also included all those individuals who held the highest official post at the Central Office of Coordination and Planning (Oficina Central de Coordinación y Planificación, or CORDIPLAN) from 1959 until 1998, even though this agency was not elevated to cabinet-level status until 1974; CORDIPLAN was widely believed to have been critical in making economic policy long before 1974. The sample also included all individuals who held the top post in two of the most important public agencies, even though they were not initially elevated to cabinet-level status: president of the Venezuelan Corporation of Guayana (Corporación Venezolana de Guayana, or CVG), 1984–1998, and president of the Venezuelan Investment Fund (Fondo de Inversiones de Venezuela, or FIV), 1974–1998. Finally, I included individuals responsible for specialized economic policy concerns in their role as ministers for the following entities: International Economic Affairs, Development in the Eastern Region, Economic Reform, and Basic Production.

Table C.1 shows that this sampling procedure yielded a total of 174 economic cabinet posts held by a total of 132 individuals (not shown on the table) over the period of two-party dominance. There are more posts than persons because some individuals held more than one ministerial post, sometimes even within the same administration. The economic cabinet posts represent nearly half (42.2 percent) of all cabinet posts during the two-party political period.

TABLE C.1. Economic cabinet posts

Presidential administration	Number of cabinet posts	Number of economic cabinet posts	Economic cabinet posts as a percentage of total cabinet posts
Betancourt (1959–1964)	35	16	45.7
Leoni (1964–1969)	35	16	45.7
Caldera I (1969–1974)	32	13	40.6
Pérez I (1974–1979)	51	22	43.1
Herrera Campins (1979–1984)	45	18	40.0
Lusinchi (1984–1989)	56	22	39.3
Pérez II (1989–1993)	70	26	37.1
Velásquez (1993–1994)	27	11	40.7
Caldera II (1994–1999)	61	30	49.2
Total	412	174	42.2

The sample of federal legislators on whom I collected biographical data included all those identified by business leaders and several experts on state-business relations as having been businesspeople before being elected (they are among the interviewees listed in appendix A). Each of these interviewees graciously agreed to review a list of all 1,899 members of congress from 1958 to 1998 in order to identify the individuals they thought had been businesspeople. For each of these 1,899, when possible, they also identified the name of that person's firm, primary economic sector, and any affiliation with one of the nation's major economic conglomerates. Those interviewees willing to complete this task included business leaders from a range of business sectors. Most had at one time served as president of one or more business associations.

Table C.2 indicates that this sampling method produced a list of 135 individuals in the federal legislature who were sufficiently visible as businesspeople for the interviewees to recollect them as such. Many of these individuals were elected multiple times, holding on average 1.6 elected posts as federal legislators with a maximum of seven terms in office. As table C.2 indicates, these 135 individuals collectively held 236 posts as federal legislators, or 12.4 percent of the total positions in the federal legislature during the two-party period. Although we might anticipate that the interviewees would have been more able to recollect individuals in the recent past, table C.2 illustrates that these posts held by businesspeople were fairly evenly distributed across all years in which Venezuelans elected their federal legislators.

		TABLE C.2. Business-identified federal legislators		
Year elected	Number of federal legislators	Number of individuals identified as businesspeople in their first legislative post	Number of legislative posts occupied by businesspeople	Percentage of legislative posts occupied by businesspeople
1958	184	21	21	11.4
1963	225	18	28	12.4
1968	266	26	38	14.3
1973	247	20	32	13.0
1978	243	14	33	13.6
1983	244	19	40	16.4
1988	246	6	24	9.8
1993	244	11	20	8.2
Total	1,899	135	236	12.4

For each of the political leaders in both samples I compiled a professional biography drawn primarily from biographical dictionaries (Fundación Polar 1997; Gavalda 1962; Gran Enciclopedia de Venezuela 1989; Guía Industrial 1971; Hernandez and Parra 1999; M.S. de Venezuela 1972; Maldonado Parilli 1989; Mezquita and Compañía 1953; Perry 1965; Quién es Quién en Venezuela 1988; Ramírez 1983; Who's Who in Venezuela 1989) and a privately maintained archive at Venezuela's National Library. The biographical materials in this archive included curriculum vitae that the archivist had personally solicited at the time of political appointments, as well as biographical sketches published in national newspapers.

To code individuals in the sample for whom I could not locate a biography in the above manner, I pursued a number of other strategies, such as contacting former politicians directly and reviewing newspaper issues from the time of their appointment, Web sites from business associations, and other sources (e.g., Filiberto 1974). To these sorts of biographical data I added political leaders' service as members of a corporate board for any of the companies that were publicly traded (1976–1998) and any information regarding prior business experience recollected by at least two of the business elites I interviewed.

I compiled professional biographies on individuals holding 93.1 percent of all 162 economic cabinet posts. In only two administrations did the percentage of economic cabinet posts with complete biographies fall below 90 percent. I assembled professional biographies on the policymakers filling 88 percent of the economic cabinet posts during the Herrera Campins administration (1979–1984) and on those holding 83 percent of the economic cabinet posts during the second Caldera administration (1994–1998). I also compiled biographies on 112 (or 83 percent) of 135 federal legislators that interviewees had identified as having been businesspeople before becoming federal legislators. Collectively, the 112 legislators held 195 posts during the course of the two-party period or 82.6 percent of all posts (in the federal legislature) that my interviewees had indicated were filled by businesspeople.

Using the procedure described in Roderic Camp's seminal studies of elites in Mexico (Camp 1989, 2002) and consulting with him (personal communication via e-mail, February 16, 2008) so as to facilitate a comparison with his data on Mexico, I coded political leaders as having had significant prior business experience if they had one of the following types of professional experiences *prior* to holding each political post: serving as president or board member of a business association, holding an upper management or executive-level position at a business enterprise, or being president or member of a board of directors at a private business enterprise. I excluded prior experience as a professional serving the private sector, such as working as an accountant or lawyer.

I coded political leaders as having had prior ties to a conglomerate if they had had upper management or executive-level employment at any of its major affiliates or served as a member of the board of directors for one of its major affiliates. In addition, those who had dedicated their professional services, such as legal services, to a particular economic conglomerate were coded as having a link to a conglomerate.

APPENDIX D.

ELITE OUTLIERS

I coded all elite outliers according to their economic interests and their access-based reasons to assist Chávez as described in the main text using numerous prior descriptions of each individual (Hellinger 2003; Ortiz 2004; Santodomingo 1999; Zapata 2000). I supplemented these descriptions with information from campaign insiders that I interviewed and an exhaustive search for articles referring to the elite outliers by name in a number of electronic newspaper databases. These included the LexisNexis News Library, the Biography File of the Reference Library on LexisNexis, and the online archive of *El Universal*. For a coded list of each elite outlier, see Gates 2007, 16. The analysis presented here, however, draws on additional sources and codes for two distinct ways that political prominence might generate reasons to assist Chávez: fear of political reprisals as well as fear of prospective businocrats (Capriles Méndez 1992; Colitt 1997; Zapata 1997, 2000).

I then list each combination of economic interests and access-based rationales by the number of elite outliers with that combination. Sorting data in this manner enables one to see if, and how, variables combine to generate particular outcomes. In this study, for example, I find that a combination of dependence on the state with at least one access-based reason to assist Chávez typifies most elite outliers (see table 5.2). Thus, it would seem that state dependence on its own cannot explain why individual business leaders would have believed their chances of gaining access to Chávez were better than with other candidates.

Such findings illustrate one of the advantages of the qualitative comparative analytical techniques developed by sociologist Charles Ragin (1987). His approach, unlike conventional statistical analysis, does not assume that each variable operates independently of the others. Relaxing this assumption allows for the possibility that variables produce a particular outcome only under certain conditions or in combination with a particular value or characteristic of another variable. It therefore helps the researcher see how and when variables combine to produce a particular outcome.

Another advantage of sorting and analyzing the data in this way is that it allows for the possibility that there may be various paths to a common outcome.

In this study, for example, I have described several profiles of elite outliers. In addition to the elite outliers who exhibited the profile of the state-dependent businessperson with an access-based reason to assist Chávez, there were non-state-dependent elite outliers. Surprisingly, all of these outlier elites, even the protectionists, had access-based reasons to assist Chávez. We can think of these elite outliers, then, as taking a different path than state-dependent business elites to the same decision. In my earlier analysis of elite outliers (Gates 2007), I come to similar conclusions using the more formal analytical technique that Ragin developed.

NOTES

Chapter 1. The Unlikely Election of an Anti-neoliberal

1. This estimate includes left-of-center presidents who criticize but do not reject neo-liberalism outright (Ellner 2004; Panizza 2005, 729). In 2006, experts classified nine (or 60 percent) of the governing parties in fifteen Central and South American countries as left or left-of-center (González and Queirolo 2008). Since then, two additional countries classified in 2006 as governed by the Right (El Salvador and Nicaragua) have elected presidents classified as belonging to the Left. Surveys also suggest that between 2004 and 2006, Latin Americans shifted their ideological orientations leftward (Seligson 2007, 84).

2. In the weeks prior to the election, Acción Democrática switched its endorsement from that original candidate, Luis Alfaro Ucero, to the more promising candidacy of political independent Henrique Salas Römer.

3. The first poll showing that Chávez had pulled ahead of the early front-runner (Irene Sáez) was conducted in March 1998 (Buxton 2001, 200). It revealed that 30 percent of Venezuelans intended to vote for Chávez and only 24 percent intended to vote for Sáez.

4. A study of business leaders confirmed this so-called Chávez effect (Olivares 1998). It revealed that 62 percent of business leaders thought the recent electoral developments (*coyuntura electoral*) had affected the investment climate negatively, while only 12 percent thought of it as having a positive effect. This study of 133 company presidents and high-level managers was conducted in February 1998. Of these 133 individuals, 59 percent were Venezuelan and 41 percent were foreigners operating in Venezuela. They represented a range of sectors, with the highest concentrations being the 11 percent in the financial sector, the 10 percent in the petroleum sector, and the 7 percent in manufacturing.

5. Cuban intellectual Marta Harnecker, for example, argued that the Left would make political progress only if it were to set aside anti-imperialist goals in favor of more realistic goals, such as countering neoliberalism (Harnecker 1999).

6. Castañeda's plea for a left-center political strategy rested in part on his assessment that the Left was hampered by its lack of an economic project that would be an alternative to the neoliberal economic paradigm. Latin America's Left had championed socialist revolutions and more broadly "the role of the state in economic and social policy" (Castañeda 1990, 480) and was guilty by its association with Cuba's model of state control over the economy (Ellner 2004, 11). But the Sandinista loss and the fall of the Soviet Union made the call for socialist revolution less tenable. Both burst the assumption that once won, socialist revolutions would not be reversed voluntarily by the people. The latter, in particular, undermined the Left's claim that there was a coherent alternative economic model, albeit one that would always need to be adapted to particular contexts. Furthermore, the state-led development that had dominated Latin America for several decades

and with which the Left was routinely associated appeared to have failed to produce sustained economic growth for the region. Thus, Castañeda concluded, the Left was able to advocate only a nuanced version of the existing neoliberal economic project, one that sought more social spending and debt relief, a greater role for the state in the economy, and less privatization and trade opening (Castañeda 1990, 482). This position, he argued, would garner insufficient support unless the Left built an alliance with the region's political Center (Castañeda 1990, 482; 1993). He argued that a center-left coalition would permit the Left to win elections and thereby temper the neoliberal economic project (Castañeda 2001).

7. In essence, then, he advocated an approach adopted by the communists during the 1930s and 1940s in their popular-front strategy (Ellner 2004, 14–15).

8. The founding father of AD, Rómulo Betancourt, shared the communist movement's appreciation for the working class. In his plan for a multiclass party, he asserted his appreciation for the historical role that the working class might play in achieving the plan's development and social justice goals (Ellner 1999, 120). Not surprisingly, then, the communists joined him in forming his own party, the Partido Democrático Nacional (PDN, or National Democratic Party) in 1936.

9. Scholars contend that AD party leaders doubted the PCV's commitment to democratic principles (Alexander 1982) and feared that including the PCV would undermine their chances of securing U.S. approval (Myers 2004, 25).

10. Feeling that the AD had betrayed their earlier commitment to a long-term progressive transformation of Venezuela's economy and social structure, many on the Left instigated an armed insurgency against Venezuela's fledgling democracy (Alexander 1964, 101; Martz 1966, 174–83). These leftists included members of the PCV as well as the leftist wings of the traditional parties (Ellner 1999, 135), such as the youth wing of AD (Alexander 1964, 101; Martz 1966, 174–83). The first AD split-off was the Movimiento de Izquierda Revolucionaria (MIR, or Movement of the Revolutionary Left), which formed in 1960. The second was the Movimiento Electoral del Pueblo (MEM, Electoral Movement of the People), which split off in 1967 (Ellner 1999, 133). Both eventually competed in the electoral arena.

11. The party's leadership came from individuals on the Left who were willing to condemn the Soviet invasion of Czechoslovakia in 1968 (Ellner 1988, 41–63).

12. Explaining why an outcome occurred in a context least likely to produce that outcome "greatly increase[s] the plausibility of the alternative theoretical understanding [the case] suggest[s]" (Rueschemeyer 2003, 311). It also "fulfills a crucial role in the development of theory, because it is precisely the anomalous cases, the ones that do not conform to the theory, that lead to the expansion of the theory's range of explanation" (Emigh 1997, 673).

Chapter 2. Explaining Chávez's Election

1. Since the 1960s, scholars have admired the exemplary statecraft of Venezuela's party leaders, praising how party leaders brokered the democratic transition through a political pact, and admiring the institutions that channeled demands from key societal groups into the formal political arena, which anchored one of the region's few democracies (Levine

1973; Martz 1966). Indeed, scholars believed that some of Venezuela's political institutions (such as the business community's peak associations and corporatist unions) were ideally suited to channel the demands of those likely to oppose neoliberal reforms (Haggard and Kaufman 1992). Moreover, many scholars were optimistic that the efforts, albeit limited, to decentralize political power within the democracy during the 1990s would enable Venezuela's political establishment to regain the public's confidence (Crisp and Levine 1998; Levine 1998; Levine and Crisp 1999).

2. Calculated based on the CPI available at http://www.icgg.org/corruption.cpi_ olderindices.html (accessed December 12, 2007). Venezuela's CPI score was 3.2 on a 10-point scale, in which a 10 indicates countries with the greatest transparency and therefore the lowest perceived levels of corruption. According to this score and related ranking, 79 percent of the other ranked nations were more transparent than Venezuela during this period. As such, this ranking indicated that 79 percent of the other ranked nations were perceived as having less corruption than Venezuela.

3. Venezuela's CPI score sank further, to 2.5, during the 1988 to 1992 period, and it hovered there until the elections in 1998.

4. This ranking was calculated based on CPI data available at http://www.icgg.org/ corruption.cpi_olderindices.html (accessed December 12, 2007).

5. A Gallup poll from June 1977 confirms that dissatisfaction with the regime went hand in hand with the perception that corruption was rampant. In this 1977 poll, 70 percent of respondents already believed that the highest levels of the administration were corrupt, 57 percent claimed there were "very serious irregularities," and more than a third (36 percent) were unconvinced the government was doing anything to combat corruption ("Venezuela: Colonel" 1977). In 1984, Venezuelans thought that the government (specifically, corruption in government) was responsible for Venezuela's large foreign debt (Templeton 1995, 87): 36 percent blamed bad administration of the nation's funds and 33 percent blamed administrative corruption specifically. Moreover, when asked who bore responsibility for the economic crisis in 1984, 62 percent of respondents thought the previous government bore a lot of responsibility, while close to half thought the present government bore a lot of responsibility (Templeton 1995, 88).

6. Before then, about a third of the population thought another party might have been able to do a better job than the existing government. But after 1983, less than 20 percent thought so (Templeton 1995, 86).

7. In 1985, for example, 67 percent of poll respondents said they had little or no confidence in the honesty of those who managed public administration (Templeton 1995, 89). But that same year, a striking 86 percent blamed the crisis first and foremost on corruption (Templeton 1995, 89). A large majority of the public (74 percent) placed secondary blame for the crisis on bad administration of natural resources, and 50 percent blamed a decline of moral values. During the 1990s, the vast majority blamed "Venezuela's dependence on oil, economic mismanagement and political demagoguery" on corruption (Romero 1997, 20). Furthermore, 64 percent blamed the crippling financial crisis that gripped the nation during most of 1994 on corruption (Romero 1997, 23).

8. My narrative on the failed institutions thesis also builds on studies conducted before the 1998 election (Canache and Kulischeck 1998; Goodman 1995; McCoy 1995), which similarly sought to revise prior institutional accounts that had not anticipated the public's declining confidence in Venezuela's political establishment.

9. The scholars I cite all share the conviction that institutions played a key role, although some stress the lack of leadership or the determinacy of oil dependence as the origin of this negative institutional influence.

10. Authors variously traced the inadequacies of Venezuela's political institutions, in particular its excessive centralism, to Venezuela's oil dependence (Karl 1997; Schael 1993) or the intransigence of political leaders, who failed to enact much-needed political reforms (Buxton 2001, 226; McCoy and Myers 2004a, 7; Molina 1998; Naím 2001). Some argued that political leaders had "overlearned" lessons of their past mistakes (McCoy 1999) and could not loosen their grip on an overly centralized and elitist political process (Crisp, Levine, and Rey 1995, 150; Jácome 2000).

11. The MAS leader left his party when it endorsed Chávez. The prominent politicians in MVR were Luis Miquilena, who had been a leader in one of the three founding parties of Venezuela's 1958 transition to democracy, and José Vicente Rangel, who had been a leader of Venezuela's Left within the federal legislature (Buxton 2001, 210).

12. The economically marginalized felt abandoned by leftist leaders within the two traditionally dominant political parties as well as by leaders of leftist political parties.

13. Trino Márquez (1998) uses the verb *atornillar,* which literally means to screw on but has a figurative meaning which can be translated as ramp up.

14. These risk assessment specialists were with Merrill Lynch, Warburg Dillon, Duff and Phelps, Standard and Poors, and JP Morgan.

15. This interpretation is consistent with those who characterize Chávez as a populist (Roberts 2003a) or, more precisely, as representing "left-wing populism" (Ellner 2004, 27).

16. Although President Caldera did not leave office officially until February 1999, we can say the two-party era effectively ended with Chávez's election in December 1998.

17. This advisor, the first head of Chávez's political organization—the MVR—was an elder statesman of Venezuela's Left (Hellinger 2003, 29). He had been associated with Venezuela's Communist Party in the 1940s and was a longtime opponent of Venezuela's establishment political parties during the two-party era (Hellinger 2003, 29). He was well positioned to help Chávez obtain assistance from business elites because he was also a businessman. Initially the owner of a newspaper, he subsequently pursued various business ventures through which he established "connections in the banking and insurance industries" (Hellinger 2003, 43).

18. See Gates 2007, 106, for a summary of these recent studies.

Chapter 3. The Role of Anti-business Sentiment

1. The 1948 coup ousted Venezuela's first democratically elected president, Rómulo Gallegos. While Acción Democrática instigated its left-leaning governance of Venezuela in 1945 through a coup, it won resounding voter support for its leftist agenda with the 1947 election of Gallegos. In that election, 70 percent of voters supported Gallegos (Hellinger 1991, 60). Colonel Marcos Pérez Jiménez cut Gallegos's presidency short when, on November 24, 1948, he seized power, outlawed AD, and forced AD leaders into exile (Hellinger 1991, 65; Hillman 1994, 36) for the duration of his brutal ten-year rule.

2. This widespread low level of confidence in unions reflects the timing of the poll, which was conducted shortly after the bank administered by the peak union federation

failed. In the aftermath of the failure, there were rampant rumors that corruption had plagued the bank prior to its failure.

3. While earlier polls prompted respondents for whether they had none, little, some or much confidence, the 1998 poll provided only 3 options (none, little, or much). This may have contributed to the higher percentage point increases between 1995 and 1998. Other polls confirm this dim view of business. In a 1995 poll, only 14 percent thought business had performed well, compared with 43 percent who thought journalists had done well and a quarter who thought the military had performed well. When asked to rank the relative importance of business for democracy, business ranked only tenth out of twelve possible institutions (Buxton 2001, 74–75).

4. I am indebted to Alfredo Vargas and the Banco de Datos Poblacionales at the Universidad Simón Bolívar for supplying me with these data. I am also grateful to Jana Morgan for helping to put me in touch with Alfredo Vargas.

5. While "*poca*" literally means little, I translate it hereafter as "some" because it is the only intermediate degree of confidence offered as an option to respondents.

6. We can interpret the 4.6 percent of Chávez supporters (twenty-four respondents) who did have a lot of confidence in FEDECAMARAS as unlikely to simply discredit the concerns raised by business. This minority group of Chávez's supporters may have been undeterred because they were more concerned about issues other than those raised by business or perhaps even because they did not believe that Chávez would follow through on his promises, which threatened to alter the business environment in significant ways.

7. In early 1998, AD was believed to favor Luis Giusti, then president of the state-run oil agency, as their presidential candidate. By the time the party decided whom to nominate, however, falling oil prices made Giusti too unpopular to nominate (Hellinger 2003, 39–41). They nominated the longtime AD party leader, Alfaro Ucero, instead. In a dramatic display of disloyalty, however, the party withdrew its support for Alfaro Ucero within weeks of the election.

8. Other scholars have used satisfaction with political parties or the congress (Canache 2002, 82; Molina 2002, 240) to assess the failed institutions thesis. These scholars find that Chávez's supporters had less confidence in Venezuela's political parties and congress than did supporters of other candidates (Canache 2002, 82). Furthermore, a full 71 percent of those who said they would never vote for one of the traditional parties voted for Chávez, while only 28 percent of those who did not reject either of the two traditional parties voted for him (Molina 2002, 235). But these measures may capture satisfaction with nonestablishment political parties, including Chávez's own MVR (Weyland 2003, 834).

9. Based on evidence that as satisfaction with Venezuela's existing democracy increased, the likelihood of supporting Chávez decreased (Weyland 2003, 834), Weyland concludes that Chávez's supporters generally "tended to reject the way in which the political class had been running the country and to agree with the mounting criticism of the established political system" (Weyland 2003, 833).

10. It is difficult to interpret the meaning of the estimated parameters of a logistic regression model because, as a nonlinear probability model, the relationship between each variable and the outcome depends on the values of the other variables (Long 1997). Scholars have developed a number of ways to interpret the results of such models that can capture the substance of the results without being too complex but recommend the percentage

change in odds (Long and Freese 2006, 180–81). Each percentage change reported in the text should be understood as the percentage change in the odds of voting for Chávez, holding all other variables constant.

11. This finding is consistent with others (Molina 2002, 239). According to one study, 55 percent of those who are concentrated in the lower third of Venezuela's economic strata said they would vote for Chávez, while only 45 percent of those who were not poor indicated support for Chávez (Canache 2004, 39, 46).

12. In 1993, only 58 percent of poor respondents reported that they intended to vote, compared to 86 percent in 1998 (Canache 2004, 45).

13. In separate tests not detailed here, I have found that neither of the economic policy variables had a significant bivariate relationship to an intention to vote for Chávez.

14. In a logistic regression that included a different set of control variables, Molina finds that opposition to one of the central planks of neoliberal economic reforms—privatizing the oil industry—did not make people more likely to vote for Chávez (Molina 2002, 239). Similarly, Weyland finds that those who rejected privatization outright (31.5 percent of respondents) were not more likely to vote for Chávez (Weyland 2003, 833–35). Furthermore, those who were categorically opposed to privatization as opposed to favoring some privatization and those who preferred privatizing some rather than all state enterprises were not more likely to identify with one of the new parties (Morgan 2007, 90). Although Weyland finds that favoring state intervention increased the likelihood of favoring Chávez, that attitude similarly increased the likelihood of favoring Chávez's main opponent. Therefore, being in favor of state intervention did not uniquely characterize Chávez supporters (Weyland 2003, 834–35). Another study confirmed that the economic policy positions of candidates did not appear to matter to voters (Molina 2002, 239). Morgan also shows that those who favored more state intervention were not any more likely to identify with one of the new leftist parties that backed Chávez than they were the two traditional parties. Similarly, preference for a particular economic system (capitalism versus socialism) did not predict whether respondents were more likely to have nontraditional partisan identities (Morgan 2007, 90).

15. Polls that disaggregate these sentiments by class confirm that Venezuelan's economic policy preferences did not differ by class status. By 1998, those in lower economic strata were only slightly less likely to support more significant degrees of privatization (34 percent) than the middle and upper strata (41 to 42 percent) (Canache 2004, 43). Between 1995 and 1998, the gap between the rich and the poor in their assessments of state interventionism closed. While the level of support for state intervention went up, from 68 to 86 percent among those in the lower strata, it surged from 29 to 80 percent in Venezuela's upper strata during those three years (Canache 2004, 43).

16. Beginning with the 1995 regional elections, "pragmatic alliances" of parties with seemingly competing ideological positions had made it increasingly difficult to discern let alone trust a candidate's policy positions (Maingón and Sonntag 2000, 42, 60).

17. In the 1980s, Venezuelans became increasingly pessimistic about the future state of their own pocketbooks (the prospective pocketbook variable) and their nation's economy as a whole (the prospective sociotropic variable). Since then, a comprehensive review of national polls demonstrates that "never more than 25% felt that they would be better off in the near future" (Templeton 1995, 81). Moreover, in the 1980s, about a third of the population expected their personal situation to get worse in the next six months. By 1989, more

than half of the respondents expected their situation to be worse in the next six months (Templeton 1995, 82). And yet, according to the REDPOL survey, in 1998, only 35.1 percent had a pessimistic view of their immediate future. Historical trends of public opinion also indicate that this turnaround was driven by a particularly sharp upturn in optimism among those in lower social strata. By 1991, those in lower socioeconomic strata were also much more likely to say they were not at all confident that Venezuela would be prosperous in five years. Of those in the lowest socioeconomic level, 25 percent had no confidence that Venezuela would prosper in five years, compared to 9 percent of those in the highest strata (Templeton 1995, 99). Even in 1995, those in lower social strata continued to be significantly more pessimistic about the nation's economic prospects than individuals at the top of the social class hierarchy (Canache 2004, 41). Not until 1998 did the poor become approximately as optimistic about the nation's prospects as the middle and upper strata of society (Canache 2004, 41).

18. Weyland argues that voter support for Chávez illustrates the cognitive-psychological thesis (Kahnemann and Tversky 2000), which holds that people generally have an "exaggerated risk-aversion." This basic human condition of a "strong fear of losses," he argues, led voters not to act "in a simple materialistic fashion" (Weyland 2003, 825), as economic voting theories would predict.

19. The power of this model is indicated by the high value (44.77) of the likelihood ratio test of difference between the two models.

Chapter 4. The Sources of Anti-business Sentiment

1. For this period, the Chi^2 equaled 3.254 and was significant at the .10 level ($P = .071$). Thus, we can say that the probability that the difference between this administration and the overall average was due to chance is less than 10 out of 100.

2. Given that the overall average for the entire period is based on two different data sets, it is not possible to test for significant difference between the percentage of corruption cases that implicated business in Caldera's administration versus the overall percentage.

3. The directors of the Central Bank were accused of having signed off on distributing more dollars than they must have known they were taking in per the official budgets at the time, "without ever pointing out to the President or anyone else this abnormality" (Capriles Méndez 1992, 562–63). The allegations against the president and many of the former ministers from the Jaime Lusinchi administration stemmed from the fact that they had been members of the Import Commission, formed in May 1987. The commission had established the policies and priorities for authorizing access to dollars at the preferential rate and had discretionary powers to grant such authorizations (Capriles Méndez 1992, 633–35).

4. For example, the government charged the development minister with authorizing more than $8 million over what should have been authorized to one of the car manufacturing companies (Capriles Méndez 1992, 589).

5. On more than one occasion, the investigations also brought to light myriad ways that businesspeople swindled their businesses or their business partners by depositing in personal accounts outside of the country the difference between the actual price and the artificially high price that was billed (Capriles Méndez 1992, 561).

6. This case is colloquially known as the "Chinese scapegoat" case because the accused was originally from China (Capriles Méndez 1992, 554).

7. The orders to detain these executives were originally issued on April, 26, 1989, but were later revoked (Capriles Méndez 1992, 590).

8. One of these two cases involved judges who let off the hook ten former ministers who had been suspected of corruption related to the RECADI program. Although business actors were clearly implicated in their actions, there were no business defendants in this specific case.

9. In addition to seizing seventeen of Venezuela's fifty commercial banks, the government also seized "35 financial institutions that belonged to failed financial groups: 8 mortgage banks, 14 investment banks and 13 leasing companies, along with more than 1000 non-financial companies and innumerable other assets" (Krivoy 2003, 3).

10. In the wake of Banco Latino's collapse, eight other banks had suffered drastic declines in deposits as depositors rushed to withdraw their money for fear their own banks would close. With the approval of the Central Bank and government officials, FOGADE had given these banks loans to help them stay open. In June 1994, the government seized these eight banks. For more on government treatment of troubled banks, see chapter 5.

11. These actions were based on three decrees issued during the second half of 1994 (Krivoy 2002, 189).

12. Pointing to FOGADE's records, some observers dispute this claim and argue that up to 97 percent went to legal obligations the banks had to their affiliates or business clients (Krivoy 2002, 218).

13. For example, the individuals whom Caldera appointed to oversee Banco Latino after the government seized it were suspected of mishandling the administration of the bank (Krivoy 2002, 207). The Supreme Court indicated it believed that high-level government officials might also have been involved in corruption related to the administration of the eight banks receiving FOGADE funding (Vargas 1994a) when it referred the case against all directors of these eight banks to the higher corruption court. The government even launched an investigation of former FOGADE officials. This occurred at the beginning of 1995, after the government seized Banco Progreso and a review of their records indicated forged documents had been used to persuade FOGADE to continue lending the bank money. FOGADE officials were supposed to have been attending the Banco Progreso board meetings since September 1994 and should have recognized the documents as forged (Chiappe 1995).

14. Because I did not collect and code biographies of all ministers, I cannot present the percentage of all cabinet members in Venezuela who had significant prior business experience.

15. Although business confidence appears to be an ordered variable, the Brant test indicated that the parallel regression assumption was violated for several variables in the model. Thus, it was not appropriate to conduct the type of logistic regression often used to analyze an ordered dependent variable: that of an ordered logistic regression. Additional tests also indicated the dependent variable of confidence in business could not be collapsed into a simple dichotomous variable of no confidence versus some or much confidence. After calculating a multinomial logistic regression with all the variables predicted to affect confidence in business, I conducted several tests to assess whether none of the independent variables significantly affected the odds of having no confidence ver-

sus some or some versus much confidence in business, as indicated in Long and Freese 2006. I concluded that the categories of some and much confidence in business could not be collapsed into one because most of the tests for whether they could be combined were significant at least at the $p < .10$ level. For example, the Wald test, which tests for the null hypothesis that all coefficients except intercepts associated with a given pair of alternatives are equal to 0 or are indistinguishable, produced a Chi^2 value of 14.825 with a probability value of .063 for the difference between coefficients predicting some and those predicting much confidence in business. This indicated that we can reject the hypothesis that these two alternatives are indistinguishable, albeit at a fairly low level of statistical significance. In contrast, we can definitively reject the hypothesis that the coefficients were indistinguishable when comparing some versus no confidence and much versus no confidence (both significant at the .001 level). Similarly, a likelihood ratio test of combining some and much confidence (calculated with Stata software using the "mlogtest, lrcomb" command) indicates that we can reject the two as indistinguishable. This test produced a Chi^2 value of 15.535, with 8 degrees of freedom and a p value of .05. The final test compares the full model with one that constrains the coefficients for a lot of confidence to 0. The likelihood ratio Chi^2 is 15.54, with a p value of .0495.

16. The likelihood ratio test for whether we can reject the null hypothesis that all the coefficients associated with mentioning corruption are simultaneously equal to 0 was significant at the .10 level, with a chi^2 value of 4.996. This indicates that, overall, the model would be different if the variable were omitted. This variable was one of only three variables for which we can reject the hypothesis on the likelihood ratio test.

17. The importance of overall satisfaction with the political establishment in predicting the level of confidence in business was further confirmed by the likelihood ratio tests for significant difference if the variable were removed from the analysis. This test produced a Chi^2 (with 2 degrees of freedom) equaling 28.065, with a p value of less than .001. The test results, therefore, allow me to reject the null hypothesis that all coefficients associated with satisfaction with the existing democracy are simultaneously equal to 0.

18. Table 4.7 also suggests, as the social polarization thesis might predict, that the assessment of how well the country had been doing in the recent past (the retrospective sociotropic variable) distinguished those who had some confidence in business from those with none. Those with a more positive assessment of the recent past (as indicated by the retrospective sociotropic variable) were 32.2 percent more likely to have some confidence in business than none at all. Thus, as the social polarization thesis predicts, a negative perception of the state of the country does have a political impact. Here, however, I show that it had an impact on not only voting preferences in 1998 but also how people viewed a critical and influential actor in society: the business community.

Chapter 5. Dependent Prominence and Elite Outlier Calculus to Assist Chávez

1. For a complete list of outliers by verification source, see Gates 2007.

2. In contrast, Frieden (1991) contends that those with predominantly liquid assets, such as bankers, or those with assets that can be easily converted into cash, such as merchants, have a structural predisposition to favor eliminating restrictions on international

flows of capital. Liquid asset holders, he argues, have much to gain from a more open market and can more easily protect themselves from the market volatility that accompanies liberalized markets than can those with predominantly fixed assets.

3. In contrast, Silva (1996) argues that those fixed-asset sectors that traditionally produce for export (sectors such as mining and oil extraction) or manufacturing sectors with the potential to compete internationally (such as food processing) may favor reforms. The latter group includes a select group of manufacturers that have not developed their export potential as a result of trade protections but are well situated to do so because of their high level of economic concentration and attractiveness to foreign lenders.

4. In Venezuela, we would expect agro-industrialists and most manufacturers to be predisposed to favor protectionist policies. Since oil was discovered in Venezuela in 1913, Venezuela has earned much of its income from petroleum exports. Selling oil on the international market brought large sums of foreign currency into the country (Cupolo 1996; Karl 1987). This easy access to foreign currency enabled Venezuela to maintain a favorable foreign exchange rate and made it cheaper for Venezuelans to buy foreign products. However, there was a downside to this seeming advantage. The favorable exchange rate also meant that it was often cheaper to import products than to make them in Venezuela. This situation undermined the profitability of domestic producers in some industries, especially domestic food production. It was cheaper to import processed food and raw materials than to produce them inside Venezuela (Naím and Francés 1995). Many agricultural producers did not survive (Karl 1987; Thorp and Durand 1997), and agricultural production declined throughout much of the twentieth century (Cupolo 1996; Jongkind 1993; Karl 1987). Those producers who survived did so as a result of trade barriers that protected them from competition with cheaper grain, cotton, and livestock imports. Not surprisingly, after the Venezuelan government removed many of these protections in the 1990s, domestic agriculture again suffered significant losses. Thus, agro-industrialists tended to favor both a high tariff on imports, to hold back foreign competitors, and generous technical and financial development aid from the state (Thorp and Durand 1997).

5. The variation in policy preferences across the manufacturing sector may help explain why, despite its historic opposition to liberalizing trade (Mann 1989; "Venezuela Trade" 1983), the main manufacturers business association, CONINDUSTRIA, did not oppose many of the neoliberal reforms in the early 1990s (Corrales and Cisneros 1999) and did not advocate for Chávez in 1998 (Seara 1998).

6. For example, the cement industry had profited after it was privatized in the 1990s. It had been able to expand its client base to locations outside Venezuela, allowing these businesses to increase exports to Florida and to various South American countries (Colitt 1996; Gutierrez 1996; Passell 1991). Both the food processing and paper industries had been able to compete domestically against international products (Bitar and Troncoso 1990). They had even grown during the 1990s, when the economy was opened up to foreign investment and competition (Jongkind 1993). Many in these industries had been able to attract significant foreign investments (Bitar and Troncoso 1990). For information about elite outliers in these industries, see "Businessmen Weigh" 1984; Gilpin 1997; Zapata 2000, 98.

7. For example, businesses poised to invest in the telephone service industry joined with foreign multinationals to advocate privatizing Venezuela's telephone company, CANTV, in the 1990s. Those in the media, including newspapers and television networks, tended

to oppose tariffs on content and physical materials needed to produce and distribute their product (such as ink and satellite dishes). They also tended to support unregulated access to a strong local currency, the Venezuelan bolívar (VEB), in order to help them import these components for their businesses (Murdock 1995).

8. The point about construction and cement manufacturing depending on building contracts from the state is derived from research on Brazil (Samuels 2001). Because much greater portions of the private sector in Venezuela depend on the state (Baptista and Mommer 1989; Briceño-León 1990, 127; Karl 1997), I extend the definition of state-dependent sectors. I include banks because after all of the state's oil revenue is deposited in Venezuela's Central Bank, it is distributed to the different government agencies via private banks. By some estimates, government deposits account for 60 percent of bank deposits (Interview 4). Similarly, I also extend the definition of state-dependent sectors to include media outlets such as newspapers and radio and television stations because the sheer size of the state made the advertisement contracts with various government agencies a crucial piece of their business. As a Chávez campaign insider (Interview 3) pointed out, the media outlets also had to ensure that they had access to high-level government officials so that they were credible with the public. Furthermore, as an expert in Venezuelan campaign finance explained (Interview 4), those individuals with significant investments in the telecommunications industry had an additional reason to support Chávez because they wanted to streamline the regulation of the various industries (such as radio, television, cable, Internet, and cell phone services) within the telecommunications sector to make it easier for companies to diversify into new industries within that sector. A series of reforms to this effect were, in fact, implemented in 2000 (Chacón 2004).

9. I coded pro-Chávez business managers and owners as having network ties to Chávez if at least one of my sources close to the 1998 campaign confirmed that the individual had a direct relationship to Chávez.

10. I diverge, here, from my earlier analysis of elite outliers (Gates 2007). My subsequent interviews with business elites and research on the political prominence of business convinced me that the political prominence of business was more central in shaping the political calculus of elite outliers than I had initially contemplated. While the earlier work details how the business ties of Chávez's leading opponent may have given some businesspeople reason to distrust him, here I show for the first time how this access-based reason for assisting Chávez illustrates the more generalized effects of political prominence on business in Venezuela. The broader analysis of how the political prominence of business might affect business's political calculus also revealed the fear of political reprisals as an additional access-based reason to assist Chávez.

11. The president of Venezuela's state-owned oil agency, Luis Giusti, was widely viewed as the likely presidential candidate for Acción Democrática in 1997 and early 1998 (Hellinger 2003, 39).

12. Many of the elite outliers were thought to have favored Alfaro Ucero (Zapata 2000; Santodomingo 1999). Nevertheless, I coded only those who had visible advantages—widely thought to have been due to Alfaro Ucero's protection—as likely to have a reason to fear political reprisal.

13. For example, two elite outliers faced corruption charges in the early 1980s that were never fully prosecuted (Capriles Méndez 1990b, 407–8, 437–40).

14. The freefall in oil prices "dealt a severe blow to the prestige of Giusti" and his neoliberal policy to open Venezuela's oil industry to more foreign investors (Hellinger 2003, 40–41). This created a sudden opening for Alfaro Ucero to become the presidential candidate in 1998. By that time, however, Alfaro Ucero was tainted by association. He had endorsed Giusti's neoliberal oil policy and entertained the idea that Giusti himself would become Acción Democrática's presidential candidate (Hellinger 2003, 39).

15. Roger Santodomingo goes further, arguing that business leaders who assisted Chávez did so as part of an elaborate plan—not to get Chávez elected but to make Chávez appear more like a real electoral threat. By doing so, he contends, these elite outliers hoped Alfaro Ucero would look like the only candidate who could forge a consensus among remaining contenders behind a single anti-Chávez candidate (Santodomingo 1999).

16. Both Zapata (2000, 133–34) and Santodomingo (1999, 46) assert that Bernárdez Lossada was known to be linked to Salas Römer.

17. One elite outlier instigated the hostile takeover when he petitioned to name someone to the board of directors after he bought a 4 percent stake in the bank ("Buying Positions" 1990). The board denied the request, citing a rule that only those with a 20 percent stake in a company had such a right (Krivoy 2002, 194). When the elite outlier proceeded to buy enough shares to reach that goal, he drove up the price of the bank's shares, from about four to forty-two U.S. dollars a share. Unable to finance the takeover on his own, this banker sold his shares in 1991 to another banker and fellow outlier. In 1993, these two bankers took control of Banco de Venezuela and removed Bernárdez Lossada from the board (Zapata 1995, 28). The takeover roused the ire of Bernárdez Lossada (Krivoy 2002, 194) and disconcerted other bankers because the buyout concentrated the financial sector in the hands of the two bankers who led the hostile takeover and one other banker who also became an elite outlier (Krivoy 2002, 194; Mann 1994b).

18. To illustrate his point, he recounted how Tinoco expelled an individual from the Central Bank who was making it difficult for the interviewee to gain approval for reforms he was advocating (Interview 43, 24).

19. President Caldera's government had failed to help his company make foreign debt obligations (Colitt 1997; O'Toole 1999), and the businocrats Salas Römer seemed likely to put in place were close to Caldera.

Chapter 6. Politically Prominent Bankers and the Historically Rooted Calculus to Assist Chávez

1. Caldera initially nominated individuals so controversial that the senate rejected them. He then undermined the two temporary appointments to these key posts by openly sparring with them for three months. The senate did not approve new fulltime appointments to these positions until April 27. These events further stimulated anxiety that the government was uncommitted to resolving Banco Latino's crisis (García Osío, Rodríguez Balza, and Salvato de Figueroa 1998, 224).

2. For instance, experts noted with dismay that "none of the regulators nor the executive took any measure to avoid the bank reaching the precipice of not being able to meet its obligations" as required by law (García Osío, Rodríguez Balza, and Salvato de Figueroa 1998, 219).

3. The government took this action on January 16, 1994, four days after the bank declared it could not meet its legal liquidity obligation (García Osío, Rodríguez Balza, and Salvato de Figueroa 1998, 221).

4. For example, the Financial Emergency Committee or JEF agreed to lend three of these banks money in exchange for pledges from two of their major stakeholders to reduce costs, sell off bank assets, and use their personal assets to guarantee loans to the bank (García Osío, Rodríguez Balza, and Salvato de Figueroa 1998, 248). Banco Consolidado was the major stakeholder of Banco de Venezuela. Banco Consolidado in turn had major stakes in two of the other troubled banks, Banco Progreso and República (García Osío, Rodríguez Balza, and Salvato de Figueroa 1998, 247). But a failed effort to sell branches in Ecuador, Spain, and Miami made it impossible for Banco Consolidado to meet the JEF's refinancing requirements. Unable to sell off enough assets, Banco Consolidado sold its shares to the government at the nominal price of half a cent per share.

5. As of December 31, 1993, Banco de Venezuela had represented 21.6 percent of the financial sector's deposits while Consolidado had represented 7.2 percent (Krivoy 2003, 4).

6. Banco Unión, for example, had suffered similarly massive withdrawals beginning in August 1994. Banco Unión survived only after it agreed to sell half the bank for one-fifth of its worth, a paltry US$18 million, to the Colombian bank, Banco Ganadero. Banco Unión's troubles had begun when Banco de Venezuela's president agreed to promise Banco de Venezuela's shares of Banco Unión to the government bailout fund, FOGADE, without consulting Banco Unión's top executives (Zapata 1995, 22). The depositor withdrawals from Banco Unión intensified in January 1995 after the government's final spate of bank seizures (García Osío, Rodríguez Balza, and Salvato de Figueroa 1998, 256).

7. In earlier work I acknowledge these suspicions (Gates 2007, 113), but here I systematically examine how they may have shaped the political calculus of elite outliers.

8. Banco Hipotecario was Banco Latino's mortgage affiliate (Krivoy 2002, 186). Banco Popular, a small Zulia-based commercial bank, had been sold by the government to Banco Barinas in 1993. The superintendent of banks had objected to the sale after the fact but had not had time to act before the bank crisis unfolded (Krivoy 2002, 186–87).

9. The Central Bank president indicated that the banks seen as refuges included Provincial, Mercantil, and Caribe.

10. Pérez's nine businocrat appointees that had significant prior business relationships with the financial sector represented about a third of his twenty-six economic ministers overall.

11. Even though the Central Bank president, Ruth de Krivoy, was successful at instigating a set of reforms, they went into effect too late, less than two weeks before Banco Latino collapsed.

12. President Caldera affirmed his finance minister's status as the supreme authority on the bank crisis when, on June 29, 1994, he created the six-member Financial Emergency Committee or JEF and named his finance minister to the JEF. Because the JEF acquired a great deal of administrative power and authority previously held by the superintendent of banks, its formation effectively transferred the authority over the financial sector to the new finance minister (Krivoy 2002, 193).

13. Several of the finance minister's own appointments generated suspicions among bankers that government policy would benefit favored banks. Within a few weeks of taking office, on February 17, the finance minister sought to appoint five bank presidents to

a special council charged with supervising those officials responsible for administering the banks seized by the government. Although none of these individuals accepted the appointments, ostensibly because they had not been sufficiently notified before the announcement (Krivoy 2002, 140), the nominations signaled to bankers which banks had access to the president. The fact that these banks later flourished during the late 1990s appeared to many bankers to confirm these suspicions. The banks that flourished included Banco Provincial, which climbed the ranks of the top one hundred companies in Venezuela and became the third-largest Venezuelan company in 1997, along with other high-performing banks such as Mercantil, Caribe, and Venezolano de Crédito (*200 empresas* 1999).

14. The nominee for superintendent of banks had helped organize a financial services company for Grupo Orinoco, and the nominee to head up FOGADE had been the accountant for the Orinoco financial conglomerate.

15. Caldera appointed Roosen in mid-February 1994 to preside over Banco Latino after it collapsed and then, in April, to preside over the newly established JEF, which was to coordinate the government's overall response to the looming bank crisis (Krivoy 2002, 167). Roosen later led the new board of administrators of the first state-owned bank (Mann 1994c; Zapata 2000, 64).

16. At this time, Caldera also replaced the president of the Central Bank, who had resigned in protest over the government's response to troubled banks, with someone who had prior ties to Banco Mercantil, one of Venezuela's oldest banks and a bank that flourished during the late 1990s. Banco Mercantil, like Banco Provincial, grew in the midst of the 1994 bank crisis. It climbed the ranks of Venezuela's largest and most successful companies, ranking ninth and fifth in 1996 and 1997, respectively (*200 empresas* 1998; *200 empresas* 1999).

17. After having been ousted from his bank, Bernárdez Lossada had remained in the private sector as a board member of the financial investment institution Fivenez Sociedad Financiera, presided over by Vera.

18. As listed on table 6.1, these troubled banks were Consolidado, Progreso, and República.

19. After seizing Banco Consolidado but liquidating the banks from the first wave of the banking crisis, the government controlled a total of thirteen commercial banks (Mann 1994b).

20. Criminal investigations revealed a dual accounting scheme in Orlando Castro's Grupo Latinoamericana. This scheme had facilitated the transfer of more than US$350 million, much of which had been given to the bank in the form of a temporary loan by the government, to a Panamanian bank (Brooke 1995). The government charged Castro with bank fraud, embezzlement, and conspiracy in schemes related to Banco Progreso's collapse, and it sought his extradition from Miami to Venezuela in October 1995 (Truell 1996a). The following April, a New York grand jury indicted Orlando Castro, his son, and his grandson "with a scheme to defraud depositors of more than $55 million at Banco Progreso Internacional de Puerto Rico" (Truell 1996b). In February 1997, a New York jury found them guilty of bank fraud, and the judge sentenced Castro, his son, and grandson to several years in U.S. prison (Sullivan 1997).

21. As I have noted elsewhere (Gates 2007), journalists reported that Vera and Bernárdez Lossada were closely associated with the other three individuals known to be linked to Salas Römer (Santodomingo 1999, 46; Zapata 1995, 42; Zapata 2000, 133–34) and thereby

implied that they would also have easy access to a Salas Römer administration. Bernárdez Lossada and Salas Römer also served on the FEDECAMARAS board together for a time and had known each other since that time. Furthermore, Vera had known Salas Römer from the mid-1980s, when Salas Römer was a governor and Vera was head of Banco de Venezuela.

22. Caldera's finance minister fueled these suspicions when he deflected a journalist who had asked about the source of bank collapse rumors by saying he did not know but that the journalist should ask García Mendoza (Zapata 1995, 16).

23. Note that this figure excludes two individuals indicated in table 4.1 as having primary interests in the financial sector because their ties were not to commercial banks. One was the president of an insurance company and the other was the president of an investment firm. Both nonetheless had also had negative experiences with the bank crisis due to their close personal connections to executives at seized banks (Zapata 2000, 61–62).

24. The total of thirty-five banks excludes three banks that were subsidiaries of other large banks but that are listed in table 6.1 among the troubled banks.

25. While the proportion of failed banks that produced an elite outlier is high, we might still wonder why the remaining failed banks did not produce an elite outlier. There are several possible reasons. First, there is the possibility that these banks did, in fact, produce elite outliers whom my campaign insiders could not verify. Second, in at least one case, failed banks might not have produced an elite outlier because the bank failure left its former leaders without enough resources to enable them to be notable contributors to the 1998 presidential elections. Most of the remaining failed banks were smaller banks. Third, the former executives and shareholders of failed banks may not have become elite outliers because they moved out of the country and made no plans to return. Journalists at the time reported that many bankers began new lives in Miami and Costa Rica. Perhaps some decided not to reinvest in Venezuelan politics. Fourth, some former bankers had less reason to suspect the government treated them unfairly. For example, the president of one failed bank was a member of the sitting president's struggling political party. Indeed, his political identification with the president fueled speculation that his bank, Banco Andino, had been favored by the government because it granted the bank additional time to raise capital before finally proceeding with the seizure (García Osío, Rodríguez Balza, and Salvato de Figueroa 1998, 252–55; Zapata 1995, 197). Another bank that failed but did not produce an elite outlier, Banco Metropolitano, was led by President Caldera's son-in-law (MacGregor 1998). Despite the bank's failure, it seems unlikely that the president's son-in-law would have believed the government acted intentionally against the bank's interests.

26. The president of one of these banks reportedly became skeptical about the government's handling of the bank crisis after he attempted to save another bank that faced liquidity problems before the government seized it (Zapata 1995, 10, 37).

Conclusion: Theoretical Implications of Chávez's Election

1. For Moisés Naím (2003), Venezuela exemplifies the petro-states, which he defines as "oil-rich countries plagued by weak institutions, a poorly functioning public sector, and a high concentration of power and wealth." In a similar vein, Roger Cohen (2007) denounces the centralization of power that oil has engendered in Venezuela. Thomas L.

Friedman (2006) chronicles the recent retreat of newer petro-states from democracy as evidence that abundant oil categorically undermines democracy, as it has, in his view, in Venezuela.

2. Scholars acknowledge, nonetheless, that resource wealth, such as wealth derived from oil, on occasion facilitates conflict resolution (Englebert and Ron 2004; Wick and Bulte 2006) and that even the presence of "loot-seeking rebels" in resource rich societies does not necessarily appear to prolong wars (Humphreys 2005).

3. Of these scholars, Thad Dunning (2008) advances perhaps the most ambitious theory of variation in regime type among societies with oil wealth. He identifies two conditions under which oil wealth tends to promote democracy rather than authoritarianism, as it has in Venezuela: when a nation's economy is not dependent on oil production (i.e., is less resource dependent) and when inequality is extreme in parts of the economy not connected to the public sector. Under these conditions, he contends, the nation's elite will be more willing to tolerate democracy, as they did, he argues, in Venezuela.

4. As noted previously (Gates 2007, 107), in some countries, the state extracts revenue from the oil industry by taxing foreign firms. In other countries, the state extracts revenue from the oil industry by virtue of its direct ownership stake in the state-owned oil entity. When Venezuela democratized (1959), Venezuela's oil industry was run by foreign oil companies. In 1976, however, the state assumed ownership of the industry in a process often referred to as nationalization.

5. Some authors focus on ways that oil impacts a nation's economy and politics other than via an enlarged state (Naím and Piñango 1984; Urbaneja 1992).

6. Many scholars behind the corruption thesis (Pérez Perdomo 1992) as well as the social polarization thesis (Ellner 2003; Roberts 2003b) share this view. While most do not necessarily adopt the broader theory of the petro-state, some have. Dunning (2008), for example, uses the social polarization interpretation of the Venezuelan case to illustrate his theory of the conditions that foster or destablize democracy in oil-rich nations. He writes, "I argue that the decline in oil rents as a source of public finance produced the social-structural base that was necessary for the politicization of social class in Venezuela and for the emergence of redistribution as a salient dimension of political conflict" (Dunning 2008, 154).

7. Rents are sources of income that do not come from domestic constituents and are therefore not based on productivity levels. They can include foreign aid as well as revenue from taxes on extracting and exporting valuable natural resources such as oil or minerals. Some scholars stipulate that states collecting more than 40 percent of their revenue from rents qualify as rentier states (Luciani 1990), while others define only states collecting upwards of 80 percent of their revenue in the form of rents as rentier states (Moore 2004, 15). Regardless, Venezuela's experience conforms to this pattern of a negative relationship between oil revenue and taxation. As oil revenue increased in Venezuela, from 6 percent of the federal government's revenue in 1924, to 60 percent in 1958, to 80 percent in the 1970s, multiple attempts to raise personal income taxes failed (Dunning 2008, 48).

8. This effect—the effect of rentier states on the business community—may be particularly important to examine in the subgroup of oil-rich societies that, like Venezuela, have a significant business community. While nearly all nations with abundant oil tend to become rentier states (i.e., states that are dependent on their high level of oil-related

revenue relative to total revenues), not all *economies* with abundant oil are dependent on oil-based production (Dunning 2008, 19). Venezuela embodies this seeming contradiction. Although Venezuela exemplifies a rentier state, oil production generated less than 30 percent of the gross domestic product even during the 1970 oil boom (Dunning 2008, 20).

9. The negative effect of overvalued currencies on domestic private sector production is often referred to as "Dutch disease" because it was first observed in the Dutch economy. See endnote 4, ch. 5.

10. Even treatments of cases (such as Libya and Tunisia) that appear to conform to the prediction that political elites in petro-states are unlikely to survive fiscal crises illustrate that these results owe not so much to the nature of an oil economy as to the particular fashion in which such economies become integrated into the world economy and in which their state is structured (Anderson 1986).

11. In Kuwait, business elites as a whole forged an alliance with state bureaucrats, in opposition to their common opponent: Islamic political movements. This alliance enabled the Kuwaiti regime to exercise fiscal restraints when they were warranted and to introduce market-oriented reforms that might otherwise have been opposed by key segments of the business community.

12. Shi'i suspicions of the Sunni may also be traced to the Sunni invasion of Bahrain more than two centuries ago (Moore 2002, 51).

REFERENCES

200 empresas más grandes: 1996–97. October 15, 1998. http://www.dinero.com.ve/ranking100.html. Accessed April 2005.

200 empresas más grandes: 1997–98. September–October 1999. http://www.dinero.com.ve/136/portada/cuadro200.html. Accessed April 2005.

Aguero, Felipe. 1995. Crisis and Decay of Democracy in Venezuela: The Civil-Military Dimension. In *Venezuelan Democracy under Stress,* edited by J. McCoy, A. Serbin, W. Smith, and A. Stambouli. Coral Gables, FL: North-South Center, University of Miami.

Alexander, Robert J. 1964. *The Venezuelan Democratic Revolution: A Profile of the Regime of Rómulo Betancourt.* New Brunswick, NJ: Rutgers University Press.

———. 1982. *Rómulo Betancourt and the Transformation of Venezuela.* New Brunswick, NJ: Transaction Books.

Alvarez, Angel Eduardo. 1995. Cuanto cuesta un candidato? Estimaciones del costo de las campañas políticas y de las elecciones en Venezuela. *Politeia* 18:57–99.

Anderson, Lisa. 1986. *The State and Social Transformation in Tunisia and Libya, 1830–1980.* Princeton, NJ: Princeton University Press.

Arroyo Talavera, Eduardo. 1986. *Elections and Negotiation: The Limits of Democracy in Venezuela.* London: Garland Publishing.

Baloyra, Enrique. 1986. Public Opinion and Support for the Regime: 1973–83. In *Venezuela: The Democratic Experience,* edited by J. D. Martz and D. Myers. New York: Praeger.

Banco Latino to Be Privatized Following Crisis Takeover by Banking Authorities. 1994. BBC Summary of World Broadcasts, Radio Caracas TV, January 25.

Baptista, Asdrúbal. 1997. *Bases cuantitativas de la economía venezolana: 1830–1995.* Caracas: Fundación Polar.

———, and Bernard Mommer. 1989. Renta petrolera y distribución factorial del ingreso. In *Adiós a al bonanza? Crisis de la distribución del ingreso en Venezuela,* edited by H.-P. Nissen and B. Mommer. Caracas: ILIS-CDENDES, Editorial Nueva Sociedad.

Beblawi, Hazem. 1987. The Rentier State in the Arab World. In *The Rentier State: Nation, State, and the Integration of the Arab World,* edited by Hazem Beblawi and Giacomo Luciani. London: Croom Helm.

Becker, David. 1990. Business Associations in Latin America: The Venezuelan Case. *Comparative Political Studies* 23 (1): 114–38.

Beroes, Agustín. 1990. *RECADI: la gran estafa.* Caracas: Editorial La Planeta.

Bitar, Sergio, and Eduardo Troncoso. 1990. *Venezuela: The Industrial Challenge.* Translated by M. Shifter and D. Vera. Washington, DC: Institute for the Study of Human Issues.

Bond, Robert. 1987. Comment on FEDECAMARAS and Policy-Making in Venezuela. *Latin American Research Review* 22 (3): 107–10.

Briceño-León, Roberto. 1990. *Los efectos perversos del petróleo*. Caracas: Fondo Editorial Acta Científica Venezolana; Consorcio de Ediciones Capriles.

Brooke, James. 1989. Investigation in Venezuela: Catharsis or Witch Hunt? *New York Times*, August 16, D1.

———. 1995. International Business: Bank Failures Undercut Venezuelan Government. *New York Times*, March 30, D8.

Burgess, Katrina. 1999. Loyalty Dilemmas and Market Reform: Party-Union Alliances under Stress in Mexico, Spain, and Venezuela. *World Politics* 52 (1): 105–34.

Businessmen Weigh More Than They Own. 1984. *Latin American Special Reports* (London), *Latin American Newsletters*, October 26, 10.

Bussey, Jane. 2000. Bank Officers Cleared of Fraud. *Miami Herald*, April 22, 6B.

Buxton, Julia. 2001. *The Failure of Political Reform in Venezuela*. Aldershot, England: Ashgate.

———. 2003. Economic Policy and the Rise of Hugo Chávez. In *Venezuelan Politics in the Chávez Era: Class, Polarization, and Conflict*, edited by S. Ellner and D. Hellinger. Boulder, CO: Lynne Rienner.

Buying Positions for the Reform; Hostile Purchase Is Crest of Recent Acquisitions Wave. 1990. *Latin American Weekly Report* (London), *Latin American Newsletters*, November 1, 11.

C.S. 1994a. Centrífuga de dólares en el Banco Latino. *El Universal*, March 22, 1–16.

———. 1994b. Uzcátegui lo notificó a Caldera: Congreso rechaza inclusión de Roosen en la Junta de Emergencia. *El Universal*, July 1, 1–10.

Camp, Roderic A. 1989. *Entrepreneurs and Politics in Twentieth-Century Mexico*. New York: Oxford University Press.

———. 2002. *Mexico's Mandarins: Crafting a Power Elite for the Twenty-First Century*. Berkeley: University of California Press.

Canache, Damarys. 2002. From Bullets to Ballots: The Emergence of Popular Support for Hugo Chávez. *Latin American Politics and Society* 44 (1): 69–91.

———. 2004. Urban Poor and Political Order. In *The Unraveling of Representative Democracy in Venezuela*, edited by J. McCoy and D. Myers. Baltimore: Johns Hopkins University Press.

———, and Michael R. Kulischeck. 1998. *Reinventing Legitimacy: Democracy and Political Change in Venezuela*. Westport, CT: Greenwood Press.

Capriles Méndez, Ruth. 1990a. *Diccionario de la corrupción en Venezuela: 1958–1979*. Vol. 1. Caracas: Consorcio de Ediciones Capriles C.A.

———. 1990b. *Diccionario de la corrupción en Venezuela: 1979–1984*. Vol. 2. Caracas: Consorcio de Ediciones Capriles C.A.

———. 1992. *Diccionario de la corrupción en Venezuela: 1984–1992*. Vol. 3. Caracas: Consorcio de Ediciones Capriles C.A.

———. 1993. Racionalidad de la corrupción en Venezuela. *Politeia* 16:207–40.

Carmona Estanga, Pedro. 1998. Los candidatos en Fedecámaras. *El Universal*, August 15, 2-2.

Carr, Barry, and Steve Ellner, eds. 1993. *The Latin American Left: From the Fall of Allende to Perestroika, Latin America Bureau*. Boulder, CO: Westview Press.

Castañeda, Jorge G. 1990. Latin America and the End of the Cold War. *World Policy Journal* 7 (3): 469–92.

————. 1993. *Utopia Unarmed: The Latin American Left after the Cold War*. New York: Knopf.

————. 2001. Mexico: Permuting Power [interview]. *New Left Review* 7:17–41.

————. 2006. Latin America's Left Turn. *Foreign Affairs* 85 (3): 28–43.

Centeno, Miguel Angel. 1995. *Democracy within Reason: Technocratic Revolution in Mexico*. University Park: Pennsylvania State University Press.

————, and Sylvia Maxfield. 1992. The Marriage of Finance and Order: Changes in the Mexican Political Elite. *Journal of Latin American Studies* 24 (1): 57–85.

Centeno, Miguel Angel, and Patricio Silva, eds. 1998. *The Politics of Expertise in Latin America*. London: Macmillan.

Chacón, Jesse. 2004. Former director of the National Commission of Telecommunications (CONATEL) and minister for Communication and Information. Interview by VenezuelaAnalysis.com, February 13. http://www.venezuelanalysis.com/articles.php?artno=1105. Accessed September 25, 2008.

Chand, Vikram. 2001. *Mexico's Political Awakening*. Notre Dame, IN: University of Notre Dame Press.

Chaudhry, Kiren Aziz. 1989. The Price of Wealth: Business and State in Labor Remittance and Oil Economies. *International Organization* 43 (1): 101–45.

————. 1997. *The Price of Wealth: Economies and Institutions in the Middle East*. Ithaca, NY: Cornell University Press.

Chiappe, Giuliana. 1994. Superintendencia emitió resolución urgente: banqueros disponen de un mes para declarar sus bienes. *El Universal*, March 22, 21.

————. 1995. Hizo la denuncia públicamente: superintendencia encontró actas forjadas en Banco Progreso. *El Universal*, January 13, 2-1.

Christiansen, Luis. 2000. Chávez: entre el querer ser y el deber ser. Consultores 21.

Cohen, Roger. 2007. The Limits of 21st-Century Revolution. *New York Times*, December 3, Opinion, 25.

Colitt, Raymond. 1996. Brazil and Venezuela Find Togetherness: Neighbors Overcome Decades of Dissension to Develop Strong Links in Trade and Energy. *Financial Post*, July 24, 45.

————. 1997. AVENSA Turning Around. *The News*, February 10.

————. 1998. Venezuela's Unfolding Television Drama: CGC Hopes Programming Will Help It Win Latin America's Media War. *Financial Times*, March 24, 34.

————, and Thurston, Charles W. 1998. Everyone Listens to the Colonel. *Latin Trade* 6 (October): 26–27.

Collier, Ruth Berins, and David Collier. 1991. *Shaping the Political Arena: Critical Junctures, the Labor Movement, and Regime Dynamics in Latin America*. Princeton, NJ: Princeton University Press.

Conaghan, Catherine, and James Malloy. 1994. *Unsettling Statecraft: Democracy and Neoliberalism in the Central Andes*. Pittsburgh: University of Pittsburgh Press.

Conniff, Michael L. 1999. *Populism in Latin America*. Tuscaloosa: University of Alabama Press.

Constable, Pamela. 1992. Coup and Corruption: Venezuela's Leader Beats Rebels, but the Battle Is Far from Over. *Boston Globe*, November 30, 2.

Cooper, James C., and Kathleen Madigan. 1998. A Costly Credibility Gap. *Business Week*, September 7, 24.

Coppedge, Michael. 1993. Parties and Society in Mexico and Venezuela: Why Competition Matters. *Comparative Politics* 25 (3): 253–74.

———. 1994a. Prospects for Democratic Governability in Venezuela. *Journal of Interamerican Studies and World Affairs* 36 (2): 39–64.

———. 1994b. *Strong Parties and Lame Ducks: Presidential Partyarchy and Factionalism in Venezuela.* Stanford, CA: Stanford University Press.

———. 1999. Venezuela: Conservative Representation without Conservative Parties. Working Paper 268. University of Notre Dame.

———. 2000. Venezuelan Parties and the Representation of Elite Interests. In *Conservative Parties, the Right, and Democracy in Latin America,* edited by K. Middlebrook. Baltimore: Johns Hopkins University Press.

Coronel, Gustavo. 1997. El "hit parade" de la corrupción venezolana (1980–1997). *El Universal,* June 12, 1-6.

Coronil, Fernando. 2000. Magical Illusions or Revolutionary Magic? *NACLA Report on the Americas* 33 (6): 34–42.

Corrales, Javier. 1997. El presidente y su gente: cooperación y conflict entre los ámbitos técnicos y políticos en Venezuela, 1989–1993. *Nueva Sociedad* 152:93–107.

———. 2002. *Presidents without Parties: The Politics of Economic Reform in Argentina and Venezuela in the 1990s.* University Park: Pennsylvania State University Press.

———, and Imelda Cisneros. 1999. Corporatism, Trade Liberalization, and Sectoral Responses: The Case of Venezuela, 1989–1999. *World Development* 27 (12): 2099–2123.

Coup and Counter-coup: Venezuela. 2002. Economist.com. April 16.

Crisp, Brian. 1996. The Rigidity of Democratic Institutions and the Current Legitimacy Crisis in Venezuela. *Latin American Perspectives* 23 (3): 30–49.

———. 2000. *Democratic Institutional Design.* Stanford, CA: Stanford University Press.

———, and Daniel Levine. 1998. Democratizing the Democracy? Crisis and Reform in Venezuela. *Journal of Interamerican Studies and World Affairs* 40 (2): 27–61.

———, ———, and Juan Carlos Rey. 1995. The Legitimacy Problem. In *Venezuelan Democracy under Stress,* edited by J. McCoy, A. Servin, W. C. Smith, and A. Stambouli. New Brunswick, NJ: Transaction Books.

Cupolo, Marco. 1996. *Petróleo y política en México y Venezuela.* Caracas: Equinoccio/ Ediciones de la Universidad Simón Bolívar.

Davis, Diane. 1993. The Dialectic of Autonomy: State, Class, and Economic Crisis in Mexico, 1958–1982. *Latin American Perspectives* 20 (3): 46–75.

———. 2004. *Discipline and Development: Middle Classes and Prosperity in East Asia and Latin America.* Cambridge: Cambridge University Press.

Delacroix, Jacques. 1980. The Distributive State in the World System. *Studies in Comparative International Development* 15 (fall): 3–22.

Domhoff, G. William. 1972. *Fat Cats and Democrats: The Role of the Big Rich in the Party of the Common Man.* Englewood Cliffs, NJ: Prentice-Hall.

Dunning, Thad. 2008. *Crude Democracy: Natural Resource Wealth and Political Regimes.* Cambridge: Cambridge University Press.

Duno, Pedro. 1975. *Los doce apóstoles: proceso a la degradación política.* Valencia, Venezuela: Vadell Hermanos.

El Diario Venezolano "La Razon" asegura que el SCH realizó pagos a la campaña de Hugo Chávez. 2002. *El Mundo,* June 30, 39.

El Ministro del Interior: Gran parte de lo que está ocurriendo se debe al delincuencia de cuello blanco. 1994. *El Universal,* July 1, 1–12.

Ellner, Steve. 1988. *Venezuela's Movimiento al Socialismo: From Guerrilla Defeat to Innovative Politics.* Durham, NC: Duke University Press.

———. 1999. The Heyday of Radical Populism in Venezuela and Its Aftermath. In *Populism in Latin America,* edited by M. L. Conniff. Tuscaloosa: University of Alabama Press.

———. 2003. Introduction: The Search for Explanations. In *Venezuelan Politics in the Chávez Era,* edited by S. Ellner and D. Hellinger. Boulder, CO: Lynne Rienner.

———. 2004. Leftist Goals and the Debate over Anti-neoliberal Strategy in Latin America. *Science and Society* 68 (1): 10–32.

———. 2008. *Rethinking Venezuelan Politics: Class, Conflict, and the Chávez Phenomenon.* Boulder, CO: Lynne Rienner.

Emigh, Rebecca Jean. 1997. The Power of Negative Thinking: The Use of Negative Case Methodology in the Development of Sociological Theory. *Theory and Society* 26 (5): 649–84.

Englebert, Pierre, and James Ron. 2004. Primary Commodities and War: Congo-Brazzaville's Ambivalent Resource Curse. *Comparative Politics* 37 (1): 61–81.

España, Luis Pedro. 1989. *Democracia y renta petrolera.* Caracas: Instituto de Investigaciones Económicas y Sociales, Universidad Católica Andrés Bello.

Evans, Peter. 1995. *Embedded Autonomy: States and Industrial Transformation.* Princeton, NJ: Princeton University Press.

Fearon, James D. 2005. Primary Commodity Exports and Civil War. *Journal of Conflict Resolution* 49 (4): 483–507.

Fedeindustria: hay evidente mesianismos. 1998. *El Universal,* November 14, 1–13.

Ferguson, Thomas, and Joel Rogers. 1986. *Right Turn: The Decline of the Democrats and the Future of American Politics.* New York: Hill and Wang.

Fewer Than Half the States Go to AD; Left Advances as Debate on Wages Becomes Main Issue. 1989. *Latin American Weekly Report* (London), *Latin American Newsletters,* December 14, 3.

Fidler, Stephen. 1994. Caracas Takes Over More Banks. *Financial Times,* December 16, 6.

Filiberto, José Angel. 1974. *Fermín Toro y las doctrinas económicas del siglo XIX.* Caracas: Editorial San José.

Francés, Antonio. 1989. Abundancia, confusión y cambio: el ambiente en el que se desenvuelven las empresas y sus gerentes en Venezuela. In *Las empresas venezolanas: su gerencia,* edited by M. Naím. Caracas: IESA.

Frieden, Jeffrey. 1991. *Debt, Development, and Democracy: Modern Political Economy and Latin America, 1965–1985.* Princeton, NJ: Princeton University Press.

Friedman, Thomas L. 2006. As Energy Prices Rise, It's All Downhill for Democracy. *New York Times,* May 5, A23.

Fundación Polar. 1997. *Diccionario de historia de Venezuela.* Caracas: Fundación Polar.

García, María Yolanda. 1998. Fiscalía General de la República elaboró informe sobre causas seguidas a banqueros y personas vinculadas a irregularidades bancarias. *El Universal,* February 28, 1–2.

García Mendoza, Oscar. 1995. *Crónica involuntaria de una crisis inconclusa.* Caracas: Editorial Planeta de Venezuela.

———. 1998. Venezuela: mala administración. *El Economista,* July 10.

García Osío, Gustavo, Rafael Rodríguez Balza, and Silvia Salvato de Figueroa. 1998. *Lecciones de la crisis bancaria de Venezuela*. Caracas: Ediciones IESA y Fundación Banco Venezolano de Crédito.

Gates, Leslie C. 2001. Why Mexican Unions Lost Power: Globalization, Intra-Elite Conflict, and Shifting State Alliances. PhD dissertation, University of Arizona–Tucson.

———. 2007. The Business of Anti-Globalization: Lessons from Venezuela's 1998 Presidential Elections. *Research in Political Sociology* 15:101–37.

———. 2009. Theorizing Business Power in the Semiperiphery: Mexico, 1970–2000. *Theory and Society* 38 (1): 57–95.

Gause, F. Gregory. 1994. *Oil Monarchies: Domestic and Security Challenges in the Arab Gulf States*. New York: Council on Foreign Relations.

Gavalda, Antonio. 1962. *Diccionario biográfica*. Barcelona, Spain: Editorial Sintes.

Giacalone, Rita. 1999. *Los empresarios frente al Grupo de los Tres: integración, intereses e ideas*. Caracas: Nueva Sociedad.

Gilpin, Kenneth. 1997. Panamerican Beverages and Venezuelan Bottler to Merge. *New York Times*, May 13, D4.

Golden, Tim. 1992. Democracy Isn't Always Enough to Repel Attempted Coups. *New York Times*, February 9, E3.

Gómez, Emeterio. 1989. *El empresariado venezolano: a mitad de camino entre Keynes y Hayek*. Caracas: Altolitho.

Gómez, Ernesto. 1998. Chávez y el empresariado proteccionista. *El Universal*, August 5, 2–2.

González, Rosa Amelia, and Rosario Queirolo. 2008. Understanding "Right" and "Left" in Latin America. Research funded by the Small Grants for Research on Democratization of the Latin American Public Opinion Project, Vanderbilt University.

Goodman, Louis W. 1995. *Lessons of the Venezuelan Experience*. Washington, DC: Woodrow Wilson Center Press; Baltimore: Johns Hopkins University Press.

Gopian, David J., Hobart Smith, and William Smith. 1984. What Makes PACs Tick? *American Journal of Political Science* 28 (2): 259–81.

Gott, Richard. 2005. *Hugo Chávez and the Bolivarian Revolution*. London and New York: Verso.

Gourevitch, Peter. 1986. *Politics in Hard Times: Comparative Responses to International Economic Crises*. Ithaca, NY: Cornell University Press.

Gran Enciclopedia de Venezuela. 1989. *Gran enciclopedia de Venezuela*. 2nd ed. Vols. 10 and 11. Caracas: Editorial Globe and UCAB.

Grier, Kevin, Michael Munger, and Brian Roberts. 1994. The Determinants of Industry Political Activity, 1978–1986. *American Journal of Political Science* 88 (4): 911–26.

Guía Industrial. 1971. *Guía industrial y información general de Valencia, estado de Carabobo, 1970–1971*. Valencia, Venezuela: Publicaciones Valencia, CA, Cables Puvalca.

Gunson, Phil. 1996. Fugitive Banker Accuses Venezuela of Vendetta. *Guardian*, April 13, 14.

Gutierrez, Estrella. 1996. Trade-Venezuela: More Liberal Trade with Chile in 1997. Inter Press Service, December 26.

Gutkin, Steven. 1998. Venezuelan Presidential Candidate Tries to Soothe Investor Fears. Associated Press, October 9.

Haggard, Stephan, and Robert Kaufman. 1992. Institutions and Economic Adjustment. In *The Politics of Economic Adjustment*, edited by S. Haggard and R. Kaufman. Princeton, NJ: Princeton University Press.

Handler, Edward, and John R. Mulkern. 1982. *Business in Politics: Campaign Strategies of Corporate Political Action Committees.* Lexington, MA: Lexington Books.

Harnecker, Marta. 1999. *Haciendo posible lo imposible: la izquierda en la umbral del XXI.* Mexico City: Siglo XXI.

———. 2001. *Los desafíos de la izquierda.* Caracas: Alcaldía de Caracas, Instituto Municipal de Publicaciones.

Hellinger, Daniel. 1984. Populism and Nationalism in Venezuela: New Perspectives on Acción Democrática. *Latin American Perspectives* 11 (4): 33–59.

———. 1991. *Venezuela: Tarnished Democracy.* Boulder, CO: Westview Press.

———. 2000. Understanding Venezuela's Crisis: Dutch Diseases, Money Doctors, and Magicians. *Latin American Perspectives* 27 (1): 105–19.

———. 2003. Political Overview: The Breakdown of *Puntofijismo.* In *Venezuelan Politics in the Chávez Era: Class, Polarization, and Conflict,* edited by S. Ellner and D. Hellinger. Boulder, CO: Lynne Rienner.

Herb, Michael. 1999. *All in the Family: Absolutism, Revolution, and Democracy in the Middle Eastern Monarchies.* Albany: State University of New York Press.

———. 2005. No Representation without Taxation? Rents, Development, and Democracy. *Comparative Politics* 37 (3): 297–316.

Hernández, Enrique. 1994. El juez Bralio Sánchez los dará a conocer hoy: nuevos autos de detención y prohibiciones de salida por irregularidades en uso del auxilio financiero. *El Universal,* June 9, 1–22.

Hernandez, Luis Guillermo, and Jesús Angel Parra. 1999. *Diccionario general de Zulia.* Vol. 1. Maracaibo, Venezuela: Banco Occidental de Descuento.

Hillman, Richard. 1994. *Democracy for the Privileged: Crisis and Transition in Venezuela.* Boulder, CO: Lynne Rienner.

———. 2004. Intellectuals: An Elite Divided. In *The Unraveling of Representative Democracy in Venezuela,* edited by J. McCoy and D. Myers. Baltimore: Johns Hopkins University Press.

Humphreys, Macartan. 2005. Natural Resources, Conflict, and Conflict resolution: Uncovering the Mechanisms. *Journal of Conflict Resolution* 49 (4): 508–37.

Hunter, Shireen T. 1986. The Gulf Economic Crisis and Its Social and Political Consequences. *Middle East Journal* 40 (4): 598–613.

The Impatience in Venezuela. 1992. *The Economist,* February 8, 35–36.

Investigarán a calificadores de riesgo. 1998. *El Universal,* June 3, 1–16.

Jácome, Francine. 2000. Venezuela: Old Successes, New Constraints on Learning. In *Political Learning and Redemocratization in Latin America,* edited by F. L. McCoy. Coral Gables, FL: North-South Center, University of Miami.

Jensen, Nathan, and Leonard Wantchekon. 2004. Resource Wealth and Political Regimes in Africa. *Comparative Political Studies* 37 (7): 816–41.

Jongkind, Fred. 1993. Venezuelan Industry under the New Conditions of the 1989 Economic Policy. *European Review of Latin American and Caribbean Studies* 54:65–93.

Jordan, Mary, and Kevin Sullivan. 2003. Trade Brings Riches, but Not to Mexico's Poor. *Washington Post,* March 22, A10.

"Judicial Terror" Hits Foreign Companies; Warrants for Top Men in Ford, Colgate, Procter & Gamble. 1989. *Latin American Weekly Report* (London), *Latin American Newsletters,* August 3, 5.

Kahnemann, Daniel, and Amos Tversky, eds. 2000. *Choices, Values, and Frames.* Cambridge: Cambridge University Press.

Karl, Terry Lynn. 1987. Petroleum and Political Pacts: The Transition to Democracy in Venezuela. *Latin American Research Review* 22 (1): 63–94.

———. 1997. *The Paradox of Plenty: Oil Booms and Petro-States.* Berkeley: University of California Press.

———, and Ian Gary. 2004. PetroPolitics Special Report: The Global Record. Interhemispheric Resource Center/Institute for Policy Studies/SEEN.

Keller, Alfredo. 1997. Las fortalezas aparentes: el caso de los actores políticos venezolanos frente a los procesos de democratización y de reformas económicas. In *Los actores sociales y políticos en los procesos de transformación en América Latina,* edited by M. Mora y Araujo. Buenos Aires: CIEDLA.

Key, Vladimir Orlando, Jr., and Milton C. Cummings. 1966. *The Responsible Electorate: Rationality in Presidential Voting, 1936–1960.* Cambridge, MA: Belknap Press of Harvard University Press.

Kilby, Paul. 1997. Out of the Time Warp. *LatinFinance,* September 1, 41.

King, Gary, Robert O. Keohane, and Sidney Verba. 1994. *Designing Social Inquiry: Scientific Inference in Qualitative Research.* Princeton, NJ: Princeton University Press.

Kingstone, Peter R. 1999. *Crafting Coalitions for Reform: Business Preferences, Political Institutions, and Neoliberal Reform in Brazil.* University Park: Pennsylvania State University Press.

Koeneke R., Herbert. 2000. La guerra de las encuestas en las campañas electorales venezolanos. In *Opinión pública y elecciones en América,* edited by F. Welsch and F. C. Turner. Caracas: International Political Association.

Kolko, Gabriel. 1963. *The Triumph of Conservatism: A Re-interpretation of American History, 1900–1916.* New York: Free Press of Glencoe.

Kovaleski, Serge F. 1998. Oil Price Drop Hits Venezuela Hard. *Washington Post,* September 9, A21.

Krivoy, Ruth de. 2000. *Collapse: The Venezuelan Bank Crisis of 1994.* Washington, DC: Group of Thirty.

———. 2002. *Colapso: la crisis bancaria venezolana de 1994.* Caracas: IESA.

———. 2003. Case Study: The Venezuelan Banking Crisis; Epilogue. Toronto Centre, Leadership in Financial Supervision.

LaFranchi, Howard. 1998. Blew Your Coup? Some Who Failed Turn to Ballot Box. *Christian Science Monitor,* October 2, 6.

Le Billon, P. 2001a. Angola's Political Economy of War: The Role of Oil and Diamonds, 1975–2000. *African Affairs* 100 (398): 55–80.

———. 2001b. The Political Ecology of War: Natural Resources and Armed Conflicts. *Political Geography* 20 (5): 561–84.

Levine, Daniel H. 1973. *Conflict and Political Change in Venezuela.* Princeton, NJ: Princeton University Press.

———. 1998. Beyond the Exhaustion of the Model: Survival and Transformation of Democracy in Venezuela. In *Reinventing Legitimacy: Democracy and Political Change in Venezuela,* edited by D. Canache and M. R. Kulisheck. Westport, CT: Greenwood Press.

————, and Brian Crisp. 1999. Venezuela: The Character, Crisis, and Possible Future of Democracy. In *Democracy in Developing Countries: Latin America,* edited by L. Diamond, J. Hartlyn, J. Linz, and S. Lipset. Boulder, CO: Lynne Rienner.

Lewis-Beck, Michael S. 1988. *Economics and Elections: The Major Western Democracies.* Ann Arbor: University of Michigan Press.

Lindblom, Charles Edward. 1977. *Politics and Markets: The World's Political Economic Systems.* New York: Basic Books.

Little, Walter. 1996. Corruption and Democracy in Latin America. *IDS Bulletin–Institute of Development Studies* 27 (2): 64–70.

Long, J. Scott. 1997. *Regression Models for Categorical and Limited Dependent Variables.* Thousand Oaks, CA: Sage Publications.

————, and Jeremy Freese. 2006. *Regression Models for Categorical Dependent Variables Using Stata.* 2nd ed. College Station, TX: StataCorp LP.

López Maya, Margarita, Luis Gómez Calcaño, and Thaís Maingón. 1989. *De punto fijo al pacto social: desarrollo y hegemonía en Venezuela, 1958–1985.* Caracas: Fondo Editorial Acta Científica Venezolana.

Luciani, Giacomo. 1990. Allocative vs. Production States: A Theoretical Framework. In *The Arab State,* edited by G. Luciani. Berkeley: University of California Press.

Luna, Matilda. 1992. *Los empresarios y el cambio político, México, 1970–1987.* Mexico City: Edición Era, Instituto de Investigaciones Sociales, UNAM.

M.S. de Venezuela. 1972. *La biografía del mérito y trabajo.* Caracas: Editorial Cediaz Auda Casanova.

MacGregor, Alison. 1998. A Fugitive in Ottawa. *Ottawa Citizen,* March 21, A1.

Mahdavy, Hossein. 1970. The Patterns and Problems of Economic Development in Rentier States: The Case of Iran. In *Studies in the Economic History of the Middle East: From the Rise of Islam to the Present Day,* edited by M. A. Cook. London: Oxford University Press.

Mahoney, James. 2000. Path Dependence in Historical Sociology. *Theory and Society* 29 (4): 507–48.

Maingón, Thaís. 1999. Los espacios ambiguos de la democracia en Venezuela: resultados electorales de 1998. *Ciencia de Gobierno* 5:33–53.

————, and Heinz R. Sonntag. 2000. Los resultados de las elecciones de 1998 en Venezuela: hacia un cambio político. *Revista de Ciencias Sociales* 6 (001): 35–63.

Maldonado Parilli, Jorge. 1989. *Gente de Venezuela.* Vol. 2. Caracas: Miguel Angel García e Hijo.

Mann, Joseph. 1989. Venezuelans Face Heavy Foreign Exchange Losses. *Financial Times,* March 7, 6.

————. 1994a. Caldera Critics Face Wave of Security Raids. *Financial Times,* July 5, 4.

————. 1994b. Sticks and Carrots for Venezuela's Banks: Selective Assistance and Pressure Is on Offer to the Troubled Financial Institutions. *Financial Times,* August 11, 4.

————. 1994c. Venezuela Bank Head Named as Depositors Fume. *Financial Times,* February 21, 6.

Márquez, Trino. 1998. Chávez y la profecía autocumplida. *El Universal,* April 30, 2–2.

Marturet, C. Rodriguez. 2002. *Gustavo Cisneros ¿presidente de Venezuela?* http://www .soberania.info/Articulos/articulo_319.htm. Accessed April 1, 2005.

Martz, John D. 1966. *Acción Democrática: Evolution of a Modern Political Party in Venezuela.* Princeton, NJ: Princeton University Press.

McCoy, Jennifer. 1995. *Venezuelan Democracy under Stress.* New Brunswick, NJ: Transaction Publishers.

———. 1999. Chávez and the End of "Partyarchy" in Venezuela. *Journal of Democracy* 10 (3): 64–77.

———. 2004. From Representative to Participatory Democracy? Regime Transformation in Venezuela. In *The Unraveling of Representative Democracy in Venezuela,* edited by J. McCoy and D. Myers. Baltimore: Johns Hopkins University Press.

———, and David Myers. 2004a. Introduction. In *The Unraveling of Representative Democracy in Venezuela,* edited by J. McCoy and D. Myers. Baltimore: Johns Hopkins University Press.

McCoy, Jennifer, and David Myers, eds. 2004b. *The Unraveling of Representative Democracy in Venezuela.* Baltimore: Johns Hopkins University Press.

Mendoza, Ibis Helena. 1995a. Informó María Inmaculada Pérez Dupuy: dictados autos de detención contra directivos del Italo Venezolano. *El Universal,* September 2, 1–17.

———. 1995b. Procesados por caso del Banco Construcción: dictaron auto de detención a cuatro ex directivos del Intercon Financial Bank NV. *El Universal,* November 2, 1–19.

Mezquita, Garrito, and Compañía, eds. 1953. *Diccionario biográfico de Venezuela.* Madrid, Spain: Impresora en los Talleres de Blass, S.A. Tipográfica.

Mine, Douglas Grant. 1992. Venezuela Mired in "Culture of Corruption." Associated Press, August 23.

Mintz, Beth, and Michael Schwartz. 1985. *The Power Structure of American Business.* Chicago: University of Chicago Press.

Mizruchi, Mark S. 1982. *The American Corporate Network, 1904–1974.* Beverly Hills, CA: Sage Publications.

Molina, José. 1998. Electoral Systems and Democratic Legitimacy in Venezuela. In *Reinventing Legitimacy: Democracy and Political Change in Venezuela,* edited by D. Canache and M. R. Kulischeck. Westport, CT: Greenwood Press.

———. 2002. The Presidential and Parliamentary Elections of the Bolivarian Revolution in Venezuela: Change and Continuity (1998–2000). *Bulletin of Latin American Research* 21 (2): 219–47.

———. 2004. The Unraveling of Venezuela's Party System: From Party Rule to Personalistic Politics and Deinstitutionalization. In *The Unraveling of Representative Democracy in Venezuela,* edited by J. McCoy and D. Myers. Baltimore: Johns Hopkins University Press.

Moncada, Samuel. 1985. *Los huevos de la serpiente: Fedecamaras por dentro.* Caracas: Alianza Gráfica.

Moore, Peter W. 2002. Rentier Fiscal Crisis and Regime Stability: Business-State Relations in the Gulf. *Studies in Comparative International Development* 37 (1): 34–56.

———. 2004. *Doing Business in the Middle East: Politics and Economic Crisis in Jordan and Kuwait.* New York: Cambridge University Press.

Morgan, Jana. 2005. Failing to Represent: The Collapse of the Venezuelan Party System. PhD dissertation, University of North Carolina.

———. 2007. Partisanship during the Collapse of Venezuela's Party System. *Latin American Research Review* 42 (1): 78–98.

References

Morris, Stephen D. 1991. *Corruption and Politics in Contemporary Mexico.* Tuscaloosa: University of Alabama Press.

Murdock, Deroy. 1995. Venezuela's Attack on the Press. *Washington Times,* June 15, A21.

Murillo, Victoria. 2000. From Populism to Neoliberalism: Labor Unions and Market Reforms in Latin America. *World Politics* 52 (2): 179–212.

Myers, David J. 1998. Venezuela's Political Party System: Defining Events, Reactions, and the Diluting of Structural Cleavages. *Party Politics* 4 (4): 495–521.

———. 2004. The Normalization of Punto Fijo Democracy. In *The Unraveling of Representative Democracy in Venezuela,* edited by J. McCoy and D. Myers. Baltimore: Johns Hopkins University Press.

Naím, Moisés. 1984. La empresa privada en Venezuela: que pasa cuando se crece en medio de la riqueza y la confusión? In *El caso Venezuela: una ilusión de armonía,* edited by Moisés Naím and Ramón Piñango. Caracas: Ediciones IESA.

———. 1993a. The Launching of Radical Policy Changes, 1989–1991. In *Venezuela in the Wake of Radical Reform,* edited by J. S. Tulchin and G. Bland. Boulder, CO: Lynne Rienner.

———. 1993b. *Paper Tigers and Minotaurs.* Washington, DC: Carnegie Endowment for International Peace.

———. 2001. High Anxiety in the Andes: The Real Story behind Venezuela's Woes. *Journal of Democracy* 12 (2): 17–31.

———. 2003. If Geology Is Destiny, Then Russia Is in Trouble. *New York Times,* December 4, A39.

———, and Antonio Francés. 1995. The Venezuelan Private Sector: From Courting the State to Courting the Market. In *Lessons of the Venezuelan Experience,* edited by Luis W. Goodman, J. M. Forman, M. Naím, J. S. Tulchin, and G. Bland. Washington, DC: Woodrow Wilson Center Press; Baltimore: Johns Hopkins University Press.

Naím, Moisés, and Ramón Piñango, eds. 1984. *El caso Venezuela: una ilusión de armonía.* Caracas: Ediciones IESA.

Navarro, Juan Carlos. 1994. Reversal of Fortune: The Ephemeral Success of Adjustment in Venezuela between 1989 and 1993. World Bank Project on Governance and Successful Adjustment in Venezuela.

Norden, Deborah. 1996. The Rise of the Lieutenant Colonels: Rebellion in Argentina and Venezuela. *Latin American Perspectives* 23 (30): 74–86.

Okruhlik, Gwenn. 1999. Rentier Wealth, Unruly Law, and the Rise of Opposition: The Political Economy of Oil States. *Comparative Politics* 31 (3): 295–315.

Olivares, Francisco. 1998. Clima electoral pone en alerta inversionistas. *El Universal,* April 20, 1–14.

Olmos, Harold. 1992a. Coup Struck a Chord in Economically Ailing Venezuela. Associated Press, February 2.

———. 1992b. Perez's Failure to Help the Poor, Wipe Out Corruption Triggers Coup. Associated Press, November 27.

Ortiz, Nelson. 2004. Entrepreneurs: Profits without Power? In *The Unraveling of Representative Democracy in Venezuela,* edited by J. McCoy and D. Myers. Baltimore: Johns Hopkins University Press.

O'Toole, Kevin. 1999. No Flag in Its Future. *Airline Business,* May 1, 72.

Paige, Jeffery. 1999. Conjuncture, Comparison, and Conditional Theory in Macrosocial Inquiry. *American Journal of Sociology* 105 (3): 781–800.

Panizza, Francesca. 2005. Unarmed Utopia Revisited: The Resurgence of Left-of-Centre Politics in Latin America. *Political Studies* 53 (4): 716–34.

Passell, Peter. 1991. Economic Scene: Cement Shoes for Venezuela. *New York Times,* September 25, D2.

Pastor, Manuel, and Carol Wise. 1994. The Origins and Sustainability of Mexico's Free Trade Policy. *International Organization* 48 (3): 459–89.

Paulin, David. 1998. Chávez Goals Strike Fear in Oil Executives; Venezuela's Poor See Him as Hero. *Washington Times,* October 20, A11.

Peeler, John. 1992. Elite Settlements and Democratic Consolidation: Colombia, Costa Rica, and Venezuela. In *Elites and Democratic Consolidation in Latin America and Southern Europe,* edited by J. Higler and R. Gunther. Cambridge: Cambridge University Press.

Peña, Maximo. 1998. El candidato del Polo Patriótico en el Atenea de Caracas. *El Nacional,* December 2, D2.

Pérez Perdomo, Rogelio. 1991. Corrupción y ambiente de los negocios en Venezuela. In *Corrupción y control: una perspectiva comparada,* edited by R. Pérez Perdomo and R. Capriles. Caracas: Ediciones IESA.

———. 1992. Corrupción y crisis política. Documento para Ética en la Gerencia, IESA.

———. 1999. Réquiem para el fomento: sobre la relación entre estado y negocios a través de la historia del Ministerio de Fomento. *Politeia* 23:141–62.

Perry, Olivero, ed. 1965. *Valores humanos de Venezuela.* Caracas: Olivero Perry.

Poulantzas, Nicos. 1976. *The Crisis of the Dictatorships: Portugal, Greece, Spain.* London: Atlantic Highlands Humanities Press.

Prechel, Harland. 1990. Steel and the State: Industry Politics and Business Policy Formation, 1940–1989. *American Sociological Review* 55 (5): 648–68.

———. 2003. Historical Contingency Theory, Policy Paradigm Shifts, and Corporate Malfeasance at the Turn of the 21st Century. *Research in Political Sociology* 12:311–40.

Procurador Petit da Costa: suspensión de las garantías facilitará tomar medidas contra delitos bancarios. 1994. *El Universal,* July 20, 1–10.

Public Citizen's Global Trade Watch. 2006. NAFTA Model Brings Economic and Social Pain to Mexico. Public Citizen's Global Trade Watch, October 20. http://www.citizen.org/documents/ImpactsonMexicoMemoOnePager.pdf. Accessed January 9, 2009.

Puga, Cristina. 1993. *Mexico: empresarios y poder.* Mexico City: Facultad de Ciencia Políticas y Sociales, UNAM, and Miguel Angel Porrua.

Quién es Quién en Venezuela. 1988. *Quién es quién en Venezuela.* Caracas: Editorial Quiénes somos en Venezuela.

Radcliff, Benjamin. 1994. Reward without Punishment. *Political Research Quarterly* 47:721–31.

Ragin, Charles C. 1987. *The Comparative Method: Moving beyond Qualitative and Quantitative Strategies.* Berkeley: University of California Press.

Ramírez, Juan José. 1983. *Diccionario biográfico del estado Monagas.* Maturín, Venezuela: Ediciones Gobernación del Estado Monagas.

Rey, Juan Carlos. 1998. *El futuro de la democracia en Venezuela.* 2nd ed. Caracas: Facultad de Ciencias Jurídicas y Políticas, Universidad Central de Venezuela.

Roberts, Kenneth M. 1995. Neoliberalism and the Transformation of Populism in Latin America: The Peruvian Case. *World Politics* 48 (October): 82–116.

———. 2003a. Social Correlates of Party System Demise and Populist Resurgence in Venezuela. *Latin American Politics and Society* 45 (3): 35–57.

———. 2003b. Social Polarization and the Populist Resurgence in Venezuela. In *Venezuelan Politics in the Chávez Era: Class, Polarization, and Conflict*, edited by S. Ellner and D. Hellinger. Boulder, CO: Lynne Rienner.

Rogowski, Ronald. 1989. *Commerce and Coalitions: How Trade Affects Domestic Political Alignments*. Princeton, NJ: Princeton University Press.

Romero, Anibal. 1997. Rearranging the Deck Chairs on the *Titanic*. *Latin American Research Review* 32 (1): 7–36.

Romero, Simon. 2002. Coup? Not His Style, but Power? Oh, Yes. *New York Times*, April 28, B1.

Ross, Michael L. 1999. The Paradox of Plenty: Oil Booms and Petro-states. *World Politics* 51 (2): 297–322.

———. 2001. Does Oil Hinder Democracy? *World Politics* 53 (3): 325–61.

Rueschemeyer, Dietrich. 2003. Can One or a Few Cases Yield Theoretical Gains? In *Comparative Historical Analysis in the Social Sciences*, edited by J. Mahoney and D. Rueschemeyer. Cambridge: Cambridge University Press.

Salamanca, Luis. 2004. Civil Society: Late Bloomers. In *The Unraveling of Representative Democracy in Venezuela*, edited by J. McCoy and D. Myers. Baltimore: Johns Hopkins University Press.

Salas, Carlos. 2006. Between Unemployment and Insecurity in Mexico: NAFTA Enters Its Second Decade. In *Revisiting NAFTA: Still Not Working for North America's Workers*, edited by R. E. Scott, C. Salas, and B. Campbell. Washington, DC: Economic Policy Institute.

Samuels, David. 2001. Money, Elections, and Democracy in Brazil. *Latin American Politics and Society* 43 (2): 27–48.

Sánchez Molina, Yesmin. 2000. Quienes fueron los financistas del candidato Hugo Chávez Frias? El origin de los fondos financieros de la campaña presidencial del abandera del MVR. Undergraduate thesis, Universidad Católica Andrés Bello, Caracas.

Santodomingo, Roger. 1999. *La conspiración 98: un pacto secreto para llevar a Hugo Chávez al poder*. Caracas: ALFA Grupo Editorial.

Scandal Grows over Cheap-Rate Dollars; New Twist as Uncertainty Rebounds on the Judges. 1989. *Latin American Weekly Report* (London), *Latin American Newsletters*, June 15, 5.

Schael, María Sol Pérez. 1993. *Petróleo y poder en Venezuela*. Caracas: Monte Ávila.

Schamis, Hector E. 2002. *Re-forming the State: The Politics of Privatization in Latin America and Europe*. Ann Arbor: University of Michigan Press.

Schemo, Diana Jean. 1998. Mistakes Hobble Venezuelan Economy, Experts Say. *New York Times*, September 2, A11.

Schneider, Ben Ross. 2004. *Business Politics and the State in Twentieth-Century Latin America*. Cambridge: Cambridge University Press.

———, and Sylvia Maxfield. 1997. Business, the State, and Economic Performance in Developing Countries. In *Business and the State in Developing Countries*, edited by S. Maxfield and B. R. Schneider. Ithaca, NY: Cornell University Press.

Seara, Marita. 1998. A Sector in Crisis: Cinderella; The Textile Industry. *Business Venezuela,* Venezuelan American Chamber of Commerce, October 1.

Seawright, J., and J. Gerring. 2008. Case Selection Techniques in Case Study Research: A Menu of Qualitative and Quantitative Options. *Political Research Quarterly* 61 (2): 294–308.

Seligson, Mitchell A. 2007. The Rise of Populism and the Left in Latin America. *Journal of Democracy* 18 (3): 81–95.

Shadlen, Kenneth. 2004. *Democratization without Representation: The Politics of Small Industry in Mexico.* University Park: Pennsylvania State University Press.

Shafer, D. Michael. 1994. *Winners and Losers: How Sectors Shape the Developmental Prospects of States.* Ithaca, NY: Cornell University Press.

———. 1997. The Political Economy of Sectors and Sectoral Change: Korea Then and Now. In *Business and the State in Developing Countries,* edited by S. Maxfield and B. R. Schneider. Ithaca, NY: Cornell University Press.

Sick, Gary. 1998. The Coming Crisis in the Persian Gulf. *Washington Quarterly* 21 (2): 195–213.

Silva, Eduardo. 1996. *The State and Capital in Chile: Business Elites, Technocrats, and Market Economics.* Boulder, CO: Westview Press.

Smelser, Neil J. 1976. *Comparative Methods in the Social Sciences.* Englewood Cliffs, NJ: Prentice-Hall.

Smith, Benjamin. 2004. Oil Wealth and Regime Survival in the Developing World, 1960–1999. *American Journal of Political Science* 48 (2): 232–46.

———. 2006. The Wrong Kind of Crisis: Why Booms and Busts Rarely Lead to Authoritarian Breakdown. *Studies in Comparative International Development* 40 (4): 55–76.

Snyder, R. 2006. Does Lootable Wealth Breed Disorder? A Political Economy of Extraction Framework. *Comparative Political Studies* 39 (8): 943–68.

Stokes, Susan. 2001. *Public Support for Market Reforms in New Democracies.* Cambridge: Cambridge University Press.

Subero, Carlos. 2004. Venezuela: With Me, or against Me. In *The Corruption Notebooks.* Washington, DC: Center for Public Integrity.

Sullivan, John. 1997. New York Jury Convicts Three Venezuelan Bankers of Defrauding Depositors. *New York Times,* February 20, B6.

Templeton, Andrew. 1995. The Evolution of Public Opinion. In *Lessons of the Venezuelan Experience,* edited by L. Goodman, J. M. Forman, M. Naím, J. Tulchin, and G. Blanc. Baltimore: Johns Hopkins University Press.

Thacker, Strom. 2000. *Big Business, the State, and Free Trade: Constructing Coalitions in Mexico.* Cambridge: Cambridge University Press.

Thompson, Edward Palmer. 1964. *The Making of the English Working Class.* New York: Pantheon Books.

Thorp, Rosemary, and Francisco Durand. 1997. A Historical View of Business-State Relations: Colombia, Peru, and Venezuela Compared. In *Business and the State in Developing Countries,* edited by S. Maxfield and B. R. Schneider. Princeton, NJ: Princeton University Press.

Trevizo, Dolores. 2003. Intraclass Conflict and Political Divisions among Capitalists: The Remaking of an Agrarian Capitalist Class in Mexico, 1970–75. *Social Science History* 27:75–108.

Trinkunas, Harold. 2004. The Military: From Marginalization to Center Stage. In *The Unraveling of Representative Democracy in Venezuela*, edited by J. McCoy and D. Myers. Baltimore: Johns Hopkins University Press.

———. 2005. *Crafting Civilian Control of the Military in Venezuela: A Comparative Perspective*. Chapel Hill: University of North Carolina Press.

Truell, Peter. 1996a. Too Close for Comfort? Inquiry Touches Money Laundering Expert's Backer. *New York Times*, April 4, D1

———. 1996b. Venezuelan Financier Indicted in New York: Was an Entire Banking System Defrauded? *New York Times*, April 5, D3.

Unexpected Moves in Banks Crisis: Troubled Institutions Closed, Re-opened to Pay Depositors. 1994. *Latin American Regional Reports–Andean Group (London)*, *Latin American News-letters*, June 30, 3.

Urbaneja, Diego Bautista. 1992. *Pueblo y petróleo en la política venezolana del siglo XX*. Caracas: Centro de Formación y Adiestramiento de Petróleos de Venezuela y sus Filiales.

Useem, Michael. 1984. *The Inner Circle: Large Corporations and the Rise of Business Political Activity in the U.S. and U.K.* New York: Oxford University Press.

Vargas, Alberto. 1994a. El expediente lo envió la Corte: a salvaguarda caso de los bancos que recibieron auxilio de Fogade. *El Universal*, November 1, 1–12.

———. 1994b. El XLII y el XIII: dos tribunales investigan a ex directiva del banco de Venezuela. *El Universal*, October 6, 1–19.

———. 1994c. En el Tribunal XXIV penal: se pusieron a derecho otros cinco indiciados en caso Latino. *El Universal*, May 31, 1–17.

———. 1994d. Por el caso de auxilio financiero: auto de detención al presidente de Fiveca y a otros tres ejecutivos. *El Universal*, June 10, 1–17.

Venezuela: A Tough Task. 1993. *The Economist*, December 11, 44–45.

Venezuela: Arrests Begin in the Banco Latino Scandal. 1994. Inter Press Service, March 3.

Venezuela: Colonel Courageous. 1977. *Latin American Weekly Report* (London), *Latin American Newsletters*, July 1, 199.

Venezuela: Ex-president Faces Possible Corruption Charges. 1992. Inter Press Service, July 17.

Venezuela: It's All Chávez. 1998. *The Economist*, July 4, 30–31.

Venezuela: This Little Pig Had Roast Beef. 1975. *Latin American Weekly Report* (London), *Latin American Newsletters*, April 25, 124.

Venezuelan Banking: Chaos in Caracas. 1994. *The Economist*, June 18, 88–89.

Venezuelan Trade: Door to Andean Imports Remains Only Half-Open. 1983. *Latin America Regional Reports–Andean Group (London)*, *Latin American Newsletters*, September 2, 4.

Weyland, Kurt. 1998. The Politics of Corruption in Latin America. *Journal of Democracy* 9 (2): 108–21.

———. 2003. Economic Voting Reconsidered: Crisis and Charisma in the Election of Hugo Chávez. *Comparative Political Studies* 36 (7): 822–48.

Who's Who in Venezuela. 1989. *Quién es quién en Venezuela 1988–1989: Diccionario biográfico venezolano*. Miami: Worldwide Reference Publication.

Wick, Katharina, and Erwin H. Bulte. 2006. Contesting Resources: Rent Seeking, Conflict, and the Natural Resource Curse. *Public Choice* 128 (3–4): 457–76.

Williams, Mark Eric. 2001. *Market Reforms in Mexico: Coalitions, Institutions, and the Politics of Policy Change*. Lanham, MD: Rowman and Littlefield.

Yesterday's Money. 1994. *The Economist,* January 22, 87.

Zapata, Juan Carlos. 1995. *Los ricos bobos.* Caracas: Alfadil Ediciones.

———. 1997. *Las intrigas del poder: quien manda en Venezuela.* Caracas: Alfadil Ediciones.

———. 2000. *Plomo más plomo es guerra: proceso a Chávez.* Caracas: Alfadil Ediciones.

INDEX

Note: Tables are indicated by "t" following the page number.